PASSAGEMAKING UNDER POWER:

Voyaging to the Mediterranean
on *TEKA III*

By Mary Umstot

To Bill & Sue —
life is a journey —
Enjoy our story —
Mary

BookLocker.com, Inc.
2010

To Denis, my husband, captain and co-adventurer

Also to David and Dawn, our children,
who inherited our gypsy spirit

TEKA III from the air on the Black Sea

Contents

Foreword

Author Mary Umstot and her husband Denis have taken the road less traveled but one that is infinitely more fulfilling than the standard route. Rather than taking a cruise ship or going from hotel to hotel, they have traveled in a small yacht that I built over 25 years ago. They spent 10 years part-time seeing parts of the world inaccessible to any other form of transport.

Imagine a 52-foot long-range Passagemaker-type power yacht crossing the Atlantic both ways under the command of a couple nearing 70 years of age! On top of that, it was done with such enjoyment, with great food, with new friends·and old friends, plus the energy from Mary to record their adventures through articles in numerous publications.

Sharing their adventures should appeal to most anyone with an interest in traveling, history, geography, boating or just a good yarn. Mary writes with a style that moves along and will keep the reader involved.

Hugo Carver
Knight & Carver Yacht Center
San Diego, California

A Really Dark and Scary Night!

On the night of October 13, 1997, I felt fear like I had never felt before. My husband, Denis, and I stood alone in *TEKA III*'s pilothouse, watching the wind and waves outside the windows creating quite a disturbance. As we approached Cape Flattery on the northwest coast of Washington, an outgoing tide, running about four knots from Juan de Fuca Strait, charged into twelve-foot swells coming in from the Pacific Ocean.

To enter the Strait we had to make a starboard turn near Tatoosh Island, a formidable rock formation. I stood on the port side of the pilothouse watching the waves build ahead of us, with a curly lip on each top. Scared? You bet! As we neared the point to change course, I physically moved closer to Denis and began taking deep breaths to control my fears. Denis had experienced that treacherous area salmon fishing for years, and from his intense concentration on steering the boat, appeared confident enough to pull it off. I, on the other hand, felt totally helpless. In my mind, if we did not climb that wave just right while turning, we would lose control and roll over, to be swallowed by the wave. I would never see my children and grandchildren again.

With darkness all around us, we turned as the next wave started its climb. The running lights reflected white foam from wave train after wave train on both sides of us. That's when I actually held my breath.

But we made it! In only a matter of minutes we were sliding down that big wave, heading into the Strait and safety. The image I have is of huge hands lifting me up and carefully cushioning my ride. At that point I bonded with my boat!

An hour and a half after that momentous turn, we dropped the anchor in Neah Bay Harbor, relieved that the day and trip were over.

We had decided to abort our trip south to the Baja that fall due to a chain of storms that filed one right after another into the Northwest, holding boats in ports for weather windows. These ports were few and far between along the Pacific Coast and days were getting shorter. Weather windows might not stay open long enough to make a passage. It took us from 6:45 A.M. to 9:40 P.M. to make it north from Grays Harbor, Washington to Neah Bay on that day. Shorter days meant traveling in the dark at both ends. And the ocean had one of its boisterous days during that time.

We experienced other episodes of bad weather during our ten years at sea. After making it through this one, coupled with the realization that the ocean had many moods, benign to boisterous, I approached each scary situation humming a mantra: *"Feel the rhythm; trust my ship."*

While this wave is in the Caribbean, imagine the same wave
at night in the story above

Breaking Out of the Box

Denis and I had boated for over thirty-five years, starting small and incrementally getting bigger. We spent ten summers cruising on a 37-foot Hershine Trawler, *PANDA,* in Puget Sound, the San Juans, and British Columbia's Gulf Islands. Venturing further from these protected waters never entered the picture. No way was she going to sea. Her hard-chine bottom reacted to any rough water by rocking the boat and in extreme cases, trying to empty the cupboards onto the floor.

We had talked about taking a trip to Alaska and maybe the Queen Charlotte Islands, but needed a seaworthy vessel for navigating the waters between British Columbia mainland, Vancouver Island, and Alaska.

I must also interject that during our marriage Denis had often expressed a wish to sail around the world someday. My response each time he mentioned it, "Can we go on a calm day?" He knew I did not like to sail, mainly because of the heeling.

My first experience on a sailboat left me unnerved. We had joined a friend on his sailboat for a sunset cruise on Lake Ontario one summer evening in 1976. A strong gust hit the sails shortly after we got underway, and it indeed looked to me as if we just might go on over. "Never mind," his wife piped from the galley, where she busily worked on snacks. "We're washing the windows!" Never to be without words, I exclaimed, "What about those on this side?" Answer: "We'll get them on the way back!" And we did.

In the 1990s, crossing the Comox Bar on Vancouver Island at the wrong tide or in bad weather freaked me out aboard *PANDA.* As the waves tossed her around, she started a severe, snappy rolling motion, each roll swaying to a greater degree than the one before. I stood spread-eagled across the cabin holding as many drawers and cabinets in place as I could until we reached calmer water. Not a fun experience! And she tended to bury her bow in heavy 4-5 foot chop, and she didn't like following seas either. She loved being at anchor or at a marina.

We could definitely use a different boat to expand our horizons and give me a safer feeling. Looking for an ocean-going vessel, we were surprised to spy one "For Sale" in Friday Harbor where we lived, and made arrangements for a tour. The boat had an unusual layout. From the galley, located on the lower level in a long hallway, a dumb waiter moved meals to the upper level for serving. The master bedroom was just a step across the hall from the stove on that lower level—handy for having coffee in bed, but the design did not "sing" to me.

Even though the couple did not sell us their Skookum, they gladly spent time with us, sharing some of their sea adventures. For example, they had been anchored in Panama when the Americans attacked attempting to capture Noriega, and showed us a video of gunfire in the harbor. With our interest peaked even more, they highly recommended Robert Beebe's book, *Voyaging Under Power*, explaining the design, construction, and benefits of ocean-going powerboats—Passagemakers.

A broker took us through another Passagemaker-type boat at the town dock. This one, built of steel with a super-high bow and one-inch thick glass in the pilothouse windows, had watertight doors with round wheel locks similar to submarines separating the two sleeping cabins. I could not have my grandchildren sleeping locked up in there. So we passed on that one as well.

Denis, a master researcher, poured over Beebe's book, absorbing ideas, and realizing the seaworthy qualities of a Passagemaker-type boat just might make his dream happen. An ocean-going trawler, with large fuel capacity for long voyages and stabilization for comfort in heavy seas would definitely get us to Alaska and back. At this point nothing had been said about world cruising, but after reading and talking, it made for an interesting thought. All he had to do was find a boat that "sang to me."

We checked out 46-foot Nordhavns, the most popular Passagemakers at that time. They were very nice boats, but a bit expensive for us, so we kept looking.

On our next trip to visit our San Diego family we searched the "Boats for Sale" Magazines. One mentioned a "Beebe-designed" boat for sale. We trooped down to Brokaw Yacht Brokers for a chat. They drove us to the marina for a tour of the 52-foot Passagemaker, *TEKA III*.

She stood proud at the dock, looking like a Coast Guard cutter with her high-flared bow. She was a ship, not just a boat! Her stern featured a covered lounging deck; open on three sides to view the scenery in comfort. I could see myself hanging out there, reading, grooving, or napping on the large cushioned area at sea or anchor. In fact, many people who traveled with us over our eleven years did just that. It also made for a super place to have potluck dinners and sundowner cocktail sessions.

TEKA III's impressive bow (Cabo San Vito, Sicily)

Already I felt good vibes about her, and I had not even gone inside.

Inside the pilothouse the 360-degree view let me see where I was going and where I had been. Standing at the helm and pretending to control the instruments gave me a special feeling of running away to sea, even tied to a dock.

Below that level is where cooking, eating, sleeping, watching movies, and socializing got done. The boat's interior wrapped itself around me—a very comfortable, encompassing feeling. Many people coming aboard to visit say exactly that: "This is a comfortable boat."

Two staterooms, located at opposite ends of the boat, would give privacy to the owners in the aft cabin and also to company or crew in the front one. Yet everyone could meet for coffee in the mid-ship galley first thing in the mornings.

While I focused on how I could live on this boat with its amenities, Denis checked out the engine room, where the Gardner engine resided. The Gardner, often used in commercial fishing vessels, is a legendary British engine noted for its robust design and extremely long life.

When other skippers learned we had a Gardner, they would say respectfully, "That engine will last longer than you will." My comment, "I'm counting on it." I enjoyed greeting him daily, "Good morning, Mr. G." And after a long passage: "Good job!"

For me the engine room had a special positive. Denis could descend five steps down from the Pilothouse to do whatever he needed to do—change oil, move fuel to the day tank, run the generator, or check the batteries, without bothering me. On *PANDA,* whenever he wanted to do anything on the engines, he had to pull up all the floorboards in the main cabin, and I couldn't even make a cup of tea until his job was done.

In addition to having a fuel-efficient engine, a Passagemaker's flopper stoppers provide stabilization to dampen the boat's roll in rough seas. At rest, two 25-foot long solid-steel poles stand upright against the boat's sides. When deployed, they are lowered to about 30 degrees above the water. Instead of a 16-foot beam, the extended poles then gave us a 66-foot stretch over the water. That alone can make things feel better—like a man walking across a high wire, holding onto a long pole for balance. But when it becomes too rough, we drop two 50-pound delta-shaped steel paravanes (fish) into the water where they ride about 12 feet below the surface. As the boat starts to roll one way, the opposite paravane comes into play and puts pressure on its side to right the boat again.

We would have to learn how to use this system, but it definitely made me feel more comfortable, considering how I reacted to *PANDA's* rock and roll. This boat started to sing choruses.

TEKA III became ours. We did some practice runs while investigating all the nooks and crannies to see what space we had; checked on and updated electronics; made major repairs on the boat including straightening and rewelding cracks in the steel flopper stopper poles, plus fixing leaks in the deck structure; purchased fuel and food toward leaving; and called up some friends to make the maiden voyage with us.

We broke out of the box with a new ship, and with it, boundaries expanded. My timidity and trepidation, "I don't do oceans and I don't do nights," would be tested and changed over the course of our journeys.

A Tale of Two Maiden Voyages

A copy of *TEKA III*'s log proved her seaworthiness. With her original owner she made two round trips to Europe from the western U.S., plus extensively traveling the West Coast. She passed the test as a very salty ship.

 We did not realize when we bought her that she'd take us on a 48,000 nautical mile adventure over eleven years, starting with our maiden voyage from San Diego to the Pacific Northwest in May 1997.

Set to go, I had to address my fears about the big trip. It would take about three weeks to make it up to the Seattle area. I calculated about 1300 nautical miles. We had hoped to port-hop on day trips most of the time, but weather could be an issue anywhere along the way. I looked at weather as "Go, stay, or deal with it!" If all looked good, go. Otherwise, stay. But if something overtook you, be prepared to deal with it. At that time I did not know what my new ship would or could do, only by reputation. And with my past experience being in protected waters, the ocean did look very different.

Cutting loose from land is a big step. First you can't see it visually, but it's there on radar. But when it's out of radar range, you have to imagine it is still there. Over time, friends have laughed at me because I insist on AAA land maps on board as well as nautical charts. Call it a secure feeling or an insecure one, but it's what I do.

Crew or not to crew is an important dimension in traveling by boat. Day trips or short hops do not require extra people. Extended ones, like this adventure up the Pacific coast, do. So who to invite? We chose friends with nautical experience. I offered my services to feed and water them, plus give them some adventure miles for their life's map.

People traveling on a boat for an extended period of time share a limited space, which can get smaller if things don't go right. The idea is to treat each other with lots of patience and a healthy dose of humor at the ready. With nowhere to escape, except hiding in the dinghy, problems have to be faced and dealt with. Someone wrote once that heated issues need three "takes"—take a walk, take a nap, or take a shower. The walk may be just around the perimeter of the boat if the weather and seas permit, but it gives the tension a break. It is like counting to ten several times before addressing the problem with a less defensive attitude.

For our maiden voyage we chose three folks and met them in San Diego, an easy connection. Bob Hermann, with years of sailing experience under his belt, and the one who gave me that sunset cruise on Lake Ontario, flew out from Delaware. Recently widowed, and grieving, I suggested a voyage on *TEKA III* as a way to heal. We had been friends with Bob and Anne many years and I told him we would cry with him if he "puddled up." That happened.

Alex and Joanne Gray flew into San Diego from Canada three days before our departure date. Alex, a top-notch marine mechanic who saved my last boat from a near-watery grave, came on board, donned his overalls, and disappeared into the engine room to meet our Gardner engine.

TEKA III's maiden voyage about to get underway made me reflect on *PANDA's* maiden voyage ten years before, her near sinking, and how we met Alex.

On a fateful night in the late 1980s, our former 37-foot trawler, *PANDA*, went on her side while anchored at Henry Bay, Denman Island, British Columbia. "We're aground!" Denis called to his mother and me. Rolling out of bed, quickly dressing, we lowered the dinghy, climbed in and rowed a short distance to shore to assess the situation. Time: 3:40 A.M.

We had anchored too close to shore, and during the night current and wind had pushed us onto the sloping sand drop-off. Denis just thought when the tide came back in, she would right herself and all would be well. He had in the past purposefully tipped other boats to clean their bottoms, and nothing adverse happened.

While we watched, the starboard engine self-started, as if saying, "I'm getting out of here!" I asked Denis what that meant. He explained that salt water had probably caused a short between the starter and ground, just like turning the starter switch on, and "we were in trouble." He jumped into the dinghy, rowed back to the boat, retrieved the outboard engine from the railing, secured it on the dinghy and roared off to a Canadian Naval Cadet Training Ship anchored further out. Mother-in-law and I just took up waiting positions on the beach in the dark staring at the shape of a forlorn boat leaning way over.

The cadets radioed the Coast Guard Auxiliary in Comox, the nearest town, for assistance. Three men came out after organizing supplies like bilge pumps and ropes. Alex was one of these men; Duke Warren, another. Cadets came over as well. Unsuccessful with their efforts to pump out the water in the engine room, the men took Denis and his mother back to town to get additional supplies and find her a hotel room. That left me alone on the beach to guard against any salvage attempts until the men returned, about 3 P.M.

As daylight came on the scene I spent time watching items float up and out the portside door, turn left and float off the back of the boat. It seemed almost comical—like the "Grapevine" dance. I got busy with the dinghy and rescued what I could, watching out for activity nearby. A rowboat brought a family to check on me. They lived not too far away from my dilemma and responded to a little girl's plea to take a picnic lunch out to that lady. I greatly appreciated the sandwich and the companionship during my crisis. A large engine roar let me know a big ship had come onto the scene—the real Canadian Coast Guard. They had heard the "Mayday" distress call from the Cadet Ship earlier and just dropped by to see if I was okay. Since they could not bring the big ship any closer, I rowed out toward them and relayed what had happened and was due to happen. They laughed. "I bet your husband is in the pub," to which I replied, "He'd better have his mother with him." They gave me water and an apple, promising to keep an ear out for my returning rescuers.

When my rescuers returned and studied the situation in broad daylight, they noticed the trawler's significant design flaw. Engine room vents were located below the rub rail and thus easy access for water to go straight into the engine room. They had to work fast as the next high tide would take the boat under, so first tried to place duct tape to plastic pieces around the vent openings. The tape did not stick to the diesel coated sides, so the plastic could not work. Industrial paper towels were useless as well, so what to do? Denis found some Bounty Paper Towels on board. So as a last ditch effort, they tried stuffing them inside the louvers of the engine room vents to dam the water. As everyone knows, Bounty is portrayed as the "quicker, picker-upper." It worked. The boat began to slowly rise to its upright position as we held our breath. Once we saw the success of the operation, everyone cheered, on land and on the boat.

We were towed back into Comox. Alex began immediately to work on the engine, followed by us spending the next year putting the boat back into shape, at the same time fighting with the insurance company. Alex was a good man to have on our side then and now!

The image of our former maiden voyage drama was on all our minds as we began a new one.

Leaving San Diego our first stop was Catalina Island. Shortly after our arrival the harbormaster came alongside, not only to help us tie up bow and stern to the buoys provided, but actually board us. He asked the location of the head, disappeared down the stairs and dropped a green pellet into the toilet. Returning outside again, he announced if he saw anything green in the water by our boat he would know we had flushed to the outside. They are very strict about any discharge polluting their harbor. We obeyed. Otherwise we'd pay a huge fine!

The Santa Barbara Channel starts at the notorious Point Conception, running between the Channel Islands and the mainland. It is affected by winds and waves coming around that point, which accelerate each afternoon. We were not aware of this phenomenon until we found ourselves in the midst of it. Traveling west toward the point we could see the swells beginning to build, then the wind picked up to about 40 knots and the water became turbulent with steep 8-foot waves slamming into the bow and spray blowing everywhere. We bashed and crashed around as we approached the Point. A commercial fisherman came up on our port side. We called over the radio. "Does it get better up there?" He laughed. "You're new here, aren't you?" He advised us not to try going around the point at that time. There was an alternative. We could anchor in a calm area just before and behind the Point; wait until early morning when the winds and seas were calmest, and have a safe passage, avoiding the Cape Effect. Not knowing how the boat would react making a turn in those conditions, Denis held his breath, but *TEKA III* performed well. We stayed put for the night, and had an easy trip the next morning, very early. A good-sized sea lion spent the night on our swim bridge and greeted us loudly as we cranked up the engine.

After Point Conception we stopped at Morro Bay. To enter we had to cross a nasty bar. Conditions were okay to go in through the breakwater yet it took us a while to get the flopper stopper poles secured before approaching. In Morro Bay we witnessed photos of the 70-foot motor yacht, *MOJO*, being bashed by huge breaking seas at the entrance to the harbor in 1978. This boat had hosted three Presidents and many Hollywood famous people. That fateful day George C. Scott and his wife were on board. They survived, but the photos of the severely damaged boat made chills run up the spine. The U.S. Coast Guard considers this bar one of the most dangerous in the nation. Hazardous bar condition warnings are posted 40 days each year, and in the winter 18-foot waves climb over the breakwater. Twenty-one lives were lost between 1979 and 1987. A sobering thought for additional trips in and out of Morro Bay. So far, so good.

Monterey Bay offered us another challenge—fog. Dense fog! We had radar, an early GPS system, but no electronic chart plotting to assist us in navigating. We did put Bob out on the bow to listen for foghorns and watch for anything moving in our direction. The fog lasted until we were almost into Monterey Harbor. Holy Smokes! What would be next?

Crab traps—minefields of them! During April and May, Dungeness crab fishermen drop hundreds of traps 400-500 feet below the surface and leave them there to retrieve later. All that is seen on the surface is the small buoy marking the start of the line. When the seas are calm they are easily spotted and avoided in the daytime. At night or in rough water, it is another matter. One does not want to get one of those lines wrapped around a prop. You are dead in the water until it gets unwrapped. For us dragging the flopper stopper paravanes in the water, we had additional ability to snatch a line. In those cases, we could more easily get loose, but no one wanted to dive in cold water and cut line from around the prop. Paying attention is the name of the game.

Crab trap lines and discarded fishing nets are not only problems for boaters, but wildlife as well. On our passage north we overheard a sailboat off the Washington coast call the Seattle Coast Guard to tell them about hitting a whale. After the initial thump, everyone on board scrambled to find out what happened as they stopped forward motion. When they saw the baby gray whale near the bow they realized it had something wrapped inside its mouth and around its head, causing distress. The whale appeared to be very tired from struggling to release itself from the mess, and did not resist when the boat came alongside and the people tried to help. While someone gathered a video camera to tape the event, others worked with knives to cut the offending lines and free the baby whale. All of this was discussed between the boaters and Coast Guard, with others in VHF radio range listening in. Finally free, he swam off. The Coast Guard requested a copy of the tape.

San Francisco Bay offered us a fantastic view of the Golden Gate (actually rusty red) Bridge looking up from the water level, while attending to ship traffic and watching out for the fast and furious currents around the bridge pylons. Sea lions ruled at Pier 39, taking over a whole area on one side of Pier 39. Obnoxiously smelly, their barking could really give one a headache fast. We at first tied up on the side they were on, but pleaded for another assignment and received one on the other side of Pier 39. Hooray!

San Francisco town offered much for the tourist exploring by foot and cable car. Dim Sum, a Hong Kong Chinese specialty, proved very authentic. We could say that after eating many dim sum meals during our four years living and working in Hong Kong.

Between San Francisco and Friday Harbor, Washington, there are not many places to tuck in. Therefore we made two planned overnight runs between ports, and one unscheduled one. That time we had anchored behind a point to break the north wind, only to have the wind shift 180 degrees in the middle of the night. Waking up, we quickly retrieved the anchor. Alex and I stood at the bow to point out a way through the minefield of crab traps. Dick Thompson, who replaced Joanne in Santa Cruz, stayed in the pilothouse with Denis, supposedly to relay our hand signals regarding the traps. No matter which way we pointed, Denis did not change course, and

Dick stood there smiling. He had gotten up so quickly he had not inserted his hearing aids and what we had said to him had not registered. Fortunately we had no problem escaping the anchorage. Now the wind and sea behind us made for a smooth ride north and we all stayed up until morning.

My first overnighter experience happened north of San Francisco. Denis, Alex and Dick waited for me to decide if I was ready to do a night watch or not, and which three hours would be mine. I chose the 3-6 A.M. shift so I could witness dawn and sunrise. There is something dramatic about the dark slowly being taken over by light, and finally a burst of color as day replaces night. So with the seas behaving, weather looking benign, and the full moon enticing me to go for it, I did. Unfortunately the moon stayed behind us that night, illuminating where we had been, not where we were going. It would have been much nicer to have it lead the way.

With this overnight experience out in the Pacific Ocean my proclamation of not doing oceans or nights began to unravel. This set the scene for many more 3-6 A.M. shifts in the captain's chair over the next ten years of ocean travel, and finding courage to trust myself as a mariner.

What happens on a night watch? You monitor the instruments and keep a two-hour log. You look out for other ships, visually, and by radar. You listen for VHF radio calls. You marvel at the phosphorescence in the water as you push through it. You listen to the wind and feel the ocean lift and move you along. All in the dark! It is spooky to look out the port and starboard windows and see only the running lights reflecting red and green. And from the front windows, nothing shows up except the glow from the instrument panel. It made me feel very alone. Yet not far away, asleep, were two others to assist if needed, but the call was mine. Things unseen that would go bump in the night worried me. And what about a rogue wave? You cannot see that coming. Denis had two rules: (1) No one could go out on deck alone at night, no matter how much the stars winked at you. That alone eliminated the chance of a MOB (man over board) situation; (2) if a ship showed up on radar approaching us within a two miles range, he wanted to know about it. Wake him up!

Learning to trust my ship and myself came with time and experience. There were interesting events that happened during my "O-dark-hundred" shift on passages during voyages and I will include them as the story goes along. Some were humorous, some scary, and all very interesting.

We arrived safely in Friday Harbor less than three weeks after casting off from the dock at San Diego, confident of the boat's seamanship, also having earned some confidence in ourselves as seafarers.

Our daughter, Dawn, insisted we contact her every night along the way and we did. She put it this way, "I don't care if you are at anchor, on passage or tucked into a marina, I need to know where you are and if you are safe. After all, I am the first name on the EPIRB!" An Emergency Position-Indicating Radio Beacon, registered to a particular boat, sends out signals to satellites relaying the boat's position to the Coast Guard. In such a distress situation, the Coast Guard has valuable information to assist in locating and rescuing the boat with a problem. Dawn is registered as the first person for the Coast Guard to contact in case our Beacon is activated.

As Alex left for home, he told us to "Keep the slimy side down and shiny side up." Good advice! I am sure someone else might also have said, "Keep the pointy end up front."

An Aborted Trip

Before leaving the Northwest for a cruise down the Pacific coast to Mexico later in that year, we took time to circumnavigate Vancouver Island in British Columbia. Protected by the Inland Passage on the east side, and open to the wild and wooly Pacific Ocean on the west, such a trip is considered good preparation for world cruising because of the varied conditions one would encounter. We were not planning to go world cruising at that time, but figured it would constitute a real good shakedown for us and the boat. Rain and fog were our constant companions for most of that summer as we adjusted to life at sea on *TEKA III* as a couple.

Some memories of that trip include spending three days and nights anchored up the inlet from Nootka Sound where Captain Cook had explored many years ago. We finally moved on when I expressed a need to see the rain falling on a different set of trees. Before that episode we had gone up another inlet to Sea Otter Cove one afternoon, and with no place to anchor, attempted to tie to a very large round steel buoy set up for much larger boats. A boat came over to us, one man jumped from their boat onto the buoy, and I threw my line to him. Otherwise we would not have been successful in staying there for the night. The men on board were beach loggers, combing areas for cedar logs to retrieve and sell for cash.

Before going around the north end of Vancouver Island, we anchored one night near an abandoned Coast Guard Station on Hope Island to wait before crossing the Nawitti Bar. On August 16, 1997, we left our anchorage to cross the bar one hour before high slack tide. With no combers or breakers coming in from the sea, we crossed safely. On another trip we re-crossed the bar from the ocean side with a low swell, incoming tide, and calm winds. This bar is notoriously wicked because of the depth change. On the ocean side, it is very deep, shallowing up to 12-feet inside the bar. It is easy to imagine breaking waves of 50-feet or more piling up during heavy winter storms. Although we had been through many rapids on the inside passage to that point, this one needed special attention. At the right tide it was a piece of cake, yet the depth sounder showed us the problem in bottom changes. (Note: The abandoned Coast Guard Station looked as if people had left because of a plague. Looking in the windows we could see furniture still in place.)

Cape Scott looked very foreboding stuck off a point of land with waves crashing all around and rocks strewn everywhere according to the chart. We deviated way out to successfully miss them. Hurricane force winds have even been reported in the summer at Cape Scott. One way to look at it—next stop, Japan—so the ocean has a long way to work up some mischief.

After Nootka Sound, and almost to the bottom of Vancouver Island's Pacific side, is Barkley Sound, a beautiful group of islands and inlets, with many places to drop the hook and throw in the fishing line.

Our first attempt to go south to Mexico ended shortly after it began. We had waited until late September 1997 in order to celebrate birthdays before leaving Seattle. Winter storms had begun tracking in six weeks earlier than normal. We arrived at Neah Bay on September 29, only to stay put a week while the weather just howled out in the ocean, and we listened to the VHF conversations between the Coast Guard and vessels in distress caught out in it. One sailboat dragged itself back into the harbor with its sails torn to shreds—a pitiful scene, but no one was hurt. However, another boat had a crewmember requiring evacuation to Seattle with a sliced-off fingertip, which needed reattachment.

Finally a weather window allowed us to leave Neah Bay, but passing the Coast Guard station yielded a VHF call requesting information about us and our destination. Perhaps they were making a new list of potential problems. Leaving the Strait of Juan de Fuca and entering the Pacific, sea swells of 10-12 feet on the stern made for a dramatic scene during the night passage. First the boat rises up, the white foam at the crests reflect in the running lights, then the waves swoop the boat forward as it moves on, leaving the pattern to begin again. We had left Neah Bay in company with a sailboat, *ARIEL*, and together we planned to go into the Columbia River—across the notorious bar! They had made the trip several times before and assured us they could lead us very easily through the ordeal, especially since we were aiming to be there at slack tide. Canadian tuna fishermen also left, heading to their fishing grounds.

Somewhere along the Washington coast our engine developed a problem. It made a gasping sound, as if trying to catch its breath. Denis went right to work and changed all the Racor fuel filters. But the problem had not been fixed. The filter on the engine itself also had to be replaced. He had not replaced one on this engine before, and never had at sea—an active sea at that. The Canadian tuna fishermen were also out in the same area and Brian Asp on *OCEAN BARON* discussed the problem over the VHF radio with Denis. Armed with this knowledge, Denis turned off the engine, descended the five steps into the engine room, and started to work. I knelt on the pilothouse floor, watching through the engine room door opening, totally focused on Denis at work, while trying to keep control of my fears. I don't remember hearing the wind or feeling the boat rocking. I must have blocked them out. In fifteen minutes he had changed it out. That might have been the longest fifteen minutes of my life, shallow breathing that is. When I saw him breathe normally, I let out a whoosh too. When he came up into the pilothouse again, everything seemed wrong. We had to check the compass as shore lights were on the wrong side of the boat. Sure enough we had rocked totally around, bouncing up and down without engine power to control our direction. After reporting to the fishermen we were okay, we were off again. And that is exactly why I didn't want to do oceans and nights!

The folks on *ARIEL* had slowed down to wait and by the time we caught up with them, we had arrived at the Columbia River mouth. The whole night had been pitch-black, with no moon in sight. Also waiting for us was a ferro-cement boat, *SPARTACUS*, three young males without experience and without charts on board, wanting to tag along.

The entrance is tricky, so we reviewed our plan. After passing the "CR" offshore buoy, about 5 1/2 miles southwest of the channel, the next marker is Whistle buoy #2, situated between the North Jetty and South Jetty. At that buoy you begin a northeast tack. Between whistle buoys #4 and #6 is the South Jetty—part of it was actually submerged. You need to keep alert and follow the buoy numbers, and at #8, turn right. If you cut between #6 and #10, a possibility of running aground on Clatsop Spit arises. After #12, the channel turns southeast into the Columbia River itself. You are across the bar.

Problems come when large ocean waves break across the spits, or outgoing river currents are encountered. Having engine problems, running out of fuel, or just being inattentive can cause severe problems very quickly. Many vessels have been lost going across the Columbia Bar. It deserves its reputation. The Coast Guard has its training facility there with "roll-over" vessels for heavy weather rescue.

Needless to say we were concerned we did it right, being led or being the leader.

That is indeed what happened. After Buoy 2 the lead boat somehow became disoriented and went out of the channel. They had been shining a searchlight behind them to let us know where they were. Bright lights like that can create problems with night vision, and perhaps that is why they drifted over.

We had no chart plotters, and using paper charts plus radar, tried to locate our bearings. I shone my spotlight out the starboard window searching until I located a marker. When I saw one and confirmed the number, "There's #6!" we cheered before dousing the spotlight. We had crossed the submerged South Jetty, and crept along the channel in the dark in radio contact with the other ships, so they could then follow us.

After #8 we became confused. Apparently we were seeing the range markers on Sand Island, but because we were so worried after messing up, we interpreted the red on one side, green on another, and white higher up as a very large ship coming out of the River straight at us! The heart rate accelerated and the knees knocked until we realized it was not a ship, thankfully.

After passing #12 and the end of Sand Island, the skies were beginning to lighten, a Coast Guard boat cruised past us as we began taking in the flopper stopper poles, and we breathed a very heavy sigh of relief. But before we got to the marina, we had to rescue *SPARTACUS* as they ran out of fuel. We towed them to an abandoned pier. That's the last we saw of them.

We moored at the Port of Astoria Marina with *ARIEL*, *OCEAN BARON*, the Canadian fishing boat that helped us with our engine problem, and many others waiting for better weather to continue on.

Daylight hours were dwindling as we got further into October. As more storms rolled into the area, we decided to abort and try again the next year. At the first window we headed north, stopping overnight at Gray's Harbor. Another fifteen hours put us at the mouth of Juan de Fuca Strait, the turn for Neah Bay and Puget Sound. It was this trip with its pitch-black night and 12-foot waves meeting a 4-knot current at the entrance to Juan de Fuca Strait that I called the scariest of nights at the beginning of my story. That's the night my ship saved me from a potentially bad situation. I knew then and know today this ship can take care of me!

After returning to Puget Sound we took the boat into Canada and left it with Alex in charge, and organized a land trip down to San Diego. Using *Charlie's Charts of the U.S. Pacific Coast*, we checked each and every port along the way. Three marks showed our evaluation for future reference: "Okay—can do," "NO, don't even try," and "Maybe?"

We had a Coast Guard boarding experience on re-entering U.S. waters near the San Juan Islands late March 2008. We saw a large inflatable boat scooting across the water ahead of us and commented it was too early for whale watching. Three men in orange suits rode with the wind. Suddenly they did a U-turn and pulled right up to our port side and said, "We are boarding you." Then we knew it to be the Coast Guard. Two men came on board; one kept circling in the inflatable. The inspectors were very professional, checking all our paperwork, emergency equipment, life jackets, and life raft. One toured the entire boat with Denis. The other one stayed with me in the Pilothouse. At one point I asked the man with me, "Where is the mother ship?" He pointed at the stern, which was in winter mode with all curtains down. Leaving the autopilot in charge of the ship, I quickly dashed to the plastic window and sure enough, a 90-foot cutter trailed close behind, just like he said. We passed the inspection, but I wouldn't let them leave without taking their photo. In Friday Harbor, the next stop for both vessels, they pulled up behind us at the dock after refueling. I had just returned from picking up our mail at the post office. Walking by their bow I looked up and asked if I could take the line. "No ma'am. We have a jumper for that." Then the jumper leaned over and asked, "Is she the one?" Apparently the men inspecting us had reported their experience on returning to the mother ship.

The Wonders of Alaska

In late May 1998 we struck out north from Washington State's San Juan Islands for Alaska—a glorious trip and one worth repeating. The wildlife was fantastic and scenery awesome!

We started up the inside of Vancouver Island, stopping at Montague, Nanaimo, Comox and Campbell River on our way north. After Campbell River, approximately halfway up the island, water coming down from the north meets water coming up from the south. Strong currents result from the water exchange. Rapids, similar to what you would find in a river, develop during maximum tide flow and sometimes reach speeds of ten or twelve knots in the narrow channels between islands and mainland. The water boils and whirlpools develop. Traveling through each rapid should be done at slack water. A book of currents in British Columbia waters gives the timing to make your transit work well.

Once we encountered four rapids in a row at the beginning of Stuart Island, a famous fishing resort. We felt challenged to complete all four at slack water with a boat speed of only 7.5 knots. I remember us calculating the right time to start the trip, feeling good after three rapids, but the fourth one just grabbed our bow and pushed it mightily toward the center of the channel. The feeling of being grabbed and pushed off course by something powerful beneath the surface is awesome. Thankfully the current had just changed. After it gets going, whirlpools develop and really can swing a boat around. When that happens, a large rudder comes in handy to offset the turn, if the boat does not have a lot of speed. There have been cases where huge whirlpools have swallowed boats caught at the wrong time.

We worked our way up the British Columbia coast to Prince Rupert, the last town. From there, Southeast Alaska lay just across Dixon Entrance, which we traversed in good weather after we had sat through some 60-knot winds in Prince Rupert. Inside Alaska proper we followed the hundreds of miles of fjords and inlets, straits and canals up to Juneau and on to Glacier Bay. The bounty of the sea for the taking, and wrapping one's mind around the wonder of the scenery, made for a great beginning to our adventure.

At Petersburg we marveled at the huge tide difference, perhaps as much as 25 feet between high and low water. Tying up at high tide we could see the whole town from the dock; however, in the morning, town and water had disappeared. We looked out at mud and mud banks.

Turning into one inlet along the way north out of Ketchikan in the Misty Fjord National Monument area, we watched a bald eagle struggling in the water while heading for land. Its wings, beating hard, never seemed to get out of the water. We thought surely it would drown, but it struggled on. While watching the drama we felt as if we were in a National Geographic special, convinced the eagle was in dire trouble, and we could do nothing to help. Soon it hopped onto a rock near shore and its talons held a huge salmon. That's why it could not swim or fly!

And once, while Denis fished, he caught red snapper too small to keep. He released them, but before the fish could submerge beneath the surface, an eagle swooped from a tall tree nearby and whisked it away—twice. Following that, a mother whale swam by to show off her baby. They swam so close and so synchronized—just magical to watch. Before they were out of sight a seal popped up near the stern and looked quizzical, as if saying, *Que pasa?*" And all this happened in one bay in a short period of time.

On the way to Juneau we wandered through channels around islands. Radar showed something that looked like a city block approaching around a bend. Only when we could see it with our own eyes did we recognize that city block as a cruise ship. Fascinating stuff!

We traveled all the way up Tracy Arm to anchor in nine fathoms below Sawyer Glacier with Bill and Leslie from *SIMITAR*, where we scooped up some ice from the sound for our drinks. This spectacular location provided a place to watch bergs calving, plus large and small pieces of ice floating by on their way to somewhere, while just enjoying the scenery.

In Juneau for Denis' sixty-first birthday we took a seaplane flight over the glaciers. The pilot lived on the island next to ours in the San Juans when he was not in Alaska flying tourists around. He allowed Denis to open his window in the front to shoot pictures better. In my back seat, the cold air just whistled around me, but the flight was unforgettable, especially when he came up close to the ridge between two peaks and dropped back down over the snowfield.

Doug Thompson from Alamos, Mexico joined us for eight days in Alaska to see Glacier Bay National Park and meet his son in Elfin Cove. We called Doug our "whistler." He whistled almost all the time, not when he was nervous, but when he felt happy. The weather proved perfect to take out the lawn chairs onto the upper deck to the salon and steer using the remote control, grooving on the fantastic scenery.

We had a permit from the Park Service to spend five days in Glacier Bay National Park north of Juneau. Humpback whales abound there. All boats had to stay a certain distance from them, yet once while Denis fished from the dinghy about a half-mile around the corner from the mother ship, one whale found him, leaping out of the water very close by. That prompted Denis to crank up the engine and head back, fishing finished or not. These are huge creatures and you do not want to encounter one so close he dumps you out of your boat.

One morning we spotted a grizzly bear on shore with not one, not two, but three very cute, very active cubs in tow. I picked up the mike and radioed the Ranger to report my sighting. He laughed and said, "So, she still has all three of them. Thanks for calling." I will also remember that place as one where we had huge success crabbing for our dinners.

The mountains ringing the west side of Glacier Bay grow straight out of the water and rise thousands of feet in the air. It makes one feel very small to just look up and up to find the top of the snow-covered peaks. We were very fortunate to have super bright-blue sunny weather. Everything just sparkled! We understand how taken John Muir was with his experiences there. And realized how much one missed if their only time to visit occurred during rainy, cloudy weather.

Those icebergs not only looked cold, but the air coming off them confirmed that feeling. Right in front of a very large glacier, one that cruise ships take their clientele to for photo shots, Denis left me in the mother ship and went to take his photos from the dinghy. While he did that, I listened to the thunder behind me as the giant iceberg calved. I anticipated a tidal wave to swamp me, but it did not happen. I confess. I am a worrier. As we traveled around Glacier Park, we daily passed pieces of small bergs in the water resembling works of art—carvings of ice accented by blue within the ice itself. Once we even saw a bald eagle perched on top of a small iceberg observing his kingdom, perhaps looking for a snack, but posing grandly.

In front of Margerie Glacier

We knew what we saw was only part of the picture. More ice lay below the surface than we saw above. This phenomenon manifested itself at Reid Inlet anchorage. We had anchored maybe 500-feet from the toe of the relatively small glacier, and during the night I heard a strange moaning sound from the stern. We sleep in the aft cabin, so this moan came from just outside my window. Was there a ghost? The dinghy had been tied crossways to the boat and its outboard motor tipped up. The moan sounded to me like someone calling for help. I woke Denis and said, "The dinghy is in trouble." We both went to check. A calved berg had caught on the motor, putting pressure on the dinghy and subsequently the big boat. It took a longboat hook and much maneuvering to get the ice loose. It then floated off to look for more opportunity to cause trouble. In the morning we took the dinghy to shore. Walking around on the exposed part of a glacier is spooky. Knowing where I was made me feel unstable. Could I get back to my dinghy if something changed?

At another time we took the 14-foot aluminum dinghy on a jaunt to see another glacier, weaving through pieces of icebergs ranging from the size of an ice cube to a small house along the way. The sound that smaller chunks of ice made on the bottom of the dinghy when we passed over them sounded disconcerting—Clunk! Rattle! Bang!

After Glacier Bay National Park we went to Sitka, Alaska, a place with people, yet still a wild place. On the 5th of July we sat in a restaurant looking out the window at the dreary rain. I called the young fair-haired waitress over. "This is July. Look at that weather. What is it like in February?" She put on her special smile and answered, "I don't know. I'm from San Diego," and danced away.

Taking a shortcut through the islands back to the bottom of Chichagof Island, we went through El Capitan Passage (aka Dry Passage), an interesting channel, with a low tide and many rocks in the clear water appearing to be just below the boat. The rocks were deeper than originally thought, but it sure looked scary. Rocks are one of those hazards to navigation, and any mistake can be a fatal one regarding your boat. Concentration and attention were definitely required to make a safe passage.

On our way back to the U.S., we made a side trip out to the Queen Charlotte Islands, ancestral home to the Haida Indians, with their long houses and huge distinctive totems. Most of the totems (made of cedar) were falling down, or had fallen and in stages of decomposing. On touring one of the long houses, we learned the doors were low and small for a special reason—security. Persons entering had to bend low to pass through, exposing necks and heads for large clubs to come crashing down on them should they be not friendly or uninvited. I found this phenomenon carried out in other cultures as well—in forts of Pakistan and ancient pueblo communities like Chaco Canyon, New Mexico.

We had many days of fog, sometimes too thick to see much. Visiting totems at a place near the southern tip of Gwaii Haanas National Park Reserve, we had difficulty locating our boat when coming back in the dinghy. We began our return trip to Vancouver Island via Queen Charlotte Straits in the middle of the night in order to arrive before dark back at the tip of Vancouver Island and protected waters. Hundreds of dolphin joined us for part of our journey south, jumping and showing off for us as we passed.

A beautiful sight and a fitting farewell for our trip north!

Back in the U. S., we organized to make a second attempt at going south.

The Stormy Pacific and a Stowaway

Leaving the Puget Sound area in August 1998 worked better weather-wise going down the Washington and Oregon coasts. Even though it remained fresh in my mind from the aborted trip how rowdy that coast can get, we had an easier ride. Maybe I could say I had more sea miles under my belt as well, so could handle more this time.

Alex had joined us in Port Angeles, Washington, and Bob in Brookings, Oregon. We had a full complement of four, knew the ship, and had experienced that coast before, so felt confident. Then, lo and behold, the ocean started to act up once again.

We had planned to make a run from Brookings to Eureka, California. But by the time we got close to Eureka, things happened. We had called Eureka Coast Guard over the VHF to ask about coming into port to get out of the weather. The man on duty asked us if we had crossed their bar before. Answer: "No." Their reply indicated very significant waves were crossing the bar at that time, and with no experience we should not venture near the breakwater. We read into those comments, "Keep going."

Winds were constant at 25-30 knots, with gusts in the high 30s (gale force) during that dark night. Between Cape Mendocino and Point Arena in northern California, we estimated the swells to be between 12 and 15 feet, with wind waves on top of that. They all seemed to come from several directions at one time. After Point Arena (near Ft. Bragg) the wind still blew 30 knots or more, seas were big, but the waves were not so confused. *TEKA III* rode well, her autopilot holding the course without any problem. But it sure felt scary to be on the top of a wave as it crested, then whooshed you forward as if on a surfboard. After 35 ½ hours we tied up at Bodega Bay's municipal dock, ready to take a break.

We did well, but a sailing vessel ahead of us by a few hours, did not. They had taken water through a porthole and lost, or were losing their VHF radio capability. We overheard their transmission advising Eureka Coast Guard that they were out there and okay, but unable to radio for assistance if they needed it later. The Coast Guard asked them to make contact again in another hour. They said, "We don't think we can." The Coast Guard did call them in an hour, and in another hour, but no answer. We kept one eye out for them along the way, and did find them in Bodega Bay, safe and sound, but ready to sell the boat. They were experienced sailors, having circumnavigated the Pacific ten years before—yet this experience had soured them on cruising.

Our trip on down to San Diego went well. We spent time at Knight & Carver, builders of *TEKA III*, where they added a bulbous bow for better fuel performance. In real life it did not work as predicted, even causing loss of speed, and the bow pounded in head seas. In Spain we removed the bulbous bow—it was a costly mistake. Without the bulbous bow we regained our Coast Guard cutter appearance versus a container ship "wanna-be." It created a lot of attention, though, with people at marinas, both land and sea folks. *PassageMaker Magazine's* editor at that time, Bill Parlatore, had said he would take my picture posed on the bulbous in clear water with a glass of white wine for the magazine. When Denis decided to have it removed, I sulked. There went my chance to be a cover girl!

Susan and Paul Hosticka, from *ARIEL,* joined us in San Francisco when Bob and Alex departed. Joe Hachenberg, who had wanted first-hand experience on the San Diego to Cabo San Lucas run before he took his boat on such a trip, joined the two Hostickas for the trip down the Baja Pacific coast. Below Ensenada, the waters around Cedros Island showed us just how nasty they could get. There's wind blowing off the land, currents sweeping around the northern tip, and waves piling up for a ride similar to being in a washing machine. We found that out up close and personal. Those three were in the pilothouse with Denis, watching the action. I chose to drop down into the salon area and play cards to keep my mind off the bouncing around. Joe came down to see how I was doing. As he sat down, I looked up at him and saw a wave of green water climbing up near the windows outside. Whoa! I grabbed his arm so hard that my fingernail marks are probably still in his skin long after he left us at Cabo.

That wave also created havoc as it came on board. With the pilothouse door shut, no one could see that the boat tipped enough that the back sliding door to the aft cabin flew open, the wave charged down the stairs and ended up on Denis' bed. What an event! We attempted to dry the mattress out on the bow after we anchored, but the wind tried to blow it away. And from then on, we put the pin in the sliding door to avoid such problems again.

We met Clark and Joan Scarboro on one of the Sea of Cortez beaches the winter before. Learning they were boaters, and from the Northwest, we asked them if they wanted to be considered for crew some time. They did and flew into Loreto for the passage across the Sea of Cortez from the Baja to the Mexico mainland. Later when we met their grown daughter back in Washington, she said she scolded her parents for going off with people she just met on the beach. After all, the parents preached to her against such undertakings. We all got a good chuckle out of that. They joined us for other passages in the Mediterranean, and even got written up in a *PassageMaker Magazine* article about one of them.

Isla San Francisco in Baja

On the island of Isla Isabella between Baja and the Mexican mainland, we did enjoy the blue footed booby birds, on land where they were nesting and in the air, where they often hitched rides on the flopper stopper lines as they continued to fish at sea. On the beach at Isla Isabella local fisherman were cutting up sharks for their fins. It seems a terrible waste to such a magnificent fish.

Joan will never forget one event we shared on a night watch together. The pitch-black night suddenly erupted with a bright orange light ahead of us. Nothing showed on the radar, but my thoughts focused on a possible fishing boat with nets all around throwing all their lights on to warn me off. I sent Joan outside with the night binoculars to check things out. She came right back inside the pilothouse and said, "I can't see anything." We had forgotten to take off the lens caps. But before we could try another look outside with the glasses, the spectacular full moon burst out of the sea ahead of us. A great sigh of relief came from within the pilothouse. I had almost decided to wake Denis and report "a situation," but hesitated. He told me in the morning I made a good decision. However, in relating this story to another watch-mate, Joan Brair, a couple of years later, she started to smile at the beginning of the story. It had also happened to her, yet she had awakened her husband, John, and felt foolish at the non-emergency.

Our experiences in Mexico focused on all those check-ins and checkouts with port authorities along the way. To check-in included a visit with Ship's Documents, Crew List, and all Passports to the Immigration Office, Customs, Harbormaster and the Bank. At the bank we stood in line to pay the fee, get a receipt, and then return to the authorities to finish the paperwork. All this process could take a lot of time, and walking back and forth. It felt like too much bureaucracy, but we could do nothing but play the game and smile. The procedure repeated itself when checking out, which gave us a "Zarpe" (exit paper to show the next port). It made us want to stay on the boat and not get to see what each place had to offer on land—just drop the hook, rest overnight and start out again in the morning.

I remember anchoring at a small bay just south of Zihuatanejo, Punta Papanao, and watching a group of armed military men on the beach pile into a panga (small open boat) and start in our direction. The officer in charge came on board, carrying his clipboard with questions he needed to ask. Only one other man came too, his gun at a ready position. All of the others stayed in the panga, holding carbines and bailing the leaky panga as needed. The officer asked his questions listed on the clipboard in English; we responded in Spanish. We all laughed at that—except Chris, who grabbed my shirt and whispered in my ear, "Mary, they have guns!" I said, "Chris, smile!" Chris and Joe Thorn, friends from England with Mediterranean sailing as their background, had joined us in Puerto Vallarta for the trip down to Puntarenas, Costa Rica. This was the first of her scary experiences with us.

I did not feel fear at this encounter. It seemed to be a water version of the roadblocks we had to deal with while RV traveling through Baja. In those situations young guys erupted from sandbags alongside the highway waving for us to stop, asked questions about where we had come from and where we were going, looked inside the trailer and then let us go. I did not feel a threat then. Nor did I feel it in this boat boarding. On neither occasion did anyone point a gun directly at me. Maybe that's why I felt okay about everything that unfolded. They were doing their job and my job was to cooperate.

On one of my night watches, a boat showed up on radar at a waypoint where I intended to change course. What kind of boat? Was he fishing? Or just resting? Were huge nets out? It was too dark to tell. His boat did not move as I approached, so I lifted the radio mike. "Calling the ship at the position of latitude___ and longitude___, this is *TEKA III*. He answered, "This is Naval Mexicana" (Mexican Navy). With my poor Spanish and his little bit of English we managed to make our verbal encounter a meaningful event. Denis, off duty and asleep at the time, seemed to think the naval man might have been bored and enjoyed talking to a lady in the night. Anyway he allowed me to pass and offered assistance if I should need it later.

One other experience needs to be reported on events of the Baja Peninsula that trip. As we approached the narrow entrance to Puerto Escondido, a hurricane hole on the Sea of Cortez side, an inflatable dinghy came roaring toward us, making circles around our boat in his excitement, as we maneuvered into the bay. I called to him from our bow and asked him to let us anchor and then he could tell me his news. His name: Ralph Cadman, a retired sign painter from San Diego. He had painted the name on our boat before launching in San Diego seventeen years ago. I asked him to come on board and sign the Guest Register. In addition to that unusual encounter, Chuck Saunders saw us in Acapulco and proudly proclaimed he had taken *TEKA*'s photo for a magazine cover when she was first launched. It is truly a small world!

On the Pacific Coast in southern Mexico and Central America, there are two notorious areas for bad weather at sea: "Tehuantepec," and "Papagayo." I tried to explain both of these problems to Chris and Joe Thorn when they came on board in Puerto Vallarta. I promised them if we knew it would not be safe to do that particular passage, we would not go. I do believe in the "Go," "Stay," or "Deal with it" choices as I mentioned before. And I wanted them to be involved in the decision process.

On a map Mexico's Pacific coast curves eastward near its border with Guatemala. The skinniest part is the dangerous part. Winds generated by a high pressure system in the Gulf of Mexico and Texas zoom through the mountain passage to the Pacific Ocean toward a low pressure system. These winds create a venturi effect, making the velocity of the wind about twice what it started out to be as they charge out into the Pacific at this point. Port Captains at each end of that stretch of land have the authority to close their ports and make boats, commercial or private, stay put. On the other hand, if things look good, they can give a go-ahead. That's what happened to us.[*]

At Huatulco, Mexico on 11 February 1999, Joe and Chris began their second and most scary time on the boat. They had been checking weather updates with the Port Captain about that area. We decided to go based on the written report received from New Orleans weather advisory, and the Port Captain's verbal okay. The 4:30 P.M. Mexican weather report predicted

---

[*]   Adapted from Mary Umstot's article: "The Tehuantepecker," *PassageMaker Magazine*, Winter 1999, pp. 76-79.

northerly winds of 10-15 knots, and all ports open along the coast. His advice: "Go!" That meant we left about 9 P.M. from Huatulco and arrived at Salina Cruz near first light. Wind and chop were not too bad, so we kept going. Many shrimp boats were coming into port at Salina Cruz and maybe we should have followed them into port, despite the unfriendliness of that port to private yachts.

Winds increased to 40, 50, and gusted to 60 knots. Our wind meter only registers to 60 knots. It may have been higher. One of the sayings about traversing this area is to "stay close to shore where you can hear the dogs bark." That was our plan. Less than a quarter mile off the beach the depth registered between 30 and 36 feet. Winds closer to shore were an issue, but nothing like what could happen several miles offshore as the wind blew non-stop, building waves after waves. Vessels further out to sea had to deal with those humongous waves ready to produce havoc. Our friend, Hugo Carver, told us he spent one particular trip on a Merchant Marine vessel—a good-sized one—with waves coming over the side of his ship.

For us the wind blew the dirt off the beach so hard that the whole port side of the boat, including the mast, was caked with several layers needing to be cleaned off later, which took many days and much elbow grease. The boat listed starboard ten degrees, feeling as if some giant held his hand against the boat trying to push it over. The flopper stoppers did a great job. In-between blasts of sand we marveled at the waves near shore, cresting but not crashing—the high wind effectively blowing them back out to sea in a geyser-like action— fascinating to watch.

Two lagoons opened up into the sea and we had to go out around each opening before returning to the relative safety of the beach. Joe and Chris were worried when we had to do that exercise. Their sailboat would not have the power necessary for the job, but *TEKA III*, weighing 40+ tons, with a huge propeller and enough engine power, did fine. Waves and spray gave the impression of a hurricane on those trips out and back. Luckily there were only two lagoons. After the second one we encountered many Mexican shrimp boats anchored right in our way, those whose captains had decided to wait and not go for port. On the radar they looked like measles. As we passed through the armada, a male voice over the radio said, "Viento muy fuente (winds very strong)!" After thirty-nine hours of adventure, we pulled into the entrance to Puerto Madero, the last port in Mexico, exhausted and exhilarated by the event—we had experienced a real "Tehuantepecker." Now that weather window CLOSED! And we never heard the dogs bark.

Joe later confronted me about taking them on such a dangerous trip. I reflected back to my original discussion advising them what could come up, and when they returned to England Joe had his story published in a nautical magazine. I believe the two of them are the only people in the United Kingdom who had such a story to tell.

TEKA III's logbook described four earlier crossings with the previous owner. Only one provided the excitement of gale winds—35 knots. We had set a new record for our ship.

After Mexico we avoided Nicaragua totally, due to patrolling gunships along the coast, and made a sixty-hour nonstop trip to Costa Rica, without meeting a "Papagayo." Papagayo winds are caused by Caribbean trade winds rising over the mountains of Nicaragua and Costa Rica creating nasty sea conditions on the Pacific side. We were lucky. One weather experience felt like more than enough!

Joe and Chris left us in Puntarenas, Costa Rica; Alex and Joanne Gray joined us again. Outside the San Jose Airport Joanne stepped in a hole and badly sprained her foot. An orthopedist checking into their hotel at the same time took a look at it and gave his opinion, with instructions for elevation and ice. Alex called us on the boat and said he had good news (they were there) and bad news (the foot problem). The next day they rode a bus two hours to Puntarenas where we were anchored in the fast-flowing river. With her arms stretched over Alex and Denis' shoulders, she hobbled down the rickety dock, into the dinghy, and on out to the boat—a feat in itself. By the time we got down to Golfito, the last port in Costa Rica, she needed someone to take a look at the problem. We had to clear out of the country there anyway, so arranged for an agent to do the paperwork, plus find us a doctor. He made several "house calls" and prescribed medicine for only $40. He made us all laugh when he said goodbye. "You are very old. No running." He, of course, was maybe 30, Joanne was 60.

There, in Golfito, we became aware that a stranger had moved aboard.[*] While tied up at a poor excuse for a pier, the four-legged stowaway must have snuck aboard, climbing up the shore lines onto the boat—an easy feat. On leaving port the next day we noticed some critter droppings in the pilothouse, and they were larger than those of a mouse. Alex claimed he heard rustling on the kitchen counter during the night. Grabbing a flashlight and beaming it in that direction netted nothing, yet the next morning, behind the bread, glaring evidence of bread-munching stood out. Crumbs were everywhere. Denis also noticed one of his fish gloves on the aft deck had been chewed on too. It was time for traps. Three were prepared—cheese in one and peanut butter in the other two.

---

[*] Adapted from my article, "Rat on-board," in *PassageMaker Magazine,* Jan/Feb 2002, pp 84-87

Next morning, peanut butter not touched; cheese stolen, but trap not sprung; and a larger hole found in the fishing glove. Night two of traps: cheese in one, fish in a rattrap and in a mousetrap. He (we assumed it to be a "he" and named him "Pedro") ate the fish in the big trap but did not spring it. Mousetrap still had bait, but had been sprung. No critter either, yet more and more droppings. We discovered two holes chewed in the teak flooring on the aft deck. During the night he came inside the pilothouse through an open vent and made a dent in a bunch of bananas on the counter. The traps now had cheese in one, a cotton ball soaked in fish sauce in another and peanut butter in the third, all placed on the path we were sure he used to go back and forth to the aft lazarette (a storage cabinet on the back deck), his home. He ignored those and found the garbage bag stowed in the bow, chewing into it to locate an apple.

Day 5 we declared war! A large trap sat waiting at one of the scuppers on the aft deck. Weather doors were closed as well as pilothouse door. Joanne and I stayed in the pilothouse to cheer on our warriors. Denis had a stick and Alex a broom handle in ready. They took off the top to the lazarette and slowly began removing items—small propane tanks, buckets, crab cooking pot etc. Alex looked like a samurai with his bandana and flip-flops. They jabbed and stabbed at the elusive animal as he darted around inside the lazarette (about 4 ft long, 18 inches high and 18 inches deep). Suddenly Denis shouted, "There he is!" then jumped high out of the way as the rat leaped into the fray and expertly dodged their weapons. He raced toward the scupper, getting his tail caught by the trap, and then took a swan dive off the boat. Knowing rats can swim, Alex and I ran to the bow to make sure he did not begin to climb up the anchor line and re-board. Denis shouted again, "There he's surfaced back here by the swim platform." There a lone pelican sat looking dumbfounded.

In only a short period of time the wind and waves carried Pedro away, his nose stuck above water and his hind feet swimming as best they could. I don't know how he got loose from the trap but it stayed on board. He must have just skirted it as he passed. Wounded he may have made a good meal for a predator, or he could have been lucky and made it to safety. We will never know. It is amusing to think he found another ride and perhaps did make it all the way to the Marquesas (islands in the South Pacific).

Then we were on into Panama. The first afternoon as we were approaching an anchoring area, a small local boat came out from the village with two men on board. They had caught fish and wanted to sell us some of their catch. We had also caught fish, so declined. Then they asked if we needed anything else, gesturing at the jungle on shore. "Limons, coconuts …" "Sure." we said, and before we could confirm just what we did want, they took off in their small craft. Soon we heard the sound of machetes cracking and whacking on shore. They returned laden down. We had two whole bunches of bananas, all to ripen at the same time, a dozen limes, some papayas and avocados, and three coconuts. It was like having a jungle Safeway Store. Everything was very fresh. We gave them some money and everybody won!

Our Panama guidebook told us about a German couple who had arrived there in a steel boat, anchored, moved on shore, and made a home some time ago. Denis and Alex paid them a visit, found their rusting boat lying on its side, no longer usable, and the two of them happily living a "Robinson Crusoe" life in the Perlas Islands just south of the Panama Canal. With plenty of fruits, vegetables, and fish available, they survived quite nicely. Rum seemed to be their only request from visitors.

The "Big Ditch" and Beyond

March 1999: Reuben, our Panama Canal advisor, boarded, shook hands with Denis and me first, acknowledged the crew, Alex, Joanne, Sam and Lisa, and then pointed at a container ship approaching our port side.

"Follow him," he said.

So we untied from the Balboa Yacht Club buoy we had swung from for nine days, and pulled in behind him. Many ships go through the Canal daily, while others wait their turn either on the Balboa (Pacific) side or Colon (Atlantic) side, taking on water and fuel and supplies. Commercial and military vessels are given priority over pleasure craft, so we had to be scheduled in between the big guys. Joanne and I spent time waving at the ships as they passed us less than a hundred yards away. All of us studied the chart of country flags to learn which countries were represented in the daily parade. And all the time the harbor pilot boats running back and forth to the waiting ships created wakes to keep us rocking at the buoy.

Pleasure craft are required to have an advisor on board for the transit. Reuben stayed with us all day, leaving at Colon at the end of a long day.

Passing under the Bridge of the Americas meant we were on our way through this historical waterway, the Panama Canal, or "The Big Ditch." We had paid $750 for this trip, plus another $750 damage deposit, redeemable after a successful transit. We were all excited. Sam, a local Panamanian with transit experience joined Lisa, a backpacker with no experience. That left Alex and me to round out the four line-handlers required by the Canal authorities for the trip. Joanne watched from her special place on the aft deck, still nursing her hurt foot.

Inside the first lock, Miraflores, two tugs positioned the container ship at the front of the lock, and then tied themselves to the wall behind it. We were instructed to raft up to the second tug. Rafting to a tug, which we requested, is only one way for pleasure craft to go through. Another is to go alone, positioned center chamber, with two lines from the bow and two from the stern attached to the wall, and adjusted as the chamber fills or drains. We transited center-chamber on our return trip in January 2007, as no tugs were available.

Thousands of gallons water flow in or drain out at a remarkable rate, both from the floor and wall sides as the chamber rises or falls. Boats have to travel through three chambers going up 85 feet to Gatun Lake, travel 15 miles across the lake, before dropping down via three more chambers 85 feet to the Atlantic (Caribbean) side. Turbulence creates a challenging job for line handlers, letting out or bringing in lines to keep the boat straight in the chamber. For our first experience, the tug we nestled to took most of that pressure.

In Miraflores and Pedro Miguel locks, we did a good job getting our lines across to the tug. Denis stayed in the pilothouse and kept the boat going. Reuben stayed with Denis to advise of future moves, as he kept in radio contact with each lockmaster. After the gates were opened in front of the container ship, and its huge propellers started churning, "prop wash" added to the turbulence already in the chamber. We knew it would happen and watched the water swirl around inside the lock as the ship started forward. At the appropriate time we untied from the tug and repositioned behind it.

When Reuben talked to the lockmaster on the other side of Gatun Lake, he learned if we kept up a speed of 8 knots crossing the lake, we could make the locks going down the same day. Otherwise it meant spending the night on the lake. They were to hold the cruise ship so we could get in front of it.

Crossing the lake we all ate heartily of lunchmeat sandwiches, chips, cookies and pop. While munching we watched the surroundings pass—trees, swampy water, plus a wildlife research station off to one side. On this trip there were no monkeys or alligators. They showed up on the return transit.

At the next to last lock we made a mistake and ended up with damage to our boat. Reuben had recommended coasting up to the tug. The wind caught us and we couldn't correct. Our boat turned sideways in the lock as the stern line missed on its toss to the tug, and the tug boat's crew tied the bow line too tight. We rammed the tug. Needless to say the tug stood firm. We cracked our teak cap rail. Embarrassed, we had to report it to the Port Captain on Colon side: our friend, Doug Finley. We had met him in Monterey, California on our maiden voyage to the Pacific Northwest two years prior! He and Rueben spoke over the VHF at that lock and Doug said he would meet us after we had finished transiting.

In the meantime we had the cruise ship to experience. We were first in the lock and it followed and followed. People stationed way up on the ship's bow stood waving and filming as the ship crept up on us. At first we could see them, and then we couldn't, only seeing the white very large, very impressive bow right behind us! Holy Smokes! The cruise ship had been under control of what are called "donkeys" (locomotives that pull the ships through the lock) and we hoped their brakes worked really well. No problem.

Entering Colon Harbor, Doug came out in the Harbor Pilot Boat. As he set foot on board I exclaimed, "Doug, you should have seen it!" He said, "I did!" Cameras in each chamber video all activity and he had seen the whole thing. We chose not to make a claim. Since we did not damage the canal we were entitled to our damage deposit refund and received it a couple of months later.

In Colon Denis and Alex had to do the checkout paperwork, and found the town very inhospitable, even dangerous-looking. The people hanging around on the streets looked predatory, and given the opportunity might cause trouble. Denis and Alex did their business in a quick and orderly fashion, and returned to the boat.

From Colon to the San Blas Islands, our next stop, would take more than one day. We chose to drop the hook in Portobello, a famous place for two reasons: pirating, and a way station for getting goods from the Pacific to the Caribbean overland before the Canal. Three forts stood guard. One still remains for visitors to meander through and pretend the pirates were coming to steal the gold shipment that just arrived. Portobello means "beautiful harbor" and it certainly had the characteristics.

The San Blas Islands, along the eastern side of Panama between the Canal and the Columbian border, are a cluster of coral-ringed atolls. It is amazing to see a place still pristine and beautiful without a Club Med, high rises, or cruise ships coming in to drop off their passengers to shop and tour. Kuna Indians independently rule their beautiful untouched sandy islands, harvest their family-owned coconuts, fish from the surrounding waters, and sell their special "molas" to cruisers.

Kuna Indians offering their molas for sale

Molas are exquisitely embroidered pieces of artwork. These 18" x 18" pieces are designed to be framed for pictures, made into pillows, or attached to blouses as decoration. The women hand-stitch these very colorful molas, representing animals and scenes in their environment—lobsters, crabs, turtles and birds—all done without a pattern. As soon as you anchored, dugout canoes approach from the nearby village, paddled by a man, with at least one woman, maybe two in the canoe. They stopped at your boat, grabbed their large buckets filled with folded molas, and climbed on board. Once they find a spot to show their wares, the molas were opened up carefully, and lovingly shown to you for inspection and purchase. With so many to choose from, the decision sometimes took a long time. If there were two ladies with items to sell, one waited patiently for the other to put things away and then make her mola presentation. We purchased several from these pleasant unassuming ladies, and made throw pillows for the boat, plus pillows for the grandchildren as well.

If we chose not to buy, they did not get upset; just packed up and left. Most did not speak English, but we understood what they wanted. A sign they were doing well became obvious when the man bringing them out to our boat ran an outboard engine instead of paddling.

We had heard one of the persons selling was actually a male, but his features were so soft and feminine looking, he passed easily as the other gender. His voice also sounded as melodic as a woman's. With that reputation, plus the fact he did excellent work embroidering his molas, most cruisers bought something from him.

Going to shore to walk around the village gave us insight as to how they lived. The children were polite, the place had no litter, and there was no smell. We found the latrine to be an outhouse covered with palm branches stuck out over the water. A plank allowed access to it and the tide took the remains of a visit out to sea.

Cruisers anchored in protected lagoons, having entered between coral openings, and then marveling at the clear water and sandy bottom. Anchored in ChiChiMe one afternoon, a fast dinghy came around the corner. Who should be arriving, but Lonnie and Mark Philbrick, friends from *HALE KAI* that we had not seen since leaving Port Angeles in 1997, our aborted trip! There is one special anchorage that cruisers call the "swimming pool," due to its clear water. Not far from another anchorage people washed clothes and their hair in a fresh water inlet.

Local sailing boats in the San Blas Islands

Some cruisers first just came to see, and then stayed a long time in those idyllic conditions. If they needed to re-provision supplies, they made a trip to the one small island with an airport. Daily runs to Panama City, a short hop away, did the trick. Alex and Joanne flew back to Canada from the San Blas via Panama City.

We continued on, but had a rough passage up to San Andres and Providencia, islands off the coast of Nicaragua that actually belonged to Columbia. Up until that time we had other people with us to help with night passages. This time we did it with only ourselves, and made adjustments to on and off duty segments as necessary, to keep going and still feel okay. When you are tired, you can make mistakes. At first I asked Denis to sleep in the pilothouse when I had the watch. He tried but couldn't rest well enough. Another approach to being close to me and yet able to stretch out and relax, he chose to sleep in the salon. That worked much better. A funny thing happened on this segment—flying fish committed suicide on the boat during night passages, maybe attracted by the running lights on the boat. In the morning (after my 3-6 shift), we counted 14 dead on the port deck. Too bad they were not edible.

For this ride we expected moderate trade winds coming in from the East, which turned out to be quite strong. Therefore, six foot waves actually showed up as twelve foot ones, right on the beam and quite uncomfortable. We were in touch by radio with *HALE KAI* during the night, and that made us feel not so alone. As you can see, my nights and oceans are mounting up.

During the first night we spent anchored inside Providencia's reef, the anchor dragged, having grabbed more grass than sand, losing its grip on the bottom. We slept right through it. That is, until we heard a loud clunk and bounced out of bed to see our starboard flopper stopper pole had connected with sailboat rigging—the last sailboat in the anchorage. Next stop: the reef! They heard it too and we met outside to see what the noise indicated. After a quick hustle, we re-anchored in a better spot. No damage had been done to the sailboat when we checked in the morning. From that experience we decided to purchase another Garmin GPS and position it in the aft cabin where we sleep, for anchor alarm and peace of mind. We can set it to alert us if the boat moves past a certain point from the anchored position. No problems since.

After we rounded the tip of Honduras and started a down-wind run toward Guanaja, one of the islands belonging to Honduras, the wind and waves changed to come from the stern, a much better ride.

Hurricane Mitch had prowled through the Caribbean only four months before we arrived off the coast of mainland Honduras. Guanaja Island suffered extensive damage as Mitch stalled and churned overhead for several days the previous December, knocking down or searing off trees and creating surges to overwhelm the houses along the low lying beach area. The hills beyond the village looked like a giant foot had lifted up and stomped very hard, beating the foliage off the trees as it bent them down and over. A desolate scene to say the least! Beachfront looked to be one block behind where it used to be. The people we saw seemed happy enough. Living through such a storm would give cause for celebration.

At Roatan, another Honduran island, we took passage on a ferry to the mainland and rented a vehicle with Mark and Lonnie Philbrick from *HALE*

KAI to explore the ancient Mayan city of Copan. A statue to Eighteen Rabbit, one of the Mayan Kings, stood in the middle of the main excavated area. Our guidebook had explained how to count using their hieroglyphics. Sure enough, eighteen showed up on the granite post, which matched the book's photo of the ruler, "Eighteen Rabbit." A game playing area, about the size of a soccer field, with multi-layer spectator stands, had been excavated. Our guide, a self-proclaimed Indiana Jones, (complete with a live small lizard—attached to his ear lobe as an earring), gave his description of the game played on that field, as we imagined the people seated in the stadium. Royalty had special seats. Commoners sat elsewhere. Indiana said the game was played with a very large, heavy ball kept in play by hitting it back and forth with the hips, shoulders and knees (hands, feet and heads were not allowed, nor were sticks or bats, to move the ball). Tournaments continued on and on, eliminating one contender after another until the final champion emerged, who was happily taken and ceremoniously sacrificed. In other words, the winner lost!

The U.S. Corps of Engineers were busy along the main roads rebuilding bridges to replace those lost in the massive landslides from the hurricane's rain. We saw kids swimming in the rivers, as well as women washing clothes on rocks, and men giving their cars a bath. After that trip we returned to the boat, checked out of Honduras, and crossed over to the Rio Dulce in Guatemala for a trip up that famous river.

Hurricane Mitch had left its mark there as well. All channel markers were gone and with a shallow bar to cross, we had to tiptoe across it, taking soundings carefully based on a latitude/longitude position we had in our material. There was not too much extra water to spare, but we did not go aground. People in Livingston, the town at the mouth of the Rio Dulce made extra money by going out to rescue folks stranded on the bar, so maybe putting up the markers again may not be a desired activity. We found a marina up the river for the boat to stay in while we traveled; I made a quick visit to the States to see Dawn and family; Denis hit the highlands of Guatemala—Atitlan, Chichicastenango and Antigua—to cool off. Temperatures along the river were a stifling, muggy 95-plus degrees.

We blew through Belize, anchoring at two atolls, which we deemed not as pretty as San Blas. The Blue Hole, made famous by Jacques Cousteau, did not keep us as we are not divers. We moved on to Isla Mujeres, Mexico, where marina personnel arranged for all the officials to visit the boat, so we could easily report into Mexico without traipsing all over town to the different offices. No problem with that arrangement, with the exception of the female Agricultural Inspector. She did not inspect any food that I recall, but asked for a $20 (U.S.) tip. Denis said he would pay her, but he requested a receipt. She jumped up from her seat in the pilothouse, said firmly, "Adios

Senor," found her very high heels she had left at the door, and stomped off the boat. Guess she did not have her receipt book with her. That is the only place to date we suspected a bribe by an official.

From the Yucatan peninsula where Isla Mujeres is located, we started home to Florida with Dave and Donna Ropp on board, skirting the north coast of Cuba on the way. We arrived in the dark at Dry Tortugas in the Florida Keys, toured the famous fort the next day, and then worked our way up to St. Petersburg.

Bob Hermann rejoined us for the ICW—Intra Coastal Waterway, west and east sections. Moving across southern Florida to the East Coast via the Okeechobee Waterway, we had to go through only one lock. What a mouth dropper when the gates opened and a lone manatee (no boats) started swimming toward us. If he had to wait for the gates, what other critters did it happen to as well?

As we anchored one night in a side channel, alligators came over to investigate us, their round eyes peering above the water as they cruised close to the boat. No swimming here. In Lake Okeechobee, we stayed in the well-marked channel to avoid going aground. The depth was only eight feet; we drew six with our keel, so had to be aware at all times. During the day a huge squall came and encompassed us with wind and blowing rain so hard we could not see. Slowing down our speed and watching the radar saved the day. As soon as it came, it seemed to leave. Yet the wind meter charged up to 60 knots as it passed.

Once on the Atlantic ICW, the waterway took us north to Jacksonville from Vero Beach, a trip 250 miles over 3 days. There we stored the boat for the hurricane season up the St. Johns River, near where we had grown up and family still lived.

We had departed Friday Harbor, Washington on May 23, 1998 for Alaska, and tied up to the Ortega dock in Jacksonville, Florida, on June 9, 1999—an over 9,600 nautical mile trip during those twelve and a half months.

Next stop: the Bahamas!

Lure of the Bahamas[*]

"The elephants are marching!" reported my husband, Denis. He had climbed up to a third floor vantage point at a Ft. Lauderdale Beach building, and returned to announce that giant square waves meant we stayed in port another day. A prudent sailor waits and watches for a weather window to cross the Gulf Stream, a powerful "river" in the Florida Straits. This "river-in-the-ocean" flows north at a rate of three knots or more, day and night, in every season. At its narrowest point between Miami and Bimini, it is 44 miles wide and 2500 feet deep. Even winds of 10-15 knots from the north meeting that fast current can result in steep waves and treacherous conditions. "Screaming-northers" with 20 knots or more can create impossible situations. The Gulf Stream commands respect.

Our window opened December 27, 1999. Bob Hermann had crewed with us from Jacksonville back down the ICW to Ft. Lauderdale to make the Bahamas trip. To use the current in our favor, we first motored south to Miami Beach before turning into the Stream. Adjusting our course as needed, we pointed *TEKA III*, toward Great Isaac Rock Lighthouse on the other side. Passing the Lighthouse we watched the GPS creep up from the usual 7.5 knots to 9.1 with the Northwest Providence Channel current. Highly decorated (for Christmas) cruise ships passed us in each direction. We arrived in Nassau Harbor about 9 A.M., twenty-six hours after leaving Ft. Lauderdale breakwater.

Immigration and Customs completed all necessary clearance paperwork at the marina. We paid $100 for a 180-day cruising permit. We purchased some fresh conch from a friendly fisherman and a local man at the dock provided me with his "family recipe" for conch salad. Our Bahamian visit began in earnest.

Witnessing New Year's Eve "Junkanoo" parade became the highlight of our Nassau time. Junkanoo, a Caribbean Mardi Gras, developed as a celebration during the pre-emancipation days when slaves were allowed special Christmas-time holidays. Two Junkanoo parades are held now—once on the day after Christmas and again on New Year's Eve. Actually it's

---

[*] Adapted from my article, "Lure of the Bahamas," in *PassageMaker Magazine,* October 2000, pp 146-157

early morning on New Year's Day—about 2 A.M. when the parade begins. It lasts until mid-morning. The clamor of bells, whistles, musical instruments and goombay drums coming down the street create a real electric feeling in the crowd. The people swayed with the music and everyone cheered loudly for their favorite group in the competition. Awards are given for best music, costumes and dance.

After our mail arrived via our mail-forwarder in Florida, supplies gathered, chores finished and charts studied, we cast off. Two miles past Porgy Rocks, we set our course to pass between the Yellow and White Banks on our way to the Exumas. The Spanish had named the Bahamas, the "gran bahamar" meaning the great shallow seas. We were to experience what it took to successfully navigate these waters.

First, we had to learn how to "read the water," keeping in mind *TEKA III* needed six feet of water beneath her. While good charts are a must, visual navigation is still essential. If the chart and the visual don't match, believe the eye—sand does move around. With good light we could easily see when dark blue water changed to green ahead of us, indicating shallow water. The depth sounder confirmed the message. To pass safely through reefs, bars and other questionable places, I put on polarized sunglasses and talked to my husband via two-way radio from a vantage point outside the pilothouse. We always tried to use sunlight to our advantage—behind us or overhead. I watched diligently for trouble, especially dark shapes indicating coral heads near the surface, aware that at times cloud reflections made the water look dark and suspicious. We traversed between the Banks with minimum depth of about ten feet. Our first experience kept my eyes busy and my tension up.

Our first stop was Allan's Cays (pronounced "keys"), a very beautiful, but popular anchorage, famous for its population of iguanas. We found all the good sandy anchoring spots already occupied, leaving only the channel where all the sand had been scoured. Three attempts at anchoring failed, so we gave up and went to the next cay. Alas, the sun at 4 P.M. appeared dead ahead of us. It made reading the water unusually hard since we had to detour around a large rocky patch before turning into Highborne Cay. To insure success, we retreated back west first before making the turn south and eventually into the open roadstead anchorage on Highborne's western side.

The next day we dinghied back to Allan's Cay. Many iguanas living there mosied out of the bush and down to the shoreline to greet us. Right after we beached, a second dinghy pulled up beside us. A French Canadian couple climbed out, offering lettuce and cookies as treats for those animals. At one point, the man had an iguana taking the lettuce right out of his hand.

After exploring Highborne by water—looking for a snorkeling spot with staghorn coral that we never located; purchasing a lobster for $10 from a local fisherman; and several walks on shore; our attention turned to the impending weather change. Weather savvy is crucial for water travel in the Bahamas. Each morning, over single-side band radio, the Bahama Air and Sea Rescue Association (BASRA) in Nassau relayed weather reports from NOAA in Florida, as well as, Nassau's Met Office. That, along with information garnered from our on board weather faxes, indicated winds were shifting to northwest with the approach of a strong cold front. We needed to find shelter before the front's arrival the next day. We chose Norman's Cay anchorage, about two and a half hours south. The anchorage had good wind protection from almost any direction.

During the day of quiet before the front's arrival, we went on shore and absorbed some of Norman's history. Decaying resort buildings, broken-up roads, a derelict dock, and cargo plane rusting away in the harbor were silent tributes to the drug smuggling bonanza days. In the 1970-80s, Norman's claim to fame came from Medellin cartel smuggling cocaine plus marijuana from South America and Jamaica. Gun-toting guards chased cruising boats away, but DEA agents disguised as broken-down boaters set up surveillance. Arresting pilots, confiscating shipments, and making raids on the cay choked off all cash flow by 1983 and the kingpin, Carlos Lehder, went to prison in the U.S.

Our gale arrived on Day Two at Norman's. The winds howled, registering over 30 knots and gusting past 40, for 48 hours. Almost everyone had out two anchors—Bahamian moored. We all posted a vigilant anchor watch. Early in the storm a trawler near us started to drag. An announcement over the VHF gave everyone a "heads up" to make sure that boat wasn't in danger of hitting and damaging them. After several attempts the skipper managed to reset his anchor and everyone collectively breathed again. We wondered who would be next. Watching the wind gauge during the dark hours became more dramatic than daytime. By sunset everyone's awareness focused on positions, either sketching out distances from objects using radar measurements, eye-balling other vessels' positions, setting anchor alarms, or all of the above. Our 75-lb. CQR anchor with half-inch chain had been buried in a four-foot high sand ridge (confirmed by diving on it). During the night it dropped off the ridge, sliding us back one whole boat length. It reset. We adjusted our eyeball position.

Two dramas unfolded during our gale—one right at the anchorage; the other several miles away. About 2 A.M. a voice on the VHF shouted, "A catamaran is loose in the anchorage!" We saw it like a ghost ship slipping along the shoreline. Spotlights came on from other boats. Life surfaced on the runaway boat's deck to start their engine. Slowly they moved back to re-anchor. Dropping the anchor meant more trouble. The current apparently allowed the anchor line to drift between the pontoons and catch on the propeller, stopping the engine. They were helpless, rapidly drifting back out of the anchorage, heading for the rocky shore. We all watched the shadowy figure. Luckily it bypassed rocks and grounded hard on a sand bar. There they stayed until high tide the next day when they freed the line, floated off the sand bar and motored back to safety in the anchorage.

The other drama involved a mail boat with fifteen persons on board. Mail boats are used throughout the Bahamas to move supplies, mail and people between places. This vessel had gotten into trouble on the Yellow Bank en route to Nassau. BASRA immediately sent their vessel, *LADY POWELL,* to assist. A USCG helicopter joined in the rescue, along with a Bahamian Naval boat and one private cruiser from the dock at Highborne. The boat sunk, but all the people first got into lifeboats and then were picked up by the Navy or the helicopter. It must have been a very scary experience in the gale and in the black of night knowing help was on its way, but not when it would arrive.

When the wind blew itself out, we experienced another phenomenon—the current. While the wind blew, all our bows pointed into it. Now, with less wind, the current had us all waltzing around each other, sometimes coming close only to sail away for another circle—spooky to witness at 4 A.M.

Later that morning we motored down to Shroud Cay and anchored in an open roadstead again. Three German flagged vessels shared this rolly anchorage for the night. On the rising tide we dinghied through the island's mangrove swamp to the Exuma Sound side and hiked up a 50' hill to Driftwood Camp. This camp had been Ernest Scholte's hermit homestead in the 1960s. Then DEA (Drug Enforcement Agency) personnel took this great lookout to observe air traffic in and out of Norman's. Today cruisers take mementos from their boats to leave at the top of that hill. It does remind one of a place Robinson Crusoe would like.

Exuma Park, a very special place, was not to be missed. Created by an act of Parliament in 1959, and supervised by The Bahamas National Trust, it is one of twelve National Parks in the Bahamas. It's the world's first-ever land- and sea-park, and the first marine fishery reserve in the region. The Park encompasses 176 square miles, boundaries extending 23 miles north to south and four miles out west and east. Within this twenty-two mile range, rules state that nothing living or dead can be removed. Exuma Park's Warden, Ray Darville, enforces the "no take" policy, coordinates scientific research, handles public relations, maintains existing facilities and oversees new construction. Along with the Bahamian Defense Force, he patrols the

Park for illegal activities—drugs or smuggling. He has eyes and ears available to report suspicious activity and a fast boat to check things out. Poachers, locals or cruisers, are not tolerated. Cruisers certainly pay fines and can even have their boats confiscated. Whereas other places have experienced heavy fishing pressure, the Park's "no take" policy has resulted in an abundance of marine life.

At Warderick Wells, the Park Headquarters are 21 mooring buoys in a narrow, horseshoe shaped channel. Attached to a well-set mooring buoy gives one a safe feeling, especially after the gale at Norman's. Once on a buoy, it's yours until you leave. Anchoring is allowed at other locations, but not at Warderick Wells Park Headquarters.

Tied to the buoy at Exuma park

Before taking a buoy at Warderick Wells, we spent one evening anchored at Emerald Rock, followed by three at South Anchorage. The South Anchorage is another part of Bahamian history—pirates. This well-positioned cove hid even large 12 foot-draft pirate ships waiting for Spanish galleons to sail by on Exuma Sound. Edward Teach, "Blackbeard," and Calico Jack Rackham used this cove. The two famous women pirates, Mary Read and Anne Bonney, sailed with Calico Jack. Three islands just south of this anchorage salute these former buccaneers—Read, Bonney, and Teach. On shore within the anchorage, a trail leads to an opening in the bush called

"Pirates' Lair." There one can stand and imagine a group of swashbucklers spread out on their mats resting, smoking, eating, plotting and even counting their treasure from the last raid. A fresh-water well still stands in the clearing. Tall cabbage palms, not indigenous to the Bahamas, and a certain type of grass usually found only in the Gulf Coast areas of Louisiana, grow here. Perhaps they originated from seeds that got rubbed off the pirates' mats.

On Warderick Wells Cay are many trails. Boaters who want to stretch their legs can definitely do so here. On one trail, the remains of the Loyalists' part of the Bahamas history are evident in very thick stone walls to keep livestock penned in, plus wells and remnants of old stone houses. Loyalists, Tories loyal to the Crown during the American Revolution, had moved to the Bahamas to escape persecution.

Boo Boo Hill, overlooking the anchorage, is reported to be the site of burial for a boatload of missionaries who were wrecked off the coast at this location. Today, boaters climb the hill for a spectacular view and leave mementos with their boat names as evidence of their passing.

Snorkeling can be done right inside the mooring area. Two small mooring buoys have been placed for dinghy use. Some people elect to do a "dinghy float" instead. They swim over the reef with one hand holding onto the dinghy for safety in the current. Other snorkeling and diving spots, including Brad's Reef and Danger Reef, are a dinghy ride away in calm water. A huge grouper lives at Danger Reef. Divers have fed him enough that he now greets new faces with an inquisitive look.

Front number two came in while we were there. This one had less wind, but lots of rain. We used a PVC pipe to collect over 100 gallons of rainwater from our upper deck right into the water tanks. Other boaters also filled their inner tanks or portable ones on the deck. Collecting rainwater keeps the water issue under control. Although we have a watermaker on board, we saved about eight hours running our auxiliary engine by collecting 100 gallons of rainwater. If you don't have a watermaker, it costs about 60 cents a gallon to purchase R/O (reverse osmosis) water—a nice savings of sixty dollars in our case!

The wind blew so hard it stretched the mooring line straight out. Each mooring line had been checked recently by a diver, so we felt safe. Based on our Norman's experience we were again concerned when weather reports said, "strong" cold front approaching south Florida.

After a week on the buoy, we decided to move on toward Staniel Cay and make arrangements to see the Super Bowl. The Staniel Cay Yacht Club dock was our home for two nights. Our first grounding occurred on the way in with the sun in our face making for poor visibility. It is said, "You haven't been to the Bahamas if you haven't grounded once." We just came to a sudden stop on sand, missing the slightly deeper area by a hundred feet or so. Oh well, no damage done, except for being witnessed by folks on the dock and other boaters anchored nearby. Within an hour the tide had raised us up enough to maneuver out of our predicament.

Once tied up we checked out the two small grocery stores, The Pink Store and Isles General. Stores have very limited stocks since everything is brought in by boat. Fresh vegetables are almost non-existent, unless the mail boat has just been there.

That night we joined several boating friends at Happy People Marina for barbecue dinner and Super Bowl on their satellite TV. Exciting game! No one left early.

The next morning at low-slack tide, many dinghies gathered at Thunderball Grotto, of James Bond fame. Three small mooring buoys had about ten dinghies suspended from them. Masks and flippers on, more than twenty-five people swam toward the cave opening and on inside. The cave seemed smaller than the one in the movie, but still impressive. It had several holes in the roof, sending shafts of light inside. Flippers seemed to be everywhere one turned. Sergeant Majors were the most prominent fish. So used to people feeding them bread, they swam really close and even nibbled fingers extended out to touch them. Within twenty minutes or so, everyone had returned to their dinghies, having explored enough and realizing the current would pick up with the tide change.

Making plans to move the following day, we took advantage of our very new experience inside Thunderball Grotto and invited others over for an evening with the movie, *Thunderball.* Downing pasta and popcorn, eight of us enjoyed this early 007 adventure, instantly recognizing scenery from Nassau to Staniel Cay.

We backtracked to a beautiful anchorage at Cambridge Cay in the southern end of Exuma Park. The Seaquarium and Rocky Dundas caves offered more chances to snorkel. We also had our own aquarium right off the swim platform as a four foot barracuda showed up every morning and hid in the dinghy's shadow watching, waiting for a possible handout. Cambridge was one of the best of our anchorages with good protection, moderate currents and delightful beaches all around.

On to Black Point, we met Willie Rolle and his "Garden of Eden." He has spent many years collecting driftwood and making sculptures which capture one's imagination just as clouds do. He has ballerinas dancing, dolphins jumping, a monkey shaving, a woman thinking and so many more. A garden grows in and among the driftwood pieces that surround his small home. In the Bahamas they call it "pot-hole farming." Any depression in the coral rock is ripe for sticking a mango tree or okra plant or tomato bush in to grow. The depression catches rainwater or dishwater and the rock holds the heat for nourishment.

Willie told us his grandfather had been a rum runner during Prohibition in the U.S. Along with pirating, drug smuggling, and blockade running in Civil War times, rum running also provided prosperity in Bahamian history. Between the years 1920 and 1933 fast powerboats ran rum from Bimini and Grand Bahama over to Florida, and large schooners sailed to Rum Row just off New York and New Jersey with their cargo. Willie claims as a small boy he went with his grandfather on some of these trips.

We had wanted to spend more time in the Black Point Settlement, but another weather front threatened and we needed protection once again from the northwest wind. Just fourteen miles further south we entered the cut between Big Farmer's Cay and Little Farmer's Cay, anchoring about mid-way between. This had been the stage for the 5F's the weekend before—Farmer's First Friday in February Festival. Cruisers descend on the small village and enjoy mixing with each other and the locals with games and contests and just plain fun. We were not there to personally participate, but other boaters just raved about it.

Although we met mostly sailboats along our way, an interesting powerboat shared this anchorage with us. *FARE THEE WELL*—a St. Pierre dory designed into a trawler—hailed from Kingston, Ontario. Whereas *TEKA III* drew six feet; the dory's draft measured only eighteen inches. This is perhaps the ideal trawler for cruising the Bahamas.

At Lee Stocking Island we wanted to take a tour of the NOAA marine research station. Apparently not much was happening at the time, so they closed down the education office, but did allow boaters to come ashore on their dock and take advantage of the pristine secluded beaches and many hiking trails for stretching legs.

Right after we set our anchor there, a local boat came by selling green peppers and nice looking tomatoes. The boat driver, Captain Red, mentioned he owned a restaurant and bar in Barraterre, across the "flats" about five miles away. We were hesitant to take the big boat there—water was very shallow—so asked if he would come and get us for dinner the next night. He agreed and said he could take quite a few in his boat. The next morning we hailed some friends on the VHF about this "field trip" and before we could catch our breaths, we had twenty-one anxious to partake. Since Captain Red's radio didn't work, another boater acted as a go-between. Yes, he could make two trips and get us all to his "Same Ole Place" restaurant. The menu choices were boiled crawfish (lobster), grouper, fried chicken or grilled conch. To facilitate serving us, we had to choose in the morning. That way he knew what he had to gather from the sea and the dishes were all ready to put in front of us when we arrived. Bahamian rice and peas plus coleslaw accompanied our main course. While Captain Red returned to the anchorage with the first load, the rest of us swayed or danced to the Caribbean music played on tapes at the bar. A late rising moon and low tide made for an interesting ride in his 21-foot open craft pushed by a 200 hp Yamaha. We actually bumped at one spot where the water got very lean. And that's with drawing only a foot or two while on a plane.

Before leaving Lee Stocking anchorage, Captain Red supplied another excursion. He came by after breakfast and took Denis to observe local Bahamian-style fishing. While Denis watched the operation, Red's partner, donned in full wetsuit, dropped overboard, dragging a 125-foot hose with him. A gasoline-powered compressor on the boat supplied the diver with air. Breathing through a regulator, he used a spear gun called a "Hawaiian sling" and a lobster hook for his hunter-gathering. He brought the lobsters up to the boat two or three at a time. Fish were stunned and floated up to the surface where Red maneuvered the boat to collect them. After two hours, the haul consisted of over a dozen lobster, and 15-20 fish, grouper and hogfish. Back at the anchorage we bought some of the catch. Other boaters did too. Captain Red had a profitable morning and we all had super fresh fish for Valentine's Day dinner.

We trolled from Lee Stocking to the cut entering Georgetown. Denis did manage to hook a large wahoo on the line, which we lost to a shark. After a good fight, Denis reeled in a ten-pound head only. He felt something hit as he fought the fish. We brushed it off as the food chain in operation. Too bad, though.

So, five and a half weeks after leaving Nassau, we arrived at Georgetown, a winter destination for many cruisers. Some come in November and stay until spring, year after year. Eileen Quinn, a Canadian songwriter and cruiser herself, writes songs reflecting boaters' lives. She calls it, "Music for sailors and normal people." Her song, "Tar pit Harbor," captures some of the Georgetown phenomenon. In it she says, "Tar pit Harbor has sucked down my anchor and with it my will to be free. There's some what goes sailing. I seem to go anchoring, stuck in the muck this side of the sea." (1997 CD *No Significant Features*).

Every year cruisers in Georgetown set up a Regatta for the first week or so in March. Plenty of planning goes into this festival and boats just keep coming for the event. By the time we arrived, February 17, boat count had climbed to 389. One week later, official count totaled 447. Fortunately Elizabeth Harbour has room for all, from Hamburger Beach to Volleyball Beach to Sand dollar Beach along Stocking Island to anchorages in Red Shanks, and right off the town at Regatta Point, Kidd Cove or Peace and Plenty Hotel. There's also a small marina.

Georgetown, initially established August 1792, has much to offer cruisers. It's a place to have mail forwarded; replace supplies and get repairs made; have fun trying the different restaurants; dive or drive to explore local scenery, walk the beaches, and attend all the scheduled or impromptu social events.

The dinghy dock at Exuma Markets remained packed all day— sometimes upward of 100 craft! Passage into Lake Victoria and that dock took you under a stone bridge through a narrow channel. At times nurse sharks shared this channel. Speaking of sharks, a hammerhead had visited several boats within the Harbor our first week there, but then disappeared. Large manta rays swam through occasionally.

Each morning the cruisers' net offered up to date information on Regatta events—how to sign up, where to show up for picnic table building in the park; times for softball and volleyball practices or games; Mail Call and Faxes waiting; a category called "Boaters' General" in which people could ask for assistance ("where is?" "I need help with..."), request sharing a cab to the airport, put in a plug for story telling in the evening on VHF or America's Cup Sailing Race on satellite TV; advise of a conch horn clinic; and report lost or found items. Local merchants and community news were also included in the morning net. A "Thought for the Day" concluded the program.

The week we spent waiting for our daughter, Dawn, son-in-law, Larry, and granddaughter, Megan, to arrive went by very fast. Along with taking care of regular business, we worked on our auxiliary motor problem and attended seminars. The first one, given by an ex-merchant marine, described how to be pro-active when encountering larger vessels (container, cruise, naval ships) on the water. Bruce Van Sant gave hints on safe passages south of the Bahamas. In addition we listened to and participated in an Eileen Quinn concert, joined some "Sundowners" and walked the beaches.

When the family arrived, we took advantage of a weather window and made our way out the south end of Elizabeth Harbor, heading to Conception Island, forty miles east. It's a beautiful place—another land park. Fishing is permitted here and the beach is outstanding. The island is only three miles long and two miles wide, surrounded by shoals and reefs. Christopher Columbus is reported to have stopped here also in 1492.

Here we saw more birds than we had seen all along our trip (except for seagulls in Nassau). Early in the morning a call from overhead caught our attention. We looked up to see many red-billed tropicbirds on their morning feed, swooping along with their long tails fanning out behind. We also saw one kingfisher and one very large oystercatcher on our ride up the mangrove creek. On shore, a large conch shell marched along, making neat tracks of its trek. Turtles swam ahead, behind, and beneath our dinghy. Also, barracuda and reef sharks lurked in the shallows looking for an easy meal.

Snorkeling around Conception was not up to our expectations. The reefs had been hurt by Hurricane Floyd. Sand had covered many coral heads, which would take time to recover. Not only had the coral been damaged, but we saw fewer fish. We did manage to catch two mahi-mahi (locally called dolphin fish) between Conception and the Exuma chain.

From Conception we made our way back to Nassau via Black Point, Cambridge, Warderick Wells and Highborne. Our family guests departed in Nassau and we set our sights on Eleuthera, but only anchored one night, at Royal Island. At the anchorage an abandoned estate house invited us to come ashore and poke around. We put it off until morning, but left the anchorage without even taking the dinghy down as a weather window with southerly winds to cross over to Abacos islands occurred. Our passage was good although the southeast seas of 6-7 feet put our paravane stabilizers to work. We were concerned about the bar for entering (North Bar Channel) since it faced southeast. However the waves seemed to flatten as we approached land and with a mid-tide, we encountered only a minor swell and had an easy, smooth entrance.

Sandy Cay, just inside that channel, had been recommended as a "must" for snorkeling. We anchored behind it and rolled from the swell most all night. In the morning we headed to the beach, gear in tow. On shore we found trees uprooted or extremely bent, a broken up dinghy way up on shore, coral rock exposed where sand had been at surface level, shells smashed, all compliments of Hurricane Floyd. There had been four mooring buoys in place for dinghies at the snorkel reef. No more. With the weather closing in and choppy water on the reef, we elected not to go snorkeling. Since that time another boater claims the reef is still okay.

Marsh Harbor is the crowded center of cruising in the Abacos. There were over fifty boats anchored in this well protected, but smallish harbor. In contrast to shore facilities in the Exumas those in the Abacos are much more like the U.S. Lots of nice restaurants, stores, marinas and repair facilities make it seem like an extension of Florida. The offshore islands of Man-O-War, Elbow Cay, and Green Turtle Cay are settled with descendants of the Loyalists and reminiscent of New England. Most of the Bahamians in New Providence and the Exumas are black. Here they are mostly white.

At Man-O-War we met Lola in her golf cart, selling her homemade bread and we promised to come early for cinnamon rolls the next morning. We got another feeling about Hurricane Floyd seeing the twisted tall fences and lights around the ball playing field near the beach. Elsewhere trees were uprooted and the cemetery had graves relocated (one skull is now showing in a grave that remained in place), and beach sand washed away. Elbow

Cay, Turtle Cay and Man-O-War suffered from being closest to the heavy winds near the hurricane's eye.

Instead of taking our vessel to Hopetown with marginal depths and limited anchorage, we elected to use the local ferry system. From Man-O-War one ferry took us back to Marsh Harbor and then another completed our journey to Hopetown on Elbow Cay. We explored the village and its magnificent lighthouse built by the British in 1864. As a symbol of Bahamian maritime heritage, it is one of the last three oil-burning, hand-wound lighthouses in the world. A lighthouse keeper must climb 101 steps to the top every two hours to hand crank the weights operating the beacon. What a view from the top!

Hopetown's beaches were devastated. Today, bulldozers moved sand back up the slope and work continues to mend the homes that didn't topple down with the wind, rain and sea surge. A sign in Vernon's grocery at the checkout counter says, "I've talked enough about the hurricane." People did what they had to to survive. Mother Nature is tending to her job of new birth. Some people said her job started in earnest only two weeks after the storm. Bougainvilleas are blooming in grand style.

Baker's Bay at the north end of Great Guana Cay, and known for its beaches, became home for a day. At one time cruise ships set up a land-base recreational site (Treasure Island) here. The abandoned buildings, especially the outdoor theater, let one know this was intended to be a grand place. But it has been left to deteriorate since the early 1990s. They even had a channel and turn-around area dredged for cruise liners to enter and anchor. The well-marked channel is used today by boaters negotiating entrance into the Whale Cay passage—an oft-times nasty crossing. Most boats do not have a shallow enough draft to go over "Don't Rock" passage. That means leaving the banks for a two mile stretch of ocean, with swells and waves dead abeam. This is exacerbated by the deep drop off into the Atlantic quite close by, causing waves to build as they come up on the bank. An early morning passage with slight wind and swell is recommended. Our trip across went without a hitch. One story we heard explained how one cruise ship nearly floundered attempting the passage under wrong conditions, causing the company to close down operations on Treasure Island. Fortunately Baker's Bay offers good protection while one waits for a good time to go.

At Green Turtle's New Plymouth Village we stopped only long enough to visit Albert Lowe Museum. Our guide, Neil Roberts, talked about the early Loyalists settlers, his family's history there, the hurricane that devastated the area in 1932, Princess Margaret's visit after the War, and the first "mobile home" in the Bahamas. The house he now lives in used to be located near the point. They floated the home around to the inner bay and rolled it up on logs to its current position making it a mobile home. Walking the narrow streets past neat clapboard and brick homes we felt we were back in old New England.

North and west took us to the top of Great Abaco Island and a small anchorage at Crab Cay for the night. Great Sale Cay took us forty-two miles further west. There we spent a blowy, blustery night before going west to Memory Rock and south to West End, where we would be in place for a weather window to cross the Florida Straits.

That opportunity came the very next morning. What we wanted was a southerly wind. It started off southeast at 15-20 knots, but clocked to southwest and decreased to 10 before we reached Lake Worth Inlet. Wave heights actually decreased in the Gulf Stream—quite the opposite from those in a north wind.

In ninety-seven days we traveled over 1,500 nautical miles, 913 of them round-trip to Bahamas from Jacksonville, Florida. Eighty-three of those days were spent in the Bahamas. We traced the Exuma chain; briefly toured the Abacos; checked out Conception Island; and spent time in Nassau and anchored one night off an island in Eleuthera. In the Exumas the ratio of powerboats to sailboats seemed to range between 10 and 20 percent. Many more powerboats were in the geographically closer Abacos.

The lure of the Bahamas is its closeness to the U.S.—tropical islands within reasonable reach. There bright sunshine, clear water, and beaches where you can squeeze white sand between your toes, invite you to lose those winter blues. People are friendly. There's no language problem. U.S. dollars are interchangeable with local currency. Crime, with Nassau as an exception, is very low. (Several dinghies were stolen from boats anchored in Nassau Harbor.)

Along with an up close and personal geography lesson, and experiencing the "gran bahamar" sensation of less water at times below the keel, there's also the possibility of witnessing green flashes at sunset—we saw three.

The East Coast—Tip to Tip

Fourteen states, winding Intra Coastal waterways (ICW), bridge tenders, oppressive summer heat, tug boats at night, lobsters plus fog left indelible marks in our memories of traveling the East coast from southern Florida to northern Maine.

Fog and lobster pots were definite hazards to navigation in Maine. Watching fog swallow us was spooky! Electronic charts, radar, and GPS helped us navigate our course so we did not go astray. Yet those instruments could not point out any lobster pots in our way. And there were hundreds. Lobster fishermen not only dropped their traps alongside channels, but actually across channels where boats traveled in and out of harbors. We could see the buoys marking them in normal conditions, but not in fog, which happened frequently that summer we cruised in Maine.

Fishermen would regularly check their traps by driving skiffs right up to toggled buoys (two buoys linked together for easy pick up), grab the line with a hook, and pull up the trap, and the next trap, and so on. All those lines in the water were targets waiting to be caught by boats passing through the minefield. For us, we had not only the prop to worry about, but the two flopper stopper lines, plus the bulbous bow. As careful as we tried to be, we caught several on the bulbous bow. We knew exactly when that happened too as the second buoy line stretched way out alongside the boat. Putting the engine in neutral allowed the line that had been caught to float off again. If lines were caught on the bow, they did not get back under the boat and catch on the prop. Yet it happened once and we needed a diver that time.

We have fog in the Northwest, too. Maine reminded us of home. Wild rocky shores, islands, evergreen trees, plus a large rise and fall of the tides were the similarities. Instead of Dungeness crabs though, we ate Maine lobsters at several places. Our most memorable one was the Chinese Restaurant in Boothbay, where we ordered lobsters in garlic sauce Cantonese-style. Our mouths still water thinking of that dish.

The SSCA (Seven Seas Cruising Association) had a rendezvous in Maine that summer and we participated in the fun and festivities, plus joined the membership. At that function we met Terry and Marie Blackburn, who owned the sailboat, *ZELDA*, plus Charles and Robin Weisneth, of *ROBIN LEIGH*, who talked about crossing the Atlantic in the future.

In our anchorage we met Steve and Linda Dashew, owners of *BEOWULF* then, now of *WIND HORSE* fame. They came by dinghy to inquire about our flopper stoppers, and then invited us over for a drink. After showing us around their elaborate vessel, Linda mentioned they were finishing up a book. I asked what kind. She went to the front cabin and returned with their already published weather book. I thumbed through it and said to Denis, "We should have this book."

He said, "Mary, we do." Not to be left speechless, I asked Steve to autograph our copy. He agreed, only if I read the chapter on 500 millibars before he came over in the morning, pen in hand. He signed it, "Mary and Denis—nice to share the anchorage and trade visits—Steve and Linda Dashew."

We keep their book handy on the salon shelf for reference. It is truly a "guide to forecasting and tactics."

It took maneuvering tactics getting from Florida to Maine to negotiate the rivers, sloughs, inlets, and inner bays of the ICW. First, there were hundreds of bridges in the way. Land traffic had priority. Bridges can be raised up or swung out as necessary. Sailboats with their tall masts required openings most all of the time. With our 34-foot high mast, we could sneak under some of them, but the first time we did it, we had someone on the upper deck, someone on the bow, and Denis looking up from the pilothouse window, each holding his breath as it looked like a "touch and go" situation.

Most bridge tenders are very pleasant. However, there are a few grumpy ones. In calling over the VHF requesting an opening is when you find out which kind is on duty. Some bridges are on a set schedule so the tender just tells you to wait. Others not so restricted. South Florida has the most bridges in a row and it can be stressful trying to gauge speed and timing of next opening to make several in a row. Otherwise you continue to reposition your boat, often against current and tide, until the next opening, sharing time and space with several other boats and chatting across the water about life in the slow lane.

My most favorite bridge tender story is from Florida. A French woman on a sailboat called ahead to the bridge tenders using a sensuous voice, "Bridge tender, we are a French boat. I do not speak English. Open the bridge, please." That worked apparently. She used it again and again. We tried hard all day to catch up with that boat and see this "Bridget-Bardot" lass.

The ICW in Florida, Georgia, North and South Carolina and Virginia had inlets to the ocean, which needed almost constant dredging to keep them free. If people wanted to pop out into the ocean at one point to speed up their trip, they could. The ICW took time to do, but it ran all the way from Miami to the Delaware River in protected waters for those who liked that kind of trip.

Sometimes it became quite shallow, and we did go aground once in Georgia by misreading the channel markers and not agreeing on the proper move. As soon as we stopped dead in the water a boat passed us, showing us the right place to have gone at that decision point. Oh well, we threw out the anchor so we stayed put until the tide came back in, which thankfully came soon. One other time we could have made a huge mistake by getting too close to a dredger at one of the inlets. We were rounding a bend when the boat ahead of us called over the radio, "*TEKA III*, make a U-turn now! We tried to pass a dredger working to clear the area and went too far over. We are stuck, but all right. You better wait to pass." We turned around and snuck up on the situation, and then waited for the dredger to swing away from us in order to pass safely. It is most imperative to stay inside the channel at all times.

At a dock in Savannah, Georgia our attention focused on a trawler passing us—*DAISY*, hailing from Port Townsend, Washington. We made immediate radio contact just to ask, "Are you really from Washington State?" Answer: "Yes, meet us in Beaufort." We did and enjoyed shrimp and grits at breakfast, a Southern tradition.

The rivers of Georgia and South Carolina gave one the feeling of being Huckleberry Finn in the old South, lazing down the streams just watching the sky, mossy trees and marshes all around. Beaufort and Charleston, South Carolina, plus Beaufort, North Carolina reminded us so much of growing up in the South with southern drawls heard everywhere and large, spacious white mansions seen along the riverbanks—like those seen in the movie *Gone with the Wind*.

Denis and I grew up in Florida, so were surprised to find we had lost our ability to deal with the oppressive heat and humidity that June we spent in the Chesapeake Bay. We ended up buying an air conditioner for the pilothouse to make life more comfortable. It remains in place today, more of a decoration and dust catcher than an air conditioner. Originally wanting to go upriver to see Washington, D.C. from the water did not materialize. It had been so hot that we elected to continue north faster than planned to find cooler weather.

Once we passed through the C&D Canal and Delaware Bay into the Atlantic, we had open sea and coastline to deal with until New York City. We have a photo taken from our boat looking across the Hudson River toward the Twin Towers on June 30, 2000. Things there will never be the same after September 11, 2001, a date to be remembered forever when those

Towers disappeared from the face of the Earth. Going down the East River we went under the Brooklyn Bridge and marveled at the "skyscraper canyons" in Manhattan. From water level, looking down the streets of Manhattan with tall building lining each side, it resembled a deep-sided canyon one can see out West. Continuing on, we whisked through Hell's Gate Rapids by the Rikers Island prison popping out on the north side of Long Island. After Cape Cod, we pointed the bow even further north to accomplish our mission of cooling off.

The view of the New York skyline in 2000

We enjoyed our time in Maine but in order to make Chesapeake Bay in a reasonable amount of time, had to leave before the weather changed. Passing Atlantic City, New Jersey on the Atlantic Ocean, I met a vessel coming out of Delaware Bay at night. The radar showed two images close together on a direct path toward me. A visual check through the pilothouse window told me the first one was a tug and its mast lights indicated it towed something. So I radioed the vessel to work out his intended path versus mine. The gruff, gravelly voice on the other end of the VHF said in no uncertain terms, "Captain, watch out for my barge!" I did.

Block Island, off the shores of Rhode Island, provided us shelter from a tremendous gale one night. We rode well, but watched as *ZELDA*'s dinghy, tied to her starboard side, bounced up and down, trying to fly away, but somehow did not. We had enough boats at anchor there to have a potluck party sometime after the storm. Four dinghies were tied up at our stern when everyone had arrived with their dinner dishes to share. At 10 P.M. when people started leaving, only three dinghies were there. The search began with spotlights and people checking everywhere. Fortunately the anchorage area is almost entirely enclosed, and that kept the dinghy within range of being chased down and captured.

Back down in the Chesapeake area, this time on the Eastern side, fall colors were coming on and the geese were gathering, either to stay there for the winter, or go further south. At Chesapeake Bay's southern end, with Norfolk's miles of ships in port or making their way to sea, plus Newport News, home to Langley Air Force Base, we caught a glimpse of our military might.

While making our way back to Jacksonville we thought seriously about doing an Atlantic Crossing ourselves. We knew *TEKA III* could do it. She had made two round trips to the Mediterranean with her original owner, Rod Swanson. But the question to entertain here: Were we ready? We weighed the pros and cons of a trip to the Med, and decided we could do it. *ZELDA* and *ROBIN LEIGH* were still planning such a trip, and indicated they were interested in being "sister ships" for such an adventure in 2001.

I shared our plans with my sister, Louise Holbrook in St. Petersburg. She shook her head and said in her best Southern accent: "That's the stupidest thing you ever thought of doing.... What about icebergs?"

In telling our daughter, Dawn, about the upcoming trip, she responded at first with, "What!?" Followed by, "I want Greece!" Son, David, said he knew we were going, but not sure when. Both kids know we have gypsy feet. Denis' parents, in their nineties, wished us well, but didn't seem overly excited.

That winter in Victoria, British Columbia, we connected with Alex and Joanne Gray for Christmas dinner at a restaurant. There were several of us spread out around a large table right near the kitchen entrance and lots of noise around. At one point I leaned over and asked Joanne if I could take Alex to the Med with us the next summer. She gave me a wave with one hand, saying, "Take him!" I asked her again since there was a lot of interference and she had a hearing problem, just to make sure she had heard me correctly. She answered the same way. I learned later the real story. She worked as a school secretary with summer vacations. The best working season for him in the marine mechanic business was summer, so that put a dent in their summer vacations. She had always wanted to go to Europe. If we took him, she could fly over and meet him for a rendezvous. Everybody would win!

Alex flew from British Columbia to Ft. Lauderdale in mid-April 2001. Our plan was to cross the Gulf Stream from Ft. Lauderdale to the Bahamas, then Bermuda and beyond. However, when he landed, we were still in Jacksonville finishing up boat chores—300 miles away. After a quick phone call to discuss the issues, Alex decided to ride the Amtrak north and meet us the next day. Our marina, located right next to the train tracks, allowed us to calculate the timing for his arrival. About 4 P.M. I positioned myself on the bow, heard the "toot-toot" from the nearest gated crossing, and waved at each car from the engine to last one. Pasted against the window in the last car was a familiar face. From his side, Alex said the Conductor announced Jacksonville as the next stop. He walked to the window, saw a marina, saw *TEKA III*, then me! We had connected. However we still had a mission before leaving the country.

Our insurance company wanted a pre-crossing engine survey. Duggan Marine Diesel Service in Fort Lauderdale was the contact in the U.S. for British Gardner engines, so we had to make a trip back south on the ICW once the boat was ready to leave Jacksonville.

Weather became the big issue after our arrival back in Ft. Lauderdale. More elephant waves marching across the Gulf Stream kept us in port. Even the supply ships were being held up, so you know things were bad. We could not go to the Bahamas, so pointed the bow back up the ICW once again while keeping a watchful eye on weather up in the Bermuda area. When conditions became more favorable to spring out, we would take the next inlet out to sea and plot a course.

Weather faxes on board, from different sources, showed 45-knot winds and 22-foot seas near Bermuda at our halfway point up to Jacksonville. We had made arrangements with a professional weather-router, Walter Hack of Ocean Marine Navigation in New Jersey, to advise us on our crossing. His first words of wisdom during this staging process were, "Wait until conditions improved"—no sense charging into something dangerous. As much as we wanted to get going, caution counted a lot.

Alex, however, was beginning to wonder if he would ever leave Florida to begin his adventure. We expected Bob Hermann to also join us along the way.

Now, four years after purchasing the boat and putting almost 18,000 nautical miles under the keel, we had a plan. The grand adventure had taken on a new dimension, an ocean crossing. As for me, after many nights and passages, my fears were getting less as my confidence and competence grew with each experience and I had learned to trust my ship.

We had relied on fourteen friends up to then to help crew and share adventures, as well as daughter, Dawn, and her family in the Bahamas. I found companionship with all of them, and even more through meeting other cruisers, especially in Georgetown and New England.

Cruisers are a special group of people. They chose a mobile lifestyle that does not stop when land ends. They accepted challenges and easily shared ideas regarding where to go and where not to go to make a gypsy life fun. There's work involved too. Cruisers have to be self-sufficient problem solvers, able to care for a range of things that can go wrong, from plumbing to fixing hydraulic leaks to changing engine filters at sea. Leaving land meant no AAA roadside service. A non-functioning toilet on land is one thing; a marine one, another. Anticipating parts needed for jobs yet-to-be determined required some real forethought. Social events cement relationships formed among cruisers.

We spoke the same language, not only nautical terms, but the free spirit of traveling without boundaries. The only boundaries were self-imposed, but stretchable over time. The closest I had come to this kind of kinship was as an Air Force wife for twenty years. We were transient, making friends as needed, knowing we were only in a certain place for a while, but may see them again in another place and time. Civilians watched us drift in and out of their communities while keeping their roots down, and glad to be steady. Cruisers love to roam. Our land friends ask often, "When will you be normal again?" Answer: "Define normal."

So as well as finding courage along the way, I continued to find companionship. And the adventure opened up to more excitement.

The Big Blue Ocean [*]

Exiting the St. Johns River breakwater at 6:15 A.M. on May 15, 2001, awareness hit us! There would be no place to park and nowhere to hide in the Atlantic Ocean, that is, with two exceptions, Bermuda and the Azores. And they were just specks on our chart. Crossing the Atlantic is like driving from San Francisco to New York, then back to Minneapolis with only two stops, the speedometer never getting over ten miles an hour. Total mileage: 3,691 nautical miles, or 4,194 land ones. This was indeed a big blue sea.

Denis' anxieties focused on the weather, mechanical reliability, crew issues, and safety at sea. My concerns were the fact we would be alone on the high seas, maybe too far out for rescue, dodging weather, definitely avoiding illness, accidents, or medical emergencies, and trying to side-step mechanical breakdowns. Plus I would miss the family.

Those were the anxieties; the realities turned out well on all counts. I did miss the family, but we kept in contact through email on the boat. I had posited that if the leg to Bermuda went okay, I would make the entire trip with the boat. If not, I could always fly and meet the boat at the other end— Lisbon, Portugal. There I could stand on the dock and grab the lines to tie them up.

Accepting the challenge however made me a stronger person, and I joined an elite group of women who could and did make ocean crossings. So I am happy to report I didn't fly to Portugal. Why? By the time we arrived in Bermuda, I had gotten caught up in the adventure. The next leg would take twice the time, but I found we had a routine on board and seemed to stay busy all the time. Unless I chose to worry, I didn't. And I teased the guys. If I deserted them, they'd miss my "galley magic."

The guys had experienced the boat and sea time with us, so it felt comfortable to have Alex at first, joined by Bob later, on board. They told stories and jokes; I kept them well fed. They licked their plates every night. Perhaps the salt air increased their appetites. With no fast food places nearby, they were stuck with me. We did have some tension about the toilet

---

[*] Adapted from my article, "Atlantic Anxiety—how one couple felt just before their first ocean crossing," in *PassageMaker Magazine*, Mar/Apr 2002, pp *92-105*

seat. Was it to be up or down? Rough water finally dictated the position—down.

With Alex, Bob, and Denis able to figure out mechanical problems should any arise, I was not worried about that aspect. I did have concern about sickness, accidents, or any kind of emergency at sea. We had a thorough set of medications to cover everything from bee stings to toothaches to diarrhea to malaria prevention. Fortunately nothing happened at sea. Denis had three accidents in port however over the ten year journey.

Regarding weather, we were going before the hurricane season, and not going anywhere near sword fisherman in the far North Atlantic, but after seeing *The Perfect Storm*, I knew the ocean could be quite the enemy. Our experience on the U.S. West Coast showed us some heavy weather sea conditions, but we were not too far from shore, as would be the case on this crossing. I trusted my ship and my Captain, Denis, to make good decisions. The flopper stoppers worked their hearts out keeping us straight, but we did tip every now and then by a series of waves close to each other and steep. But we recovered to a stable condition soon. No water came over the bow I am happy to report.

Our trip to Bermuda covered 891 nautical miles. Crossing the Gulf Stream caused no problems and soon we were rising and falling with the six-foot ocean swells and watching the winds from the southwest. When the 15-25 knot winds clocked first to the west and then around to the northwest, seas began building—to 8, then 9, and then 12 feet, creating a rough ride, but no problem. By May 15, a cold front arrived on the scene, complete with squalls all around us. Weather faxes received on board via single-side-band radio had predicted this set of circumstances, so we were prepared to keep on going through them.

Within a few days we had gotten used to the rhythm of the sea as well as rhythm of on-board activities. There were meals to plan and cook, dishes to wash, weather faxes to study, watches to do, and logs to keep. And email the kids. The sea always started to get lumpy about time to cook dinner. I remember saying more than once, "Keep the wheels out of the ditch!"

Before crossing we had installed a computer chip in the radar, which gave us information about other ships around us. Acquiring a target image let us know which direction the vessel was going, its speed, closest point of approach, and the timing for that. We could watch the target and see what actually happened and if there would be a possible collision in the works, there would be time to correct our course or speed to make sure we remained safe.

With that in mind, on a night watch (not mine this time) a ghost ship appeared. It showed no lights, did not answer our VHF call, but did cross our bow quite close—about 100-feet away. The one on duty had to pause for reflection as we were in the Bermuda Triangle at the time. Who was on duty on this fishing boat? Did it just have the autopilot locked in and no one on watch? Anyway, that is why we have night watches. Safety first!

We had a flopper stopper block break on this crossing, damaging the teak rail and tearing the canvas below the railing. The flopper stopper line runs through a block, which changes its direction—think of block and tackle. It sure made quite a racket when it broke loose. Using only one flopper stopper worked until we could get in for repair at St. George's, Bermuda.

We arrived in St. George's Harbour (the British spelling) on Day 6 out of Jacksonville. We heard Bermuda Harbor Radio calling a vessel when we were still a few miles out. It turned out to be the boat ahead of us on the radar screen when we checked coordinates of the vessel they hailed. Bermuda is surrounded by a coral reef and Officers at Harbor Control needed to know names, call signs, home ports, number of persons on board, and life raft data, to start with, of all approaching boats. They particularly wanted to find out if charts of St. George's Harbour were on board. They did not want to come out and rescue anyone who, unprepared, messed up. We had all our information ready when they called us to report. We located the approaching markers, then channel markers, and then the entry channel. It took tight choreography to allow cruise ships in and out of the harbor, plus all the other traffic. They impressed me so much we had to schedule a visit to their facility high on the mountain overlooking the harbor. With all their ultra-modern sophisticated electronics, and high-powered radios, they must have felt like "King of the Hill."

There in the harbor we met up with *S/V ZELDA*, who came up from the Virgin Islands, and *S/V ROBIN LEIGH*, who cruised south from Chesapeake Bay. Bob Hermann, our fourth person for the crossing, arrived by plane. With our two sister ships ready, and last crewmember on hand, we left for the Azores on May 28.

Twice a day radio contact let us know each other's position. Since we kept the same speed 24/7, we ran ahead of them. They slowed down at night. By reefing in their sails, they made sure no wild winds swooped down on them and caused havoc. In the morning sails went back on full duty. With our radio contact we knew they were all right. In my mind's eye I realized if we had trouble ahead, they could catch up; likewise, we could do a U-turn and return to help them. But we needed to keep monitoring positions.

The sister ships used a Canadian weather router, Herb, whom they talked to by radio every night and received up-to-date information on the weather picture ahead. We, as I said before, used Walter Hack's forecasting service that focused mainly on advising large ships crossing the Atlantic. We compared notes between the two forecasters and at one time changed course to a more southerly direction because the Jet Stream ran south of its normal track at that time. That meant two things: it would be a longer trip, and clouds continued to gather off our port side not far away.

Our route to Flores took us 1,673 nautical miles to the westernmost island of the Azores Archipelago. For the first four days a southeast wind, averaging about 15 knots created seas no higher than 8-feet. Dolphins arrived on May 31, and again three days later. A cold front passed over us on June 1, dropping the temperature to 63 degrees. Winds changed to northwest, but still blew about 15 knots. June 2, our 44th anniversary was also the halfway point, and we celebrated with smoked salmon and a glass of Shiraz wine. A nice moon the next night followed rain during the day. We had talked about stopping the boat to go swimming at the halfway point, but conditions did not favor this activity, so it did not get done.

By the eleventh day at sea, shearwater birds and dolphins greeted us. We always think it is a good omen to have dolphins come racing across the water to run alongside, diving and surfacing to breathe and enjoying the bow wave ride. When they had had enough fun, they swam off, leaving us with much pleasure from watching and communicating with nature.

A unique phenomenon occurred when over the SSB, a long-range radio, we heard ocean fishermen talking. They were in the North Atlantic off Newfoundland, long-lining for swordfish like *ANDREA GAIL* of *Perfect Storm* fame. We were indeed in the middle of nowhere.

As we grew nearer our destination, we slowed the speed down so to make landfall in the daylight. At first we could see the image of Flores on the radar, then with our eyes, as the sky lightened. What an exciting event! I remember saying to everyone, "We found it!" The Azores is an archipelago of nine islands in the middle of the Atlantic. Easy enough to miss if you have programmed the wrong figures into the computer! Soon we saw the breakwater and made our turn into Lajes Harbor and dropped the anchor, happy to be safely stopped once again.

Flores, the island of flowers, is full of hydrangeas, pink and blue and white and shades in between, used for decorating their walkways and for field boundaries. Wild roses, red and pink, also abound along the walkways, growing alone in bushes or intermingling with the hydrangeas. There were no Club Meds here, no warm water and no sandy beaches. With a large amount of winter rain, sometimes hurricane-like storms, the islands receive a lot of water. Subsequently everything blooms and the grass is very green. The Azores had a whaling history and many men searched for whales as their occupation until recently. Now without the whaling trade, the population has dwindled, but we found our time there just wonderful.

The people there were so friendly. The first person we saw, as we walked around on shore looking for the Immigration Office, was a woman pushing her garbage cans down the driveway to the street. She waved and asked in English, "Did you have a good trip?" We were stunned, but quickly recovered to ask her about Immigration, and how she learned English. She said to just wait for the authorities. They would find us. Look for a jeep later on in the day at the pier. As for English, she lived in Santa Barbara, California for over twenty years. When she had earned enough money to retire, she returned to the Azores, bought a beautiful house overlooking the harbor, and watched for boats with American flags to drop anchor. Following that encounter we met Joe, our image of the Chamber of Commerce and local tour guide rolled into one. He first met Bob by the market, who then took him to meet us. In his truck he gave us a tour of the lakes and southern region of his island, organized a pizza party, arranged for a giant wheel of local cheese cut into thirds to share between the three ships, and just took good care of us. He had lived in the States for a while and said he keeps an eye out for American boats coming into the port and makes them feel at home.

The formal check into the country took place on the hood of a jeep parked on top of the harbor wall. The officials had no office, but did regularly check the vessels in port. Their method of contact was to flip their headlights on and off while blowing the horn to get attention, waving for the boaters to come ashore by dinghy. Our sister ships arrived two days after us, safe and sound.

One Sunday, Marie and Terry, from our sister ship, *ZELDA,* went with us to the other side of the island. We had coffee at a sidewalk café before our search for an abandoned whaling station. We walked and walked, meeting no one else while following the map from our guidebook, which was not much. Finally we found a man working on his car. Terry asked, *"Donde esta el estacion de las ballenas?"* (Where is the whaling station?) They spoke Portuguese in the Azores, not Spanish, but Terry tried. When the man did not respond right away, Terry repeated his question, exactly the same, but even slower. The man then answered in perfect English, "I understand the question; I just don't know the answer." We found the whaling station by just walking around.

Even though we had officially checked into the Azores there in Flores, we had to do it again on the island of Horta a week later. At first we anchored out and took the dinghy to the Customs dock. They proposed we pull anchor and cross the harbor to tie up at a commercial concrete sea wall after completing the paperwork. That worked for us as four people sharing one dinghy for different trips ashore made for a hassle. We could just climb out of the boat this way and do or go at will. Or so we thought.

Father's Day afternoon I took a nap, resting a new cold. Denis stepped over to *ZELDA,* rafted alongside us, for a glass of wine to celebrate the special day. Port authorities came and demanded we, both vessels, move because a large commercial ship was coming. Denis had left his bicycle on top of the sea wall. The tide had dropped so he had to climb up from the boat to get the bike. On attempting to get off, he lost his footing and fell between boat and wall, upside down! Several people saw it happen. He caught himself before losing all control. Several people assisted in getting him back on board. Gasping for breath, scared, and hurting, he waited on the deck while we tried to assess the damage. The Port Manager called an ambulance and the EMS men, or "Bomberios Voluntarios Servicios," carefully took him on a board off the boat and into their vehicle. I grabbed passports, money, and jackets, then the EMS helped me off the boat, and I rode along to the hospital.

There they had to call a radiologist in to work, since it was a Sunday. Once x-rays were taken, the doctor determined Denis had three cracked ribs and showed him the films. No one spoke a lot of English, but the staff managed to tell us where to get a prescription filled for pain. They also requested we stay in Horta a week and return for further evaluation at that time. Also, sleep sitting up. The ribs were not taped. And with my new cold, I had to be diligent and keep him from catching it. Sneezing and coughing for a person with broken ribs is not fun!

Back at the boat, *ZELDA* had moved to another spot. Denis couldn't do the boat relocating in his condition, so I told the harbormaster we would do it in the morning, as the ship still had not come into port. Early morning we went out to anchor again, with a squall coming through at the same time. Soon a harbor patrol boat arrived to tell us we were still in the way— actually the ship's turn-around area. So that makes three tie-ups. At the end of the harbor lay a giant steel buoy with *SAM'S TOY BOX,* an Aussie sailing vessel larger than us attached, but with room for us too. Their crew helped us tie up, but we had to move again when the wind died down and the buoy attempted to go beneath our boat. It had already damaged the Aussie boat during the previous night, so both boats untied and went to the fuel and Customs dock. We were #2 and #3 boats out from the shore.

By morning there were 7 boats rafted (tied up to each other in a row). Many feet stomped across our boat on the way to land during the night and early morning. So when customs opened, we drifted back from that line-up and anchored, only to be told to move once more. After anchoring again, this time very much exposed, we threw up our hands. "We've been here 4 days and had 7 lodgings!" Time to move to another island! Bob had already left by military "space-available" flight for Delaware.

Down to three persons at 06:30 the next morning we upped anchor; arriving at Praia da Vitoria anchorage at Terceira Island eight hours later. There we visited the USAF Medical Clinic for treatment. Nothing to do for the ribs except rest; however, a problem arose with an infection in the leg due to a scrape from the fall (flesh-eating bacteria?). The Air Force doctors thought at first it might be a clot and sent him to the downtown Portuguese hospital for evaluation, and perhaps surgery. An interpreter went along, supplied by the AF clinic. When she went into the room with Denis, she immediately came back out, quite a bit miffed and somewhat intimidated, being curtly dismissed by the arrogant surgeon. Apparently he spoke English and told her to go away. Analysis: no clot, just infection, treatable by antibiotics.

While in Terceira and mending from his injuries, Denis, Alex, and I took our rental car into the main town several times to take part in its week-long festivities. They included a running of the bulls—six of them with gold tips on their horns that came quite close to the people while determining which streets they could run on and which were blocked. The frightened eyes darted in all directions. One man jumped in front of one bull's path, waving a red umbrella. Needless to say, he dropped it and re-crossed the barrier very soon. Each night featured parades, which did not get started until 10 P.M. We saw the beginning of them, but not the end—way past our bedtime. Each village sent costumed men and women to dance their way along the parade route. Draped from balconies along the way were beautiful embroidered quilts—such color! It seemed as if they were vying for the best quilt among the townspeople.

After nine days of excitement and rest, we pushed on to the last island on our list. Ponta Delgada, Sao Miguel's port, had an escapee from the local prison on the day we were to leave. So when we went to the port captain's office to clear out and head to Lisbon, the police told us they had to make a personal inspection of our boat to make sure he had not stowed away. They were checking all the boats leaving the harbor. The policeman walked through the living part of the vessel, but no one, neither him nor us, thought of checking the dinghies on the top deck. After we arrived in Lisbon, I called Marie on *ZELDA* to tell her that over the VHF radio. You never know who else is listening when you are on an open communications systems like cruisers use to call each other. A male voice came over the system and told us, "We have found him. Don't worry." If he had been stowed under the canvas cover of the 14' aluminum dinghy, he would have had a sloppy journey for six days as the crossing got rough at times—10-11 foot steep waves with winds of 20-25 knots.

ROBIN LEIGH had left us by that point, continuing on to England for a special Rally. In 2004 we met Robin and Charles in western Turkey on the way to join the Black Sea Rally—both of us. *ZELDA* went on to Barcelona, then eastern Turkey. We caught up in Marmaris, Turkey two years later.

Tying up at the dock in Lisbon's main harbor, we spotted the large ship we had heard over the radio as we neared the coast. *BARRACUDA* tagged along as a "guard vessel" for ships laying cable. The captain, speaking with an Irish brogue, radioed ships getting too close to the activity and firmly told them to move a certain distance away. We went over to pay a visit. He presented a very interesting picture of their important job of keeping the areas open so the cables could be put in place with minimum problems. As we were touring, I commented that I could have brought my washing over for their dryer, which was busy taking care of the ship's laundry. My clothes hung on the upper deck drying in the sun. "Oh no," he said, "We cannot tumble-dry mixed-sexes knickers in the same load." (Very British)

We spent a week in western Portugal, as did Alex, who happily traipsed off with wife, Joanne, to enjoy a reunion and play tourist. Remember she had agreed we could take Alex as crew, but on one condition. We had to be in Lisbon on July 12 as that's when her plane landed. We marked our calendar and came in early. Alex met her with flowers in hand.

Two months transpired on the calendar since popping out into the Atlantic from Florida, but actually only 23 days at sea—6 to Bermuda, 11 to Azores, and 6 more to Lisbon. We looked forward to more land touring along our world adventure. At each port opportunities would present themselves for us to try exotic foods, attempt to wrap our tongues around different languages, and just expose ourselves to other cultures. We looked forward to the experience.

Shipping lanes off Portugal

--- - ROUTE OF TEKA III

9/11 From Far Away

A panicked voice called over the VHF radio: "Everyone in the anchorage, turn on BBC! There has been a terrible disaster in the United States!" Our anchoring at Espalmador in the Balearics coincided with the terrorist attack on the World Trade Center. We could not believe it when other cruisers in the anchorage made that announcement over the radio about the tragedy in New York City. We sat glued to the speaker, awestruck, shaking our heads in disbelief, then and for a few days after as we listened again and again to the awful news. It took three days for us to locate a newspaper. Even then, with the headlines and photos on the front page, it looked like a bad movie, not real life. While we were trying to absorb this phenomenon, locally anchored cruisers from other countries in Europe and "Down Under" made it a point to come by in a dinghy to all the Americans there and express their sympathies. What a warm feeling to help dissolve the grief.

We took the dinghy to a small island nearby with a store to find a newspaper for the printed news. On Formentara's lovely beach we walked through the crowds gathered on the sand to top off their tans. Most of the women were topless. One man had taken advantage of the clothes optional deal, stretched out on his side, and exposed everything, sporting a proud smile on his face. The three couples—from *ZELDA, GOOD COMPANY,* and *TEKA III*—kept urging one another to take a photo of this well-endowed specimen. "You take it!" "No, you take it!" but no one took it. The man watched us approach and pass; heard our discussion I am sure; and kept sunning while he waited for someone to capture his pose on film. That experience took our minds off the issue at hand, anxious for more news, yet apprehensive to receive it, and feeling helpless being so far away unable to do anything. Terry Blackburn's daughter worked near the Towers, and it took days to even find someone who knew she might be okay.

Getting to the Balearics we traveled many miles from Lisbon in Portugal to southwest Spain, Gibraltar, and Spain's Costa del Sol, now inundated by people from the north of Europe taking advantage of sun and cheaper living, complete with medical care under the European system.

In Rota, Spain, we met Carmen and Barry Blitch (he: American; she: Spanish). We saw them watching us from the marina docks and waved them over to the boat. After introductions they asked if we needed help with anything. Yes! We wanted to get a cell phone. So off we went to the phone store.

At first Carmen worked on our behalf using Spanish with the clerk, and then translating for us in English. Before long the young lady skipped the Spanish step and spoke directly with us in our language. It took a whole heartbeat to realize what had happened. They took us for lunch at an outdoor café after our phone purchase and gave us a quick tour of their place and the town. We exchanged address information and corresponded with them for several years via Christmas cards and emails. Four years later on our way to the Gran Canaries and a re-crossing, we pulled into the marina at Rota, walked into town and found their street. Looking up at all the windows on the second floor we wondered exactly which place was theirs. No luck, until a young boy walking his dog stopped when he heard us speaking English, introduced himself as Alex, and asked if we needed help with anything (similar to the original meeting in 2001). When he heard we were looking for Carmen, he said, "That's my grandma! She and Grandpa are in Florida right now." Now, what are the chances of that happening!

Coming into Gibraltar is such a sight! Lots of ship traffic to contend with of course, but the sight of that piece of rock makes an impact on the eyes and brain because it is such an icon. We took the boat around to the Spanish side, La Linea, to anchor for a few days. From our anchored spot we took the dinghy to a rickety-looking dock and locked it up there while we walked to the British side of Gibraltar. To do that, we had to obey the traffic lights and cross the active runway after showing our passports to the Immigration man at the booth. As he looked at my passport I asked him if he could stamp it. He declined. I asked, "How am I going to prove I have been here?" He answered, "Take your picture!" And we did—lots of them. I think I know the background of the term, "Gibberish," now. It seems Spanish and English are blended into a new language referred to locally as "Spanglish" or "Gibberish."

After enjoying anchorages along Spain's Costa del Sol, we aimed the bow out to the Balearics, islands 65 miles offshore. Coming out of Ensenada de los Escullos, the Spanish Guardia Civil (Coast Guard) boarded us. Their boat roared up beside us, out of nowhere it seemed, and demanded we pull up the port flopper stopper arm so they could come directly alongside. Seas were rough, so the black tires they put over the side as fenders moved up and down with each wave motion, leaving black scrape marks on our white painted side. Neither one of us was pleased when the men climbed on board, wearing heavy black-soled boots, seemingly unconcerned about any marks they would make. After checking our boat papers, they did a cursory inspection, climbed back across to their boat, untied lines joining the two boats, and roared off again, leaving us with a clean-up job.

After Espalmador, we headed up to Mallorca, a very famous tourists hangout. We had quite an experience in Puerto de Andraitx anchorage on the southwest side. During the night a storm came rolling in, directly onto the anchored boats there. Two boats sank after being pushed by waves onto the rocks near shore. We stayed safe. The inner harbor, normally reserved by the harbormaster for the fishing fleet, offered some respite in the morning, so many boats could move into safer surroundings. The one boat left out at the opening, called over the VHF radio, "Can anyone tell me how long this storm will last?" It turned out he was a solo sailor, with two anchors out and the anchor chains crossed. With the winds blowing so hard on his side, he could not manage to work out the problem and needed help. Of course, cruisers went to the rescue. It was quite exciting to watch through binoculars as Denis, and Terry from *ZELDA*, bobbed up and down in their dinghy alongside the Canadian craft, *FREE UNION*, until they could manage to board. Then it took quite a while to free him from his chain dilemma. Later in Barcelona, John Zufelt's three sisters came from Toronto to visit. They told me John related his rescue and added he wanted to buy and fly an American flag to show his respect and gratitude.

At the same time that was happening near the breakwater, a charter boat with several German men on board came into the inner harbor looking for a spot to drop their hook. At the first spot they had trouble. They ended up picking up a large hawser rope, which they released from the anchor still up in the air, and tossed it back into the water. I hoped they would not anchor near us, but they did—too close, and no matter what I said or did, they just shrugged their shoulders and pretended I was invisible. They left the next morning, as all charters have to be back to port on a scheduled day, never mind the weather. I am sure they had a very lumpy ride, and really did not care.

One thing we noticed early on in our Mediterranean travels was the ease at which Germans and Austrians (noted by their country flag) would come into an anchorage, drop the anchor and then drop their drawers. When our granddaughter came to visit in Croatia, we kept vigilant, "Megan, don't look!" Of course, she did.

On September 30, 2001, we tied to the dock at Marina Port Vell (pronounced Vey) in downtown Barcelona, where we left the boat until April 2002. Marina personnel asked us to take our U.S. flag down, so as not to encourage any problems from possible terrorists.

That winter Denis and I visited Megan's second grade class in Tacoma, Washington, to talk about living on a boat and crossing an ocean. To prepare me for what the kids wanted to know, I asked the teacher to have each student write out a question for me. In my talk I answered those questions, plus impromptu ones as well. I gave each person a wallet sized laminated photo of *TEKA III* and described the boat from bow to stern, especially mentioning the flopper stopper fish. I asked, "How many of you weigh fifty pounds?" Answer: all of them. So they instantly equated their weight to the fish's weight. In their thank you notes to me later, many drew a profile of the boat with the flopper stoppers in their extended position and the fish in the water, with the number "50" written on them.

One guy, a serious and loyal Seattle Mariners (baseball team) fan, had written the question, "Can I see my Mariners games on your TV?" "No, not at sea", I replied. A female classmate, seated on the floor next to him, offered him a solution. "My Grandma can tape them for you."

Spain: Pickpockets, Festivals, And Cruisers

"No! No! No!" I shouted at the nicely dressed twenty-something-year-old Spanish man in the Metro Subway station. He backed up, holding his hands so I could see he held nothing, and appeared as innocent as he could. But innocent he was not. He and his pal had just performed one of the many pickpocket schemes cruisers had been warned about while traveling around Barcelona.

A two-page typed handout to newcomers alerted us to many schemes. A popular one went like this: a person in front of you hesitated, bumped into you, or stumbled in getting his footing and at the same time accidentally dropped a bunch of change on the ground in front of you. If you bent over to assist in retrieving it, your hip pockets became visible and available—voila! But there is also the tried and true just sticking a hand in your pocket searching for wallets or money.

In our case both happened. Denis, Marie and I had gone to the outdoor market and purchased a drag-along trolley for transporting market goodies back to the boat. While we waited on the platform for the subway, two well-dressed young men in their twenties came to stand close by, but said nothing. The train pulled in; doors opened; one man stepped in and spilled his change all over the floor. Denis did not bend down, but the other party tried to get Denis' wallet by stuffing his hand into the front pants pocket from behind. Everything seemed to happen at once. Denis grabbed the hand so the man couldn't take the wallet out. Marie pulled on the hand to get it out of Denis' pocket. And I screamed for the thief to stop. It didn't take but a few seconds; all the while, the train did not move. At each end of the train, large mirrors allowed the driver to see along the platform. He apparently saw our skirmish and waited until it looked clear before closing the door and moving on. At that point we were just mad. The wallet was not stolen. We were okay. But what should we do? The two men had left the scene. By the time we got to the next station, where would they be? That is, if we could even make ourselves understood in Spanish to report the problem.

Other incidents happened to people in the marina. A man on the street stopped one of our cruiser friends and told him a bird had pooped on his hat. When he bothered to check his hat, the thief helped himself to the wallet, and started using the credit cards before the couple could get back to the marina and report the loss to the company. Terry Blackburn had a man in front of him on the shopping mall escalator drop money as he stepped off. Terry just climbed over him.

Gypsy women pushed closely around you as you walked, offering fake roses for sale, or asking for money while posing with a baby in their arms. All the time their free hands were working hard to get inside your clothes.

Having a car presented another problem. At stoplights tires could be slashed, and when drivers stopped to change the tire, with the trunk open, things could disappear quite easily. There were other potential problems listed on this alert circulated, but these were the ones I knew about personally in Barcelona.

We took a trip by Sants Renfe (Spanish Amtrak) to Valencia for the Falla (fal-yah) festival in March 2002, after returning from our winter stateside visit, and before starting out on our new cruising season. There we also met some sneaky fingers.

Valencia's "Las Fallas de San Jose" is an exuberant and anarchic blend of fireworks, music, festive bonfires and all-night partying. Every square throughout the city sports at least one large paper-mache statue, very colorful, satirical, and some of them almost six stories high. The artists began planning the next year's statues soon after the current ones are burned on the last night of the festival. These sculptures are grotesque effigies satirizing celebrities, current affairs and local customs; also international images, such as King Kong rescuing the young lady on the Empire State Building, an Egyptian scene, and a Super-sized Cabaret singer. These are judged for first, second, and third prize. The cabaret lady came in second out of the over 800 sculptures placed in every square in town it seemed. My personal favorite was a four-story tall bullfighter, anatomically correct evidenced by the bulge in his tight pants, with a wee red cape waving from his left hand and a haughty look on his face. What a treat to walk down the main street, around the traffic circles and down the alleys to large and small squares to see just what awaited you at each turn.

One of the fabulous fallas in Valencia

On the last night of the festival, these were all torched, about the same time. Fire prevention measures were made in the small squares with huge asbestos blankets draped from the buildings, and fire trucks close by. All the kids seemed to have the time of their life, running around, watching from balconies with their families, their eyes lit up as the fireworks started and the fallas began to burn. What a sight!

Many people crowding together, pushing and shoving to get around, could easily brush up against anyone, feel the pockets as they jostled the person, and help themselves to the contents. Denis had held his camera over his head, exposing his side pocket. Even though I had my arms wrapped around him from the rear, it happened. We had dinner with Terry and Marie before going out into the masses. Terry calmly announced he intended to put his wallet in his shorts and suggested Denis do the same. Terry had his wallet the next morning. Denis didn't, confident he'd be able to know when someone manipulated the Velcro on his pocket. He felt nothing. I saw nothing. It just happened and we were extremely lucky, only losing a little cash. No credit cards or identification were inside the wallet, on purpose. He did not miss the wallet until the morning when we went for coffee.

After those pickpocket episodes, Denis purchased a special hand-made cloth wallet (designed by cruisers) that looped through a man's belt and then dropped inside the pants at the belt level for security, yet accessible. He has not been "hit" since, and still wears it today as a travel precaution.

Another event in Valencia during our time there created emotional reactions from the participants, and those observing it. Groups of beautiful young women from many barrios within the city, colorfully dressed in local costumes, complete with mantillas, paraded solemnly through the streets toward a large square where a Madonna statue awaited. Each of the women carried a flower, either red or white, which they presented to the person in charge of creating a Madonna floral piece at least fifty-feet high. We watched from the sidewalk along the parade route at first, then from the square. When these women gave their flowers, tears streamed down their exquisite faces, showing the emotion of the moment. It took many thousands, if not more, flowers to make this robed statue of Mary, with Jesus held in her left arm, and her right arm stretched out to the masses. I have never seen anything like it. A spectacular work of art made by human delivery of special flowers.

Madonna statue made from flowers.
Note people on lower left, to show the huge size

From that experience we continued by train to Cordoba, staying at a hostel where if you did not speak of word of Spanish, you could understand the delightful lady who took care of us. A special visit there took us to Alcazar de los Reyes Cristianos (Castle of Christian Monarchs—Isabella and Ferdinand's home). In one of the rooms inside, the monarchs gave audience to Christopher Columbus, where he said, "Give me boats and men and I will find you riches across the sea."

Also in Cordoba is the Mezquita, a blend of Islamic mosque and Christian cathedral. Sounds funny, but it is really so. You can quietly sit in one corner and imagine all the prayer rugs spread out in the mosque section, knowing that just around a few columns stood an elaborate altar where the Christians worshiped. Normally conquerors tore down existing religious places when they took over, and replaced them with appropriate ones. Not so in this case when the Christians threw out the Muslims. Instead, the powers in charge incorporated the two religions. The guidebook said the Pope appeared very unhappy when he saw the end result of blending a mosque and cathedral. However, it is stunning!

A forty-five minute journey by train took us to Sevilla from Cordoba. We decided to take a bus from the train station into the city center and look for a hotel there. Studying the bus map created an international group of map interpreters—a black woman from Frankfurt, now living and working in Sevilla, plus a Chinese man on vacation from England where he studied for a Master's in Computer Science. We also asked her about a good Chinese restaurant, and three of us went off to indulge. We later returned for another meal, and the staff remembered us.

We were in Sevilla for the Easter Week activities, from Palm Sunday to Easter Sunday. Large platforms featuring scenes of Christ and Mary, his mother, were displayed inside several churches before they were paraded down the streets, accompanied by brass bands with drummers. Each float moved by only muscle power. Different sets of twenty or more men switched off at various points, without losing a step, to manpower those very heavy floats during the Palm Sunday event. You couldn't see them, just their shoes as they passed by. People with tears in their eyes reached up to touch some of the platforms and make the sign of the cross. Also in the parade were people paying penance by walking barefoot, carrying a cross, but not lashing themselves as in the past. Many hooded people, wearing tall-coned hats similar to the Ku Klux Klan of the U.S. also paraded. Some hats were bright purple, others white; all with holes for eyes and very dramatic-looking, even spooky-looking for someone raised in the South.

On to Madrid and a quick visit to the Palacio Real, where the current King and Queen live, before another train to Toledo and the old walled city on top of the highest knoll with a commanding view and good fortification system. There I got locked in the bathroom stall. The door went from floor to ceiling and only when I shut it did I notice the lock once set, could not open. It had been broken off on my side. So I listened for the sound of other women coming into the area. Nothing. Then I banged on the door loudly several times. Nothing. Then I called out and banged. Finally a woman, in English, asked, "What is the problem?" "I cannot open the door," I responded. She then easily turned the knob on her side and I was free! She looked befuddled until I showed her the broken handle on the inside. When I saw Denis again, I asked him why he did not come looking for me. He said he did not make it a habit to go into ladies rest rooms. I assured him he had my permission to in the future. If not go in, get someone else to check on me. After that experience, I hesitate to go into stalls with doors I cannot climb under or over to get out, and check the mechanism before shoving the lock into place.

Back to Barcelona via a short trip to Madrid again, and the Prado Museum to gaze at Goya, El Greco, Velasquez, and other paintings.

At Marina Port Vell (Vey) in Barcelona we really enjoyed the other cruisers, the activities they arranged, and the proximity to the downtown area. Bicycles or feet or the metro system got you where you wanted to go and back easily enough. We joined the Cruisers' BBC—Barcelona Bicyclist Club and with a group of 15 or 20 every Sunday, went in search of the perfect croissant, using up calories first by pedaling to get to our designated spot to indulge, then pedaling back to the marina. While munching on delicious bakery goodies one Sunday, I commented on a lady's red and green earrings. "Are those for Christmas?"

"No," she replied, "these are my port (red for left side) and starboard (green for right side) earrings." Silly me, missing nautical signs that easily.

Cruisers are unique. We learn from each other where to go and what not to miss. Alas, what to miss as well. I say we feed off each other and keep excitement going. Denis and I learned early on that not everyone cruising on a boat fell into the retired gray-haired category. Many had decided not to wait—do it now! Taking children along, up to four on a small boat, and home-schooling them along the way truly impressed me. It seemed they could study something one day and do a field trip the next. What a way to learn!

Each morning over the VHF, a Cruisers' Net started off our day. People took turns as Net Control. A set formula organized the processing of information. After it had been determined if anyone had a dental or medical emergency, the weather report presented the up-to-the-minute forecast, based on several sources. Then if anyone needed help in finding parts or services, all they had to do was state their case, and more often than not, someone had the needed part or knew where to get one. Now if in searching through your boat, you found items you no longer needed, they became "Treasures of the Bilge" and then offered for trade or sale—a floating flea market. Items lost or found were broadcast. Any security issues went on the table. Welcoming newcomers to the marina and wishing "Bon Voyage" to those leaving took a few minutes. And the category of any other business finished up the net for the day.

Each Sunday afternoon on E Dock, everyone took a potluck dish to share and something to barbeque on the grill, while we spent the afternoon getting to know each other. The docks started at A and went to G, with E the largest one. These docks held between 12 and 20 boats each, and the group photo taken at Easter 2002 showed over 70 people waving and smiling at the camera-person perched on a high spot nearby. Not everyone attended though, so I cannot say just how many lived, temporarily or permanently at Marina Port Vell. Most were European. Some Americans and others from "Down Under" rounded out the population. Powerboats were the minority, as not many had the range to cross the ocean on their own keel, such as we did. *SEASCAPE*, a trawler from Santa Barbara, California, had been shipped by freighter for the Med adventure. *LILJANA*, a steel trawler built in Holland under the watchful eyes of their owners, began their Med journey by cruising down the European canals south to Marseilles. These two boats became our buddy boats for the next few years, along with *GOOD COMPANY,* a sailboat from Galveston. At these weekly parties Denis always searched the food presentation for Liljana Yashruti's potluck dish, from her stash of Middle Eastern recipes. And he was never disappointed.

Barcelona cruisers Sunday potluck

Denis' back injury flared up again in Barcelona and two memories surface immediately. First, he could not walk far, so rode his bicycle everywhere, even to the end of E Dock (our dock) for the weekly potluck. I followed along, carrying a chaise lounge for him. Normally everyone sat on cushions on the concrete dock to eat and socialize. Salah Yashruti, Liljana's husband, commented that it looked as if Denis had a harem with all the ladies positioned on cushions around him in his special chair. The second image is when Salah (a retired doctor from Port Orchard, Washington) knocked on the boat and said he had come to see the "patient" before we pulled out of the marina. I asked him where his black bag was. Holding up his hands, he answered, "These are my instruments." He poked and prodded, checked for responses to a safety pin prick here and there, then had Denis promise to take it easy on the next leg of cruising. Salah would be available for consultation in person or over the VHF radio, as we traveled more or less the same routing.

We left the boat in the water while we were gone four months over the winter. With the warm water in the marina, barnacles grew spectacularly on the prop during our absence, and when we cranked up the engine to go over and be lifted out of the water, the prop would hardly turn. On the hard in the shipyard, removing the bulbous bow followed cleaning the bottom and prop of gook. Our experience with the bulbous bow had been a negative one rather than a positive one. Rather than increasing our speed, it actually decreased it. And it pounded in rough water! While removing it, we donated the lead bricks inside the fiberglass bulb to another cruiser for ballast in his trawler. He made multiple trips back and forth with a wheelbarrow loaded with another set of bricks to accomplish his plan. A good recycling event, especially for *VENTURER*.

Now, washed, polished, and new bow image, we waited for the Gulfo di Lyon mistrals to lay down to proceed north across that notorious bit of water, similar to the Tehuantepec.

France By Sea and By Land

I spun on my heels when my ears picked up one special word from my roots, "ya'll." We had tied up at the marina in Toulon on the French Riviera to explore Provence and partake of its excellent French food and wine. But first I needed to find a self-serve place to do laundry.

That heel spinning took place as I rounded a corner and passed a sidewalk café. There several U. S. Navy guys sat outside having coffee and discussing how to meet French women. I had not noticed the men at first, but when I stopped to respond, it became obvious very quickly these guys were American, and Southern to boot. I asked about their ship. It had been tucked way into the inner harbor, and if they were to be low-profile tourists, I could have blown their cover with my behavior. It is always nice to see and talk to the young men whose job it is to protect and defend. They have an important and demanding role and who knows which ones will make it home. So it is important for me to give them a "well done" pat, special smile, and "Hi, ya'll," back.

To get to Toulon we had to cross the infamous Gulfo di Lyon. We chose a direct crossing since the weather prediction looked good, and kept our fingers crossed the winds would stay down. We had a calm crossing, taking 13 hours to cover 109 nautical miles, anchoring one night near Marseilles before traveling on to Toulon.

There we rented a car and headed north and west to the Luberon Mountains and the area of Provence. We got lost a few times, but never too lost, and always psychologically refer to that as "having an adventure." About lunchtime we entered a quaint place called Cucuron and stopped to walk around, sniffing out something good to eat. La Petite Maison menu looked scrumptious, but expensive. The waiters inside wore black suits and ties, confirming the menu prices. We walked around the small village before returning and taking the plunge. We never said a word as we approached the door. Yet, at the door a very tall young man greeted us with, "Good afternoon." He knew we weren't local. (Perhaps my tennis shoes gave us away.) All the garden tables had been taken or were reserved, so he seated us inside, at a 17th-century heavy wooden table which allowed a glimpse inside the kitchen when that door swung open. We enjoyed a culinary experience we cannot stop talking about.

Mary enjoying the gourmet French food.

For those of you versed in the language, here's what we had presented to us in a most elegant manner, explained in English after they announced the individual dish in glorious French.

Mise en bouche
Risotto d'epeautre de Sault, aux premieres asperges vertes de la Vallée
de la Durance
Agneau de lait des Pre-Alpes confit au thym frais
Legumes engros morceaux confits
Fromages affinees par notre fromager
accompagnes d'une salade de saison melangee a l'huile d'olive primeur
Tarte aux premieres gariguettes, sorbet gariguette-basilic
Mignardises.

A very special meal—one that hooked us on haute cuisine!

That night we stopped at Bonnieux and watched the sun set across the valley from our small hotel room terrace. A very pleasant experience, even though it had started to lightly rain. It rained more during the early morning, but we struck off anyway. On to Menerbes, home of *A Year in Provence* author, Peter Mayle, where we bought *café au lait* and a bakery treat to get us going. We drove north from there to Murs, had a picnic lunch south of Apt, and on to Aups for the night and a special meal at the Restaurant des Gourmets.

For our last day of land touring we headed to the Grand Canyon du Verdond and drove for several hours along the rim of the largest canyon in Europe. It slices through the limestone plateau midway between Avignon and Nice. The unusually high fluorine content of the water gave the river a rich green color. We shared the two-lane road with tour buses, other tourists (on a Sunday drive), motorcycles and lots of bicycles. Boy did those people have big hearts—and large thighs! Our only disappointment was the fact that there was no place to pull off and gawk. Spotting a wide place on the winding road, we would make a temporary stop, get out and take a quick photo. Returning to Toulon we made a stop at Chartreus de la Verne, a monastery built in the 12th century and still lived in by 15 Carthusian nuns (they aren't from the 12th century). We looked forward to buying some of the nuns' homemade "pain a la farina de chataignes" (chestnut flour bread), but the monastery was closed that day. Everyone who drove the dusty road up just took advantage of a nice walk with peek-a-boo scenes of the Mediterranean to the south. No bread that day.

From Toulon we took *TEKA III* out to the Porquerolles Islands, staying three nights, until the wind shift sent us on to the next port—St. Tropez. Seas were kicking up on our trip there, so we had both flopper stoppers in the water to hold us steady. At one point a loud noise on the starboard side grabbed our attention. A quick assessment—the shackle at the extreme end of the arm (25 feet out from the boat), which connected the flopper stopper lines to the arm, had broken. When that happened, all the attending lines and flopper stopper dropped way under water. Putting the engine in neutral, we scrambled to gather in all the rope before any got under the boat and fouled the prop. Then while tossing about in 7-foot beam seas (the other flopper stopper worked hard to control the rocking on its side of the boat), we used two block and tackle systems to retrieve that 50-pound flopper stopper. We didn't want to drag it along beneath the boat, or risk losing it, or have it bang against the boat, so we had to get the potential menace back on board. Boy did the adrenaline flow! As a team we got everything under control and limped into St. Tropez Bay, where we took the dinghy down to assess the damage, and completed repairs before sunset.

Then the fun started. Weather did change. Gale-force winds (35-40 knots) were predicted by midnight. Midnight came and we bolted out of bed. The rigging started singing and the boat began bouncing up and down with OTN (on the nose) waves. And wind at that time registered only 20 knots. We had to pull anchor and relocate before wind got up to 40. A quick check of the chart showed us if we went about 2.5 miles across the big bay, we could possibly be out of harm's way. We bounced along listening to the wind creep up to 40 knots during that 1-hour trip to go 2 ½ miles. Safely re-anchored by 2 A.M. we resettled our psyches and finally went back to sleep.

Next morning arrived bright and clear. We moved back across the bay and took the dinghy to St. Tropez town where we gawked at the mega yachts in the harbor and the fashionably dressed folks strolling through town. The following morning we started to Cannes.

The Isles de Lerins stand just across from the city of Cannes, home to the International Film Festival just finishing up. We anchored at St. Marguerite just below the fort/prison where the man with the iron mask spent many a day. We wanted to visit Fort Royal while there, only to find the Museum with the mask inside was closed on Mondays. Now I will never know if the mask had a silk or velvet lining, or even who it was. Much speculation here, including was it a he or a she?

Our first evening there we watched a passagemaker-type boat flying a British flag anchor nearby. The man lowered his dinghy, climbed in and started the motor, then came over to see us. He said he wanted to meet those famous people from *PassageMaker Magazine*. We enjoyed swapping stories, as both boats were over 20 years old. He had been busy modifying his to be a live-aboard boat and cruise wherever. He told us he was president of Jacques Savoye (Automobiles de sport et de luxe depuis 1934—his grandfather started the company) and lived in Paris. His accent just flowed and I could have listened to him speak for a long time—in French or English.

The next morning we watched as the snow-covered Alps appeared with the sunrise—magnificent! Clouds had covered them the other two days and we were unaware of their presence until they showed up.

At L'Oasis Restaurant just outside Cannes, we had another gourmet meal, this time recommended by the Frenchman. Following that delight we pulled up anchor and set our sights on the last anchorage along the French Riviera—Ville Franche. It's a large harbor ringed by mountains and full of everything from cruise ships to small sailing vessels. We met up with the sailing vessel, *DUTCH TOUCH*. Peter on that boat gave the weather report for the Mediterranean Cruisers' Radio Net each morning.

After two nights there, Italy called.

Italy: Inland and Islands

Our Italian waiter touched Denis gently on the shoulder, then verbally and non-verbally as only the Italians can do, exclaimed, "Bellisimo!" On our first stop along the Italian Riviera in June 2002, we celebrated our anniversary at Santa Margherita Ligure, anchoring just below a restaurant perched above the bay. After the waiter presented us with the menu, he walked over to the large picture windows and stared out at our boat. We called him back to the table and told him that boat was ours. He broke out in a huge grin, ran to get his boss and that moment became a touching memory.

Portofino, with its busy harbor of fishing boats, pleasure craft, and mega-yachts all lined up tightly together had a Mediterranean feel about it. The homes surrounding the harbor were painted pastel colors, had balconies for openness and shutters for privacy. Cobblestone streets ran through the village. Tourists mingled with the locals, creating a melodic sound of languages to match the already colorful scene.

Portovenere had a spectacular narrow entrance just below a church and castle on the hill and a small port nearby. We anchored across the way and had a grand view all night, after having climbed up to the castle that afternoon and I had my photo taken with none other than "Mother Nature." She was quite chubby, had big breasts, may have been pregnant—all the images that one has of a mother figure. She sat on a bench, arms open, as if calling people to sit next to her.

Mary sitting with Mother Nature in Portovenere

Elba had some interesting events transpire, from a storm blowing one boat very close to us in the anchorage, to walking around the port, knowing this was the famous place Napoleon had spent many a day as a prisoner, and meeting some Thai ladies at a pizza place. They could not believe we had lived in Bangkok and we even spoke a little bit (nit noi) of Thai, and loved Thai hot food. One lady had married a local man who did not like Thai food, yet she moved to Elba and worked in his pizza restaurant to please him, taking her family with her.

At first the Port authorities in Elba would not allow us off the boat for touring the town. Someone had to be there on board at all times, something we never quite figured out. At one point they did give permission to leave for a limited time, only if we called the port office on the radio and discussed it with them first.

Porto di Roma, built at the beach where the Emperors once frolicked outside the big city, allowed us a nice place to stay while waiting for company. However we had two significant events happen before their arrival. First the costly med-moor prop wrap; second, an Emergency Room run.

Coming into the port through the breakwater, we met men in a marina dinghy to help us to our assigned spot and assist us in med-mooring. Med-mooring is done throughout the Mediterranean and is supposed to be a simple job. Instead of tying sideways, as we do in the States, the boat is tied with stern lines to the dock and secured at the bow by an underwater line pulled on board. So instead of using 52 feet of space by side-tying, we used only 16 feet. Many more boats can be accommodated using the med-moor method. What is supposed to be simple can become complicated, which we found out over our time in the Med. Wind can effect positioning. Currents get involved. Boats need to be squeezed open to make adequate space. And then there's the prop wrap, which happened to us.

The men in the dinghy pulled up to the dock and jumped out to wait while we reversed into position. No other boats had to be dealt with, so it looked as if we would have an easy job, just like in Barcelona. But while our prop was still reversing toward the dock, one of the men got ahead of the game and pulled the underwater line up that went to the bow. It got wrapped around the prop. Nothing could be done until we hired a diver to cut it away. He took quite a while to do that job too, coming up with small pieces of rope at a time. The marina men did not appear upset about our situation, shrugging shoulders and looking bored while we got untangled.

Welcome to Porto di Roma, home to a mighty surge at times, and many seagulls decorating the docks. Daily dock washing kept the staff busy. But this port, conveniently located to the International Airport, proved the easiest way to visit Rome, and strike out to explore the islands between Rome and Napoli.

Son David and his family (Denise, Soren, and Aeren), joined us on Father's Day, June 16, for eleven days to do Rome, four islands, and the Amalfi coast. But before they came we had an accident! I had taken the garbage bag out of its container in the galley to be removed for disposal. Leaving it on the floor at the bottom of the salon stairs for only a minute created the opportunity for Denis to step on one corner of the bag, and get a nasty cut on his foot. A tin can lid turned out to be the culprit. And his bare foot connected with it through the plastic bag. Lots of blood needed instant attention. One woman walking a dog down the dock answered my call for help. I had asked her if she knew a doctor. She said, "No, but I am a nurse!" She came on board, looked at the bleeding wound, and wrapped it enough to get us the Emergency Room. Americans on *GATTI FELICE* at the end of our dock had a rental car and knew how to get to the hospital, thus becoming our ambulance.

At the hospital they took Denis in right away, cleaned the wound, stitched the cut using no anesthesia, bandaged it and said, "No charge." We all went back to the marina, vowing to be more careful with the garbage contents in the future.

Once the family settled in, we made plans to visit Rome for a couple of days, going back and forth on public transportation each day. It took 90 minutes from the marina to central Rome by bus from the marina, train to metro, metro to destination stop. On the first day in Rome, grandson Soren, 12 years old then, took the opportunity to square off with one of the period-dressed Gladiators outside the Roman Coliseum for a photo op. One gladiator wore lime green (Day-Glo) running shorts along with his red centurion cape and headgear.

The Coliseum is an awesome place to visit. One can easily imagine the feats taking place on the large stadium floor at the bottom of the circular building. There is enough of the giant structure left to realize just how many people the Emperor could have at his beck and call to boo or cheer the fighter of the moment.

The best time at the Forum, across the road from the Coliseum, occurred when the boys, all four of them, wetted their whistles at the ancient water fountain, and also filled their hats before plopping them back on their heads to cool off. It had been a scorcher of a day. On the following day, another scorcher, we toured St. Peter's Church and the Sistine Chapel. Many people flocked to this enormous square to fill their hearts and minds with spirituality.

To cool off, we dropped our med-moor lines and headed out the breakwater for some island activity early on June 20. Calm seas took us easily the 64.5 nautical miles to Isola Ponza. The marina looked full; the anchorage, "chock-a-block." We soon found out why. At midnight we watched fifteen minutes of spectacular rocketry put on to celebrate the Summer Soltice, and David's 41st birthday.

Ponza's geology showed not only lava flows, ash and rocks in layers, but also my first look at large areas of white ash turned to rock, called "tuff." Quite striking! And the view of the rock above and clear water below created a sense of nature easily labeled, "awesome."

Isola d'Ischia, with its famous formidable castle, became our next anchorage. This time we had to jockey for a place to anchor with all the weekend boaters, large and small, out for fun and sun. On shore we ate pizza, panini (Italian sandwiches) and gelato (ice cream) before striking out along the cobblestone walk to the castle and across a moat bridge into the walled city. In medieval times, local citizenry fled to safety across the causeway during a siege, with maybe up to several thousand people hunkering down inside the castle. A nunnery once existed inside the castle. One of the most unique rooms in the lower area showed where the nuns were taken when they died, to sit upright in special stone chairs laid out in a circle, until they decomposed and the bones were removed. An unusual cemetery!

In contrast to such a busy harbor, Procida, the next island, stood only four miles away, but looked untouched. Sure, fishing boats were there, but not many pleasure boats where we anchored. The houses along the harbor and up the hillside near the castle sparkled in their pastel colors of blue, pink and yellow reflecting the summer sun.

Everyone knows the Island of Capri from song and movies. It is spectacular, especially with the wind and water erosion of rocks on the south side that leave an opening attracting vessels to pass through, but which takes bravado to do. What's really special about Capri? The Blue Grotto. Locals take you inside the caves in their small boats to ooh and aah at the light bouncing off the water and the blue hue around you. Denis and I had done that trip many years ago, so let David and Denise go this time while we waited outside in the big boat.

Bougainvillea, showing their many colors, bloomed everywhere along the ridge above the Amalfi coastline. In the port we chose to med-moor rather than anchor out, and that turned out to be a mistake. All boats along the concrete seawall had the bow line going down to a heavy chain stretched in the center of the small harbor. When heavy surge came around the point, it started a bouncing reaction for each and every boat attached to that chain. We were particularly worried that this behavior would somehow damage our rudder by hitting pieces of rock and concrete down on the bottom near the seawall—too close for comfort. As a result, four of us moved out to the anchorage for a rough night pitching fore and aft, but not rocking and rolling in that unsafe position. The other two were successful in locating a room on land for the night. Everyone regrouped at the bus stop in the morning to continue the adventure, this time in northern Italy. We had an appointment at Rome's International Airport, so we turned the boat around.

As an aside, anchoring in Amalfi at another time, we just missed greeting friends from Maine there on a land trip. "Letters to the Editor" section in a later *PassageMaker Magazine*, explained what happened. Our friends were having coffee at a sidewalk café, watching us anchor. We have a distinctive profile and were easily identified. They tried to call us on a borrowed portable radio. We had just turned all our electronics off, including radio, so we could rest and relax. Someone offered to take them by small boat out to see us, but they had to catch a bus, and did not have the time. So their best bet was to write a letter. Editor Bill Parlatore printed it and that's how we found out about our missed opportunity. Too bad we did not get a chance to visit with the folks from *LADY PAMELA*, but happy they took time to write the editor.

Back at Rome's Fumicino International Airport, we picked up Clark and Joan Scarboro for a three-week visit, one touring Tuscany by rental car, and two cruising from north to south on the west side of Sardinia.

Tuscany offered many vistas of sunflowers fields, wheat ready to harvest, olive, fig, and walnut groves, cut hay in rolls or bales over the landscape and lots of flowers, especially bougainvillea. There were walled cities; towers, crumbling or still standing tall; red-tiled roofs; two-lane winding roads; older women sporting their practical house dresses which let in the cool air from the top and bottom; English plus German speaking tourists; and hippies at the hot springs, who washed their clothes as well as themselves in the same pool.

Of special note were the "lay-by ladies." These women from Africa stepped out from the woods along a busy highway, dressed in city clothes, and lingered near the road waiting for a trucker or traveler to stop and make a business arrangement. We heard later on a radio interview that young women from Nigeria were brought to Italy on other pretenses, yet ended up becoming prostitutes and in a predicament that more or less imprisoned them. They lived in houses in the woods with an older woman who supervised what they ate, what they wore, and the schedule they kept. As with all prostitution, the participants were trapped, with no way to go back home and no other source of income to pay off their debts. It sounded very sad.

On our road trip we stopped in Siena to see the Duomo, one of Italy's great Gothic churches. It gleamed in the morning light as we approached. Inside were inlaid marble panels carved in the floor, black and white banded marble pillars, small chapels with ornate paintings, and a pulpit carved in marble.

Outside, the Piazza del Campo, shaped like a scallop, was paved with brick and encircled by rings of stone slabs. Eight white lines divided the area into nine segments, each symbolizing one of the nine members of trade and banking, who ruled the city during its greatest period of prosperity—13th to mid-14th centuries. Twice a year the townspeople put on a pageant for the tourists. Dressed in period costumes they paraded around the piazza, and then raced horses, with heavy betting on the outcome. Outside the Town Hall two men stood, holding birds of prey, attached to chains on their heavily gloved hands. One held a bald eagle; the other a great horned owl, with intense yellow eyes. The men and birds stood for photos before wandering from the Piazza into a nearby field where the birds were released to soar among the towers of Siena.

Returning to Porto di Roma and the boat, we purchased some provisions and waited for a weather window for crossing to northeast Sardinia. A few anchorages later we were in Santa Teresa Gallura, where we found ourselves anchored in the turnaround path for the ferry that went back and forth between Bonafacio on Corsica and this Sardinia port.

While Clark and Denis went ashore in the dinghy to buy more groceries, Joan and I stayed on board and watched the happenings. The first happening almost brought the wrath of the ferry authorities down on our heads and shoulders.[*] A ferry backed out of the channel and had to avoid us to make his turn. Our friendly waves brought only frowns and scowls from the captain, but he carried on. Then someone came out in a small boat and told us to move. Our chart had an anchor on it, indicating anchoring was okay. But not so! That ferry left, and they wanted us to move before the next one came in from across the way—one ferry crossed another about halfway between Sardinia and Corsica on their routes. I started the engine and pulled the anchor part way up while watching the ferry's approach far off the bow. At the same time I kept an eye out for our men to appear on the shoreline and get into the dinghy for their return to the boat. I had a plan—if Denis and Clark had not shown up before the ferry came within a certain range, I would pull the anchor all the way in and start circling outside the ferry's path until they showed back up. Fortunately that did not have to happen as the guys arrived in time.

Cruising down the western side of Sardinia we heard on the Mediterranean Cruisers' Net that a mistral (those gale force winds that blow across the Golfo di Lyon and keep blowing down to Sardinia) was coming, so needed to find shelter. This time we went into Alghero and med-moored to the wall in front of a medieval fort. People paraded past us all day and into the night along the promenade. One young lady stopped with her friends and I heard her say in English, "This boat is from my home state. I went to college in Tacoma (Washington)." So I walked to the stern, and asked her which college she went to and what she studied. She had graduated from University of Puget Sound and majored in International Studies. Denis taught there, and was involved in taking students to Asia for International Business course work. About that time Denis came out of the pilothouse. I asked her if she knew him. She did. What a small world!

---

[*] Adapted from my article, "Not a ferry good anchorage," *Passagemaker Magazine,* Nov/Dec 2002, pp 158-159

Med-moored to the town wall at Alghero

Several anchorages down the western side became home for a night or two on our way to the southern end, Cagliari. There we stayed at Marina Santelmo with twenty boats, including two Brit boats on their last leg of a four-year circumnavigation. Clark and Joan returned to the States, and Marvin Day, of *GOOD COMPANY,* helped Denis with a two week paint job on the decks. Every day he arrived bright and early with a smile, "Your 'day' worker is here!" We had purchased the paint in Barcelona and had a worker lined up, but he let us down by accepting another job, so we left with the paint and waited for an opportunity to use it. Marvin and Denis did an excellent job.

On several occasions at the Cagliari dock we saw three large dolphins chasing schools of bait fish toward our boat. Bait fish on the surface brought many terns to feed, flying back and forth across the bow picking up tasty morsels for themselves, and some for the baby tern posted on the teak railing up front. He waited so patiently, looking for the ones feeding him, and opened his mouth on cue for the treat to get dropped inside. That is, all but once. It slipped out while he tried to turn it in his beak, and fell into the water. He looked so funny, leaning over the side, studying the situation. But he didn't move. Soon the parent bird came with another snack and he was back in business.

Painting finished and ready to roll, we joined two buddy boats for the run to Africa. *GOOD COMPANY*, a sailboat with Marvin and Nancy Day on board, and *SEASCAPE*, a trawler carrying Joan and John Brair, plus Tipper, their nautical dog, would be our companions for this trip.

Taste of Tunisia

A large Italian Guardia Finanza helicopter dropped out of the sky and hovered just outside our pilothouse window south of Sardinia, but in international waters.

We heard it coming before we could spot it. It circled us once then hovered outside the starboard pilothouse window. The men inside just stared. Really stared. Although we could not see their eyes behind shiny helmets, the rigid posture of the head, neck and body in their seats showed their intense interest in us. The Guardia Finanza check for smuggling and we might have made a good target for close inspection. They did not call on the VHF; even though they could see I picked up the mike and pantomimed they could call me. I did not slow down or change direction, simply waited for them to go away or say something. Finally, after probably only a few minutes, they flew off. It seemed like half an hour to me.

My background knowledge of northern Africa turned out to be wrong. I thought all of it was desert, based on the *Lawrence of Arabia* movie and the WWII German General Rommel, AKA "Desert Fox." True, there is a lot of desert in Tunisia, but in Tabarka, the nearest city to Algeria in the northwest corner, it is very green and we learned it used to be the "bread basket of Rome," plus where the animals came from for the Gladiator events in the Coliseum. One day we took time to explore the area nearby—visiting ruins of ancient slave markets, temples of worship, and homes, their frescoed floors still visible, adding life to the empty scene.

Roman ruins in northwestern Tunisia

Two events happened at that port. John and Joan Brair on *SEASCAPE* had their American flag stolen right off the back deck during the night. A surprise for them to say the least! John and Tipper gave chase, but did not catch up with the thieves. The next day several young men stopped at our boat and asked if they could have our large American flag. I told them that flag was the only one I had (meaning the only large one). They did not believe me, but left me alone. I quickly exchanged the large one for a regular-sized one, hoping no one would steal it. Nothing happened.

The other time surprised me. A mother with four children stopped on her way back from the beach when she noticed we had a water hose on the back deck. She asked, *"S'il vous plait?"* pointing to the hose and then the children. I agreed she could use it. First she put her two boys, probably age 6, on the swim bridge, stripped them, rinsed them off quickly and re-dressed them. The two girls waited their turns, but Mother used towels to cover them when the swimsuits came off. They were about 12 years old and not keen about undressing in front of a lot of people. I soon realized I had two sets of twins using my water supply. I asked the mother, "Double?" (Twins?) She smiled, "Oui." The boys got the giggles and when they left, waved and grinned. My thoughts were along the lines of hoping they would remember this American's kindness when they grew up and perhaps became fighter pilots. I know that was a leap in my thought process, but it felt very real.

At our next port, Bizerte, we fueled up, survived an ATM scam, and planned a trip down into the Sahara Desert.

In Bizerte we first had to go through the clearing formalities, again. Each port wanted to see boat papers, passports and crew list to mark their books. And when you finally left Tunisia, you had to leave the boat's cruising permit with the proper authorities and have spent all your Tunisian dollars.

We had several problems at that port. Wind caused havoc with med-mooring, one of the nightmares for boaters in that dilemma. Another one was the official asking for whiskey, more than once. They knew we had liquor on board as we had to list it on the boat inventory papers. He became quite a pest until he finally was told in Arabic by John, our traveling partner, we would not do it. A bottle of whiskey in Tunisia was worth approximately $100 U.S. No wonder he wanted one.

We took advantage of fuel being cheaper in Tunisia, so put in a large order with the men at the Bizerte port fuel dock. They agreed they had enough on hand, but when we tied up at their dock, things did not work out that way. They only gave us part of their available diesel from the dock tanks, saying other boats were coming and needed to be filled too. So trucks were ordered. The first truck's fuel gleamed a turquoise color. The second one, a darker shade, and by the fourth, we wondered if we should have put on a super-filter. The fuel dock people seemed non-bothered about the discrepancy, assuming a "Just pay and leave" attitude. Our 816 gallons cost $1.17 a gallon, PLUS the delivery truck charge which we could not get out of, no matter how hard or fast we could talk.

ATMs were a blessing as we traveled in different countries. Using our card, we could get local currency easily enough everywhere. Except in Tunisia. I usually accompanied Denis to the ATM and covered him when he entered the PIN number, keeping prying eyes behind us out of the loop. The day we wanted to get money in Bizerte I could not go, having been sick all day.

Denis approached the machine, thought he had inserted his card, but did not notice it had not gone into the slot. While he spent time studying the information on the screen, most of it in Arabic, the man behind him made a distracting motion with his hand near the card. He was actually taking the card while at the same time indicating to Denis the bank had swallowed it inside. So Denis came back to the boat. We were scheduled to go to the Sahara Desert for two nights with our friends that afternoon. As soon as possible we told the tour arranger about the problem. He assured us he would go to the Bizerte bank the next morning (his friend was the manager) and find out if the card was inside the bank.

We were very fortunate the man who took the card was not a skilled crook, or that the ATMs in town did not work well for him. The bank found no card inside. When we reported our loss to the U.S. bank, they said it had been used at three different banks in a 24-hour period of time, but did not yield much cash at any one of them. Needless to say our bank cancelled the debit card to avoid other problems and wrote off the transactions. I still had my card, but it would not work in those circumstances. We learned that a second and different card would be helpful in such cases and made that happen on our return to the States next time.

When we returned from our desert trip, the two of us went to investigate how the man could have seen the PIN number. We watched people walk up to the ATM and step up on a small platform to insert their information. Just that bit of height gave the next person in line a good view of the numbers being entered. Now we knew. I should have been there.

Money on the boat provided us with enough cash for the trip to the Sahara. Leaving the boat in port, the six of us, plus Tipper, took a van south. Sand and more sand! There were camels too, wild ones in a herd seen crossing the road, and others available for a price to ride. Camels have such a haughty look about them. Heads are held high. Their eyes, batting very long eyelashes, look down scornfully from up in the air. Plus they always seem to be chewing something they might just want to spit out at you. However, Marvin and Nancy took the plunge and rode a couple of camels for an hour. The camels let one get on them when they are seated on the ground. The getting up process looks scary and they rock and roll climbing up on all fours again. Then the gait is something else as they plod on the sand with those huge feet and long legs with you saddled in-between their humps. The four who did not ride camels chose to ride in a horse-cart. It rattled Denis' back more than the camel would have while riding up and down the sand dunes. We did get to munch on some bread baked inside the sand. And visit a Berber village where "Star Wars" was filmed. The Berbers lived in houses carved out of the sand dunes, just like in the movie.

Along the way we stopped at Sfax, Tunisia's second largest city, to shop at their famous souk—a marketplace that sold most everything from shoes to silverware, headscarves to handicrafts. Tipper played All-American Ambassador that day. Most Arabs do not like dogs and in fact some are extremely afraid to be near one. When we got out of the van at one stop, a man pointed out Tipper to a young boy. The boy came near, but kept his distance and was not anxious to pet her. We all waited, including Tipper, who never growled or barked. The young boy's hand stretched tentatively closer and closer until finally he touched the dog. He grinned and wanted the old man to do it too. We had drawn quite a crowd by that time.

We did buy a few souvenirs at the souk before continuing on our way past Beduoin tents, grazing sheep and stark landscape to Bizerte. Our local guide, Salah, did an excellent job driving us 610 miles along the coast, through some desert, and back across the interior to where we originally joined him at Hammamet. He had a hard time saying "Goodbye" to Tipper, as he had bonded with her, making sure she had shade and water at stops along the way.

In Bizerte we prepared for the next leg, Sicily, then to Gaeta.

Glimpses of Gaeta

The "No Smoking" sign over his head meant nothing to the Fontera (border) policeman in Marsala, Sicily, as he puffed away, nonchalantly awaiting the arrival of a key to unlock the passport stamp box. At first the police did not want to be bothered at all, saying we could check back into the European Union (E.U.) in Gaeta, many miles north of Sicily. We insisted and persisted, complicated by the language barrier, until our passports were stamped and we were legal again.

We had an interesting experience at Sicily's northwest point, Capo San Vito, which in photos looks like the Rock of Gibraltar. There, Denis took the scuba air tank in to shore to be "topped off." The British lady running the dive shop asked him which boat was his in the anchorage. Looking down his pointed finger, she exclaimed, "Oh, the George Clooney one!" This happened not too long after the movie, *The Perfect Storm*. We did look like a Cape Cod fishing trawler with our flopper arms in their extended position.

Some land touring of Sicily showed us landscape dotted with WWII gun placements still visible, plus a whole family out harvesting grapes. They invited us to pick some grapes ourselves, and then solemnly reminded us it was the first anniversary of 9/11. In one town we walked up to a stunning statue honoring the local boys who had immigrated to Nord America before WWI, then fought and died for their new country. I felt the emotion of the people in that statue. Well done. Later we read in the guidebook that over a million Sicilians immigrated to the U.S. and Canada between 1870 and 1910.

A 12th-century cathedral at Monreale had huge mosaics along the walls and ceilings depicting stories from the Old and New Testament. Included were God creating the World, Adam and Eve, Noah and the Ark, Jacob, and the fishers of men, just to mention a few. And they were gorgeous! A mosaic of Christ with outstretched arms took over the entire front of the church. Sitting in a pew, just absorbing the beauty through all your senses, made the trip worthwhile. It reminded me of the Bible stories presented on the doors of Norte Dame Cathedral in Paris, which we learned is how those parables were taught to the masses, pictorially, just as in the mosaics.

Having spent a few days on Sicilian roads we came away with vivid images of driving and drivers. They drive fast, even in villages with very narrow streets; employ "blow and go" strategies; park very uniquely—if a spot is almost available they just point the front end into the curb, sometimes up onto the curb with one wheel; open their doors without looking; and back up as needed to make a forward move.

Back on the water we dropped the hook near the volcanic island, Stromboli, which burps daily with ash and some lava, like having perpetual indigestion. That night we watched lava roll down its sides. Impressive!

After Stromboli we encountered a strong rain system. The radar showed rain everywhere around us. At first Denis said, "We can go around it," and changed course. It turned out to be bigger than we thought, so he modified his intentions to, "we'll punch right through it!" Not a good idea as it got truly rough, including four lightning bolts, two forward and two aft in a row, striking right next to the boat. Nothing hit us, yet our friend, Marvin Day, had his sailboat's autopilot damaged by a strike right in the anchorage later that day. At the top of our mast, plus the ends of our flopper stopper arms are "porcupines" to help diffuse lightning strikes, and so far so good. Hedging my bets a bit further, I feel better anchoring amongst sailboats with very tall masts to make our 34' mast a smaller target.

Gaeta, Italy has a long history. Originally a modest settlement of peasants and fishermen, shipbuilding and sea-trade made it an important Tyrrhenian Sea port around 1700. The narrow cobblestone streets have felt many feet traveling over them, from the locals who lived and worked there, to the ship-builders and traders who flourished there, to the many foreigners who fought and died in wars throughout that area, most recently, WWII. Today the town is divided into an old part and a new part, remodeled after World War II damage.

Now Gaeta is home port for the U.S. Navy's Fifth Fleet Command Ship, *USS LA SALLE.*[*] During our time back in the States, from October 2002 to March 2003, things heated up about going to war, and the day before we returned, the coalition attacked Iraq. The first thing we noticed on arrival at the marina was the number of cruising boats flying a "PACE" (Italian for "Peace") flag. The Australian boat there flew its flag upside down in distress mode, accidentally at first, then intentionally as a political gesture. The *LA SALLE* was conspicuously absent from inside its barrier enclosure nearby.

---

[*] Adapted from my story, "Cruising the Mediterranean in troubled times," *PassageMaker Magazine*, Jul/Aug 2003, pp 68-71.

Denis asked me to go and buy a *Stars and Stripes* newspaper at the military compound gate. I flashed my military ID card to enter the small area where the newspaper boxes were located. The Italian guard looked at me funny, but never challenged me. I put my money in the slot, opened the box and retrieved a paper. When I looked at the date, I realized when the Command Ship had probably left. Newspaper date: Feb. 24; actual date, March 24. Newspapers are not replenished in the box when the ship is not in port, so it had been gone a month.

While we stayed tied up at the marina wall, two Navy vessels came into the bay. The Guardia Costiera (Italian Coast Guard), Carabiniere (a branch of the Italian Army), and Guardia Finanza (Customs) boats also stirred up the water roaring back and forth outside the marina. Two tugs helped bring the *HMS CORNWALL* and the *U.S. NAVY FRIGATE* P-40 into the sausage ring and secure them. Both vessels bristled with armor and electronics. They stayed a few days and on the last day a helicopter buzzed the entire area before landing on P-40. After the ships left, we overheard P-40 hailing a commercial ship and although we did not see it, subsequently boarded them for inspection as part of "Operation Endeavor." Very exciting to eavesdrop on such a conversation over our VHF radio!

On Easter Sunday the *LA SALLE* returned, flying the largest American flag from its mast I have ever seen on a vessel. All the families waited expectantly on shore. Cruisers in the marina watched as well, whistling, blowing horns, and waving flags as the ship arrived. It backed into place and large pontoons were set in place around it for protection so no one could get close and do damage to the ship. The men on board stood at attention on deck in their white uniforms until given the command to break ranks. Then they returned the waves and cheers from their people on shore. And they turned around and greeted us too—we had our big American flag out and waving wildly to show our allegiance and support. After twenty years as an Air Force wife, I felt a special kinship to those who serve and the ones who waited for them. My heart was full that day.

Patriotism runs high—return of USS LA SALLE to Gaeta

With our ID cards, we could walk up the hill to the U.S. Navy Support Base and use their library, do laundry, pick up supplies, or make medical appointments. One day while there we were told by a Security Officer to leave the base immediately. Not only us, interrupted from ordering a new camera over the Internet, but everyone inside the base. We had to walk outside and stand behind the barrier set up across the street to the guard post. Perhaps 100 people huddled there waiting for the "all clear" to go about our business. On the way back down the hill I mentioned this event to a woman walking toward me. She laughed. "They don't care if you are in the middle of lunch or middle of a pap smear, you have to leave!" And so it goes.

We kept abreast of the news through AFN, Armed Forces Network. On a couple of occasions they announced upcoming demonstrations, advising Americans to stay clear. One Saturday a small gathering, complete with Carabinieri control, walked to the marina, then up another street. Someone told us later that these were the people who wanted to protest, but didn't want to make the trip to Naples, 50 miles south, or all the way to Rome. Everything went off without any problem, yet it made us aware we did indeed live in "troubled times" and needed to be careful. We stayed in the marina that morning.

The marina in Gaeta had no gates or fences to keep the local people from using the quay as part of their daily evening strolls. Elderly couples, dressed up for their promenade and holding hands as they walked, gave me a warm and fuzzy feeling. Whole families would stroll together, kids bouncing along having fun while the adults caught up on each other's news of the day. The event impressed me. It seems we in America have lost this kind of camaraderie with big cities, and lots of cars for transportation. Maybe the older folks there live longer and stay together as a couple because of this daily ritual of seeing and being seen by members of their community.

One Sunday we were busy on the aft deck doing something when a family of husband, wife, and small child stopped at the stern of our boat to say *Buon giorno*. We smiled and answered back. The man pointed to his camera and our boat, and non-verbally indicated he wanted a photo of our boat. I gave him permission to take a picture. Within seconds he had passed his camera to our friend standing there, and gathered his wife and child and boarded up the gangplank. They smiled at me, then turned and smiled for the camera. Well done!

Another fun event in Gaeta occurred when ten seasoned women cruisers took a new American bride, Marsha Wood, for lunch to share their stories. Together they represented over 50 years of life on the water, and had much to tell. These ladies had raised families and worked outside the home—teacher, school bus driver, CFO, pharmacist, bank officer, CPA, psychologist, retail manager, and/or assisted husbands in their fields—before escaping to sea.

Some advice: Don't be afraid of the unknown; don't sweat the small stuff; pick your battles; be aware of the restricted space on a boat; be ready to give and receive reality checks on issues (communication in any relationship is important, whether on land or sea), be tolerant of others and other cultures; remember your favorite foods are not always available (so try the "tipico" meals when you can—no dishwashing involved either), and make your boat "homey" with something from home (take the crystal glasses if you'd like to). They stressed how easy it is to make friends with other "yachties" (cruisers). They speak the same language, have the same fears, and enjoy going and doing.

It can be said, "Don't get too attached!" as you have to leave them somewhere. Yet in another somewhere, there you may find them again. This happened several times to Ruth on *ANNAPURNA*. They met someone in the South Pacific, had a good time socializing, said, "Goodbye," and then there they were in another anchorage across the world! Wow! In our case, we first met *SIRIUS*, in Italy; saw them again the next year in Croatia, and the last time in Zihuatanejo, Mexico. We had anchored ahead of them and could not see their boat name from that angle. Becky popped up from inside their cabin, thinking I need to send an email to *TEKA III*, and her mouth fell open when she spied us right in front of them.

Other pointers from the lunch ladies included the notion that all is not "cookies and cake" out there. *BOUNDLESS* reported they had to turn around 500 miles into their Atlantic crossing, right in the teeth of a storm, as their communications failed. SAYONARA said they spent three days anchored in Force 9-10 winds (near hurricane strength), their focus so intent on the weather that he forgot her birthday. *MAD RIVER* calls ocean passages like "camping in a washing machine." There are many examples on this issue, but this gives you an idea of some really harsh ones.

Bottom line from us to her: Expand, Explore, Experience, and Keep a Diary!

Croatian Imprints

Dubrovnik, the magical city of Croatia, called us to come and explore. To do that we had to journey down to and around Italy's boot. Two images of that trip stand out—the Strait of Messina at the "toe" and a stealing experience at the "heel."

Narrow bodies of water, running fast between two pieces of land, represent images of rapids, whirlpools and mayhem possibilities. The Strait of Messina is one of these and lists a long history of ancient mariners sailing through, plus Richard Halliburton, an American adventurer, who attempted to swim across in the 1930s.

At the beginning of the strait, running between mainland Italy and the island of Sicily, we listened long and hard for the mythical "Sirens" that history books says lured sailors of old to their death in whirlpools near shore. No sirens that day. We did encounter ships—freighters, container ships, five NATO warships and numerous ferries plying the waters. They just lined up on the radar coming north, or zipped right in front of us crossing as passenger ferries between the island of Sicily and Italy's mainland. I found the experience exciting, just to travel that historical piece of water, but realized I had myself too worked up about the rapids and whirlpools. The waters in the Strait can be rowdy if taken at the wrong tide with an opposing wind in a narrow, restricted area. That holds true for any strait. With our charts and additional information we studied the right time for our passage. The 3.5-knot current going our way gave us a push on our transit. All went well, and Mt. Etna on Sicily stood out bright and beautiful as we passed by. My experience, described earlier in Canada and Alaska, had given us opportunities to perfect rapids transiting by choosing slack water and going with the current, thus avoiding extra-exhilarating rides. So I felt ready for the Strait of Messina.

At the "heel" of the boot, after traveling along the sole of the shoe for several days, we tied up to the seawall in the fishing port of Santa Maria di Leuca. There, thieves in the night stole my favorite bright-orange fender from the railing. For protection in tying up to seawalls or other boats, fenders (round or sausage in shape) are positioned over the sides of boats to cushion any impact between objects that might cause damage.

I awoke when I heard voices alongside the aft deck. I got out of bed and watched as best I could from the porthole inside the cabin. I could see several pairs of feet below the canvas curtain along the side, and heard people whispering. I kept listening and watching, ready to pounce if they leapt on board. Instead, I missed my chance to capture them in the act. They had been busily untying the fender from its post while whispering. When it came loose, they pushed on the boat to give them room to pull it up between boat and seawall, and then took off running as if the cops were after them. Too late to rescue my absconded property!

From Brindisi to Gruz, Croatia required an overnight passage. There we cleared into the country and our Cruising Permit cost U.S. $302. We only intended to stay a couple of months and continue on down to Greece, so that felt like a lot of money to shell out for a short-time cruising permit. In addition to visiting most of the Croatian islands, we managed a land trip into Montenegro with two other couples. There we enjoyed a visit to an island in a famous fjord, which is now even more famous. In the *Casino Royale* movie, "007" (Daniel Craig) recuperated on that island after his tortured interrogation by the bad guys. Denis and I almost came out of our seats in the theater when we recognized the setting, realizing we may have been the only people in the audience to know where the stars were in that scene.

Weather kept us totally involved during our two months there. In Croatia the nasty weather revolves around boras. *Boras* are the winds that come down off the high mountains so intense they take all vegetation away. Looking up as we traveled on the Velitski Canal, we were reminded of a moon landscape and super glad it was a nice day. These winds are well respected and travel is limited when boras are in session.

We dropped the hook at about a dozen different islands, with such names as Korcula, Pag, Rab, Cres, Hvar, Vis, and Mljet, and one bay called Rogoznica. The cruisers all called it, "Rosie's knickers." There are no sandy beaches in Croatia and people seem to arrive at the seaside early so as to spread their blankets or mats on the "softest" rock. However each of the islands has a castle, cobblestone streets, interesting buildings, and lots of shops.

Dubrovnik's walled city sat on a cliff dominating the scenery all around. During their recent war in then-Yugoslavia, most of Croatia escaped damage, yet some remnants (shell holes in the walls) were visible. Dubrovnik's wall sang out for us to march around and not only look out to sea, but also down on the town itself, where we could imagine the who, what, where, why and when of history made there. Some houses are still not rebuilt; all we could see were piles of rubble.

Dubrovnik walled city

While anchored (bow and stern) at the nearest island to Dubrovnik, we had a rude awakening when the wind kicked up suddenly to 20 knots right into the cove and started bucking us around. For safety sake we had to leave. The stern anchor could not be raised so Denis buoyed the line and cut it so we could escape, anchoring somewhere else temporarily. When the wind calmed down we retrieved the buoy, line and anchor. I had forgotten about this line until we recently did a stern-tie to a rock in Desolation Sound, British Columbia. I fed the line out from the boat as the dinghy took it to shore. Oophs! There were two pieces of rope, requiring a quick reconnection, then a click in the old memory storage.

Hvar Island left us with three images—one pleasant; one, unpleasant; and the other a mouth-opener. The pleasant one occurred in Starigrad, where twenty four boats carrying over 50 people gathered for a "Cruisers' Rendezvous," that Denis and I organized, getting people on land and on boats together with information on how to successfully enjoy this opportunity for fun and fellowship. We sampled the local wine, enjoyed a potluck in town and a country dinner out of town. Denis celebrated his 66th birthday there, which included the arrival of our daughter, Dawn, and her family from the States for the grand occasion.

Before leaving Starigrad, an unusual storm came through. We could hear the thunder and see the lightning just before dawn. The skies opened up and the rains really came down, hard. Everyone got up to watch the drama, not quite knowing what to expect. While we watched, water in the whole bay seemed to be sucked out of its opening, only to rush back in like a tsunami, three times. After losing about six feet of water under the boat, as measured by the eye on the seawall, enough water remained, so boats med-moored to the wall were not damaged. However, the passerelles (gangways attached to the boats used for walking ashore from the stern) were damaged. The quick up and down jolt bent the gangway attached to the boat, requiring extensive repair in some cases after the storm. Some dinghy davits close to the seawall also were affected. Everything settled back down after a few minutes, and luckily no one got hurt, but the town got flooded. Later, in discussing this phenomenon with townspeople, they told us that a similar storm ten years ago had pulled all the water out of the bay, stranding the fish on the bottom, where they flopped around like crazy. Anyway, it was scary!

Next stop was the town of Hvar on the opposite side of Hvar Island. The harbor had far too many boats in it and the port person in charge kept letting more in to anchor, directing them from his dinghy. Many left the anchorage on the morning we took our dinghy to shore and hiked up to visit the castle on the hill. On returning to our boat, we were met by that same port person in his skiff. He announced we had cut the rope to a fisherman's boat, located nearby. We disagreed in looking the situation over, as our prop is beneath the swim bridge and unable to cut like he surmised. However, he insisted that Denis go with him to the office. There he demanded Denis pay $60 to buy a new line for the fisherman. The fisherman never materialized. Denis paid reluctantly as the only other option was to fill out a lot of paperwork, wait for the proper authorities, and a diver. That left a very bad taste in our mouths for this scam after such a delightful time previously with the rendezvous.

Hvar Harbor, Croatia

Another interesting event happened in Mljet. A small powerboat came into the bay and reversed into an available anchoring space. A nude young lady surfaced, went to the bow to drop the anchor, and then walked to the stern, grabbed a rope and dove into the water. She swam to shore, climbed out, and tied the rope to a tree, then swam back to disappear inside the cabin. It was a "shut my mouth" phenomenon. But nudity was ever-present in all of the Croatian islands.

Looking for Zorba![*]

Just whisper "Greek Islands," and eyes light up. These islands have enticed thousands of people over time to come, see, play, stay a while, and take home stories and memories. Greece, with its many islands, is strategically located in the Mediterranean. To go from west to east—Italy to Turkey, or south to north—Red Sea to Black Sea, you have your choice of places to explore and options to do so. Most people focus on islands in the Aegean Sea, yet the Ionians offer interesting places too. To undertake your exploration, you can ride one of the large ferries or super-fast hydrofoils plying the waters between Athens and Rhodes with scheduled stops in the Aegean; fly from Athens to Corfu in the Ionians; charter a sailboat from one of the companies located throughout Greece, find a friend who lives on their boat and go with them, or be lucky enough to have your own vessel and the time to go where you choose.

"Calling the vessel at latitude ___ and longitude___, this is *TEKA III*. You are approaching on my starboard side. Do you see me?" On this passage to Corfu, Greece from the last town in Croatia, we had to keep constant vigilance on the high-speed ferries going back and forth between Brindisi, Italy and Corfu City. It looked as if the radar had the measles with all the images on it. Our boat does 7 ½ knots; the ferries' speeds equaled three times that. We crept off to the side during the night so as not to get in the way. However, one boat started coming up inside the tracks laid out by our boat and our buddy boat for the trip, *LILJANA*. Denis and Liljana (their boat had been named after her) had just gone off-duty, leaving Salah and me on watch duty in the two boats. I had asked Salah over the VHF radio channel what he thought. He said, "You call him, Mary."

So I did. If he intended to turn and cross between our two boats without notification, there would be trouble, and guess who would be the recipient? I must have sounded official enough because Salah said, "That's very good, Mary, but you better rebroadcast on Channel 16." I had neglected to change

---

[*] Adapted from my story, "Allure of the Greek Islands," in *PassageMaker Magazine,* Jun 2006

the channel from the one we used to communicate between ourselves to the main channel for everyone. Gulp!

I resent the message on 16 and waited. He apparently finally saw us and put on some speed before crossing my bow—to my relief. It is sometimes an unknown if the person driving the boat you are calling, can (a) speak and understand English; (b) is awake and on the job; or (c) cares. In this case, we all came out okay.

We checked into Greece at Corfu—many desks and lots of paperwork over a two hour period of time. The fees and transit log cost U.S. $167. At each port, authorities had to stamp the log, and we had to surrender it at the last port, Symi. In 2005, on a return trip, the fees had decreased to $63.44.

After spending the night below the fort out on a peninsula, we decided to move in to calmer waters, yet still had our flopper stoppers out and fish in the water. A Greek Coast Guard cutter came out from Gouvia, our new destination, and inquired what was in the water. We volunteered to raise the pole so they could see we were not fishing illegally, and did. They were quite polite, thanked us for cooperating, went back to base, and then called us on Channel 16 to say, "If you need anything, call us on Channel 12."

And our arrival in Turkish waters also netted us a visit by their Coast Guard. We had entered the bay, checking it out to drop our anchor, when a large cutter saw us from the entrance, slowing down to have a good look. It did not come into the bay, but within minutes, a smaller one had come out from the base in Marmaris to look us over as well. No one spoke to us from either vessel. By the time we had finished anchoring, a chopper came swooping down on us and did a quick fly-over. Still no radio contact. Apparently they were satisfied by then we were not fishing and returned to base. Perhaps they did not speak English. We definitely did not speak Turkish.

In Corfu, friends from San Diego, Gary and Diana Whitney, arrived. Together we spun around the island in a rental car, and practiced Greek 101 by reading all the road signs and interpreting them with our unique analysis, until something began to make sense. Our skills grew from there.

In Fiskardo, we met a lobster fisherman on his boat. His cage of lobsters looked great. We asked him, mostly by sign language and smiling, if we could buy one. "No, they were for a restaurant." Diana, not to be left hanging, asked if she could take his picture. He held up one finger, dropped down into his small boat, popped out with a clean shirt, and grabbed a good-sized lobster to be his prop for the photo.

Fiskardo, lobster fisherman

Diana, famous for her Mexican cooking, did her best with the supplies on hand to whip up a genuine South of the Border meal for us one night. She must have made a mental note about ingredients needed for future such events. The next time she came to crew, she outdid herself. In preparing meals for the two of them prior to their Caribbean boat visit, she made extra to freeze for the trip. We were impressed when they pulled an ice chest out of the airport delivery van, packed with our surprises for their Antiguan stay.

There are two ways to reach Athens from Corfu: one is the Corinth Canal, which costs money to transit, and the other is longer and more scenic around the Peloponesse peninsula, with its three fingered fjords. We chose that one. Land trips included old Olympia, where the first torch was lit; Sparta, where the fierce warriors lived and learned to fight (according to guidebooks only healthy children survived infancy, as sickly ones were thrown into the mountain ravines); and Mystras, a fascinating ancient place atop a mountain near Sparta (which we enjoyed more than Sparta).

We anchored near castles a lot—Corfu, Methoni, Monemvasia, and Navplio, the first capital. At Navplio we anchored too close to the sewer exit in the town wall. Smelly!

In Athens our first experience came with finding a marina for a few days. We had phoned the closest one to Athens while still en route, but they were not helpful. Our charts showed just the perfect spot, so we set the GPS coordinates, and were thoroughly disappointed to find it did not exist. At least not at that time—they had torn it down to make room for the upcoming Olympics. So we headed down the coastline a bit, found the entrance to a marina that looked reasonable, and pulled inside the breakwater. When we called the marina office via the VHF radio to find out about availability, they said, "No room." Denis said, "I see empty slips. Can we go into one?" Reply: "No! Go to Piraeus" (the marina closest to Athens we had already phoned). We left.

At the next marina we went inside and just floated around looking anxious. Someone came out in a small boat and asked us what we wanted. We told them. They called the office and motioned for us to wait. We floated some more. Soon the word came we could stay there, but it turned out to be way back in the corner, like the "hick" relatives. All the boats in this marina were big expensive mega-yachts and we didn't make the image, so they took our money but kept us out of sight. Not only were they expensive, but their policy of charging as of mid-night caused us to pay for two nights instead of one.

Temperatures were over 100 degrees during our stay in Athens. We moved on after an entertaining visit with a tour guide to see and learn about the Acropolis, had our new batteries delivered and installed, and gathered the next crew couple, Gary and Jean Coard. By the time we arrived at the Temple of Poseidon near the end of the Greek mainland in a couple of days, the temperature had dropped to around 60. What a relief!

Our Acropolis guide, Maria, told us how Athens got its name. The Goddess Athena and God Poseidon vied for the honor. Poseidon threw down his spear into the earth and water started rising everywhere. To cancel that, Athena threw down an olive branch. Not only did the water subside, but olive trees sprung up everywhere. They represented life; the water, death. Therefore the metropolis became known forever as "Athens."

From that jumping-off point, we stopped at nine islands while working our way to Turkey. Beautiful anchorages awaited us at each, but getting to them sometimes involved going through some rough weather. In Greece, the wild winds are meltimis. They can come on strong and last quite a while. They can put you into port or keep you there. They are nothing to mess with since each island is not too close to another.

With the exception of Delos and Rinia, that is. Delos is the birthplace of Apollo and Artemis and goes back to 2,500 B.C. Large carved lion statues (only a few still totally intact) remain on guard, lining the town's main road. Many buildings left in ruin are depicted on placards as to what they were. Rinia, just across the bay, was described as the place of birth and death for the population of Delos. We did not have a tour guide; most of them came by boat with groups from Mikonos, several miles north. So we used a guidebook and did the best we could. Delos was quite the crossroads of the Aegean in its time.

We took advantage of being held up by a meltimi in Naxos to visit the island of Santorini (Thira) by Blue Star Ferry. Santorini ranks high on everyone's list of places not to miss in the Greek Islands. It used to be a round volcanic island, that is, until 3,500 years ago when a series of earthquakes and massive explosions left a crater 6 miles long and 4 miles wide. The quake sent an ash plume sixty miles south to Crete, along with a tsunami, supposedly bigger than the Christmas 2004 one in the Indian Ocean. Historians say the Minoan people who had lived in Crete since 2100 BC were virtually wiped out. The fallout from the ash had long term negative effects on crops. The tsunami did even more damage.

Volcanic activity still exists today on Santorini, but mostly minor tremors. However, in 1956, a major earthquake, measuring 7.8 on the Richter scale, killed many people and destroyed most of the homes in Fira and Oia, the two cities on the rim.

What is spectacular today is to cruise right through the crater, either in your own boat or on a big ferry, like we did. The feeling is awesome when you look up to the rim, maybe 1000 feet above you, knowing people up there are also looking down at you. When leaving the ferry at the port of Athinios, hotel people wait to rent you a space and buses or vans wait to take you to the top. Fira is the main town in the center of the ridge; Oia, smaller, is at the north end. We stayed at a hotel in Fira, rented a car for a day, and on the last morning struck out walking to Oia along the windy ridge with long-distance views in all directions. It sure gave the impression of "living on the edge."

Santorini rim viewed from sea level

Sunsets from the rim can only be described as awesome. The Greek Orthodox churches on Santorini stand out with their blue domes contrasting dramatically with the white buildings. Postcards and posters also capture this colorful pairing, "just like the Greek flag." We were impressed by the landscape, the people, and how life goes on despite calamities.

Altogether we visited 22 islands, 17 in the Aegean and 5 in the Ionian. The Aegean is famous for its meltimis; the Ionian has to cope with earthquakes. We narrowly missed one in Lefkas. Our friends who stayed described it as being aground, but still moving and shaking around.

Several Greek islands lie quite close to Turkey. We checked out of Greece in Simi, having studied Greek 101 along the way with names of places and things, and completed many walks on the islands with the Coards. We placed our feet on paths long ago walked on by a multitude of other feet. All the time we wondered what tales the rocks and hedges would tell if they could talk. Burros lined the rock walls giving us the eye as we passed, patiently waiting their next chore. Small chapels along the way, with opened doors, invited the local people to come inside, find rest, give thanks, or just pray quietly. Apparently one priest moved from place to place ministering to his spread-out flock. We met many nice Greeks, but missed Anthony Quinn.

In Marmaris, Turkey we connected again with friends who had spread out in places throughout the Mediterranean. And with them came a celebration I will never forget—my 65th birthday. Twelve people at a long table upstairs in the marina restaurant smiled and sang "Happy Birthday," to accompany a large cake the waiter placed in front of me. Instead of candles, sparklers made the illumination. I spit all over the cake trying to blow out these "candles." A good time was had by all!

Before being lifted out of the water for winter storage, I asked our next door boat neighbor a special question. We had been side by side with the British sailboat, *SLYPUSS*, for a few days, but never talked to each other— just smiled and waved. I studied the man a lot and could not resist asking a question when we pulled out past him on our short trip to the travel lift. I called him to watch his boat so we would not hit or damage it as we passed. He put his sandwich down, walked up to my position, and then I asked, "Are you Michael Caine's brother?" He looked me straight in the eye and said, "No, I'm Michael Caine!" Then he laughed. Well, how would I know if I didn't ask?

The next year when everyone put their boats back into the water and started their cruising year, we got to know Rod and Margaret from *SLYPUSS* much better. Whenever she saw our boat profile coming into her view, she called on the VHF, chatted a minute, and then signed off with, "Michael sends his love."

Marmaris Yat Marin had an excellent haul-out system. Their yard held more than 700 boats out of the water in winter time, large and small. They wrote the re-launch date on each boat's rudder, and positioned the boats in the yard so they could be moved out in order. If someone missed their date and had to be moved to make room for the boat ahead of it to go back into the water, they were charged for another move. That sounded fair to us.

We stayed two winters on the hard there, which included a paint job for the hull. The paint crew tried to teach me Turkish as they worked. I only learned a few words, but I remembered them, for a while. The prime coat of gray stood out. If we had a couple of 50 caliber guns for the bow, we could have signed up for the Coalition.

Greek cats awaiting a meal

Losing a Cruising Mate

Cruising had its down moments as well. Here is one that happened to our sister ship from the Atlantic Crossing, *ZELDA*. The cruising community, spread out in the Mediterranean, became instantly involved.

The morning of May 17, 2004 began as usual by tuning into the Mediterranean Cruisers' Net on single-side-band radio. Instead of weather updates and status reports of boats anchored, or on passage, we heard Marie Blackburn's voice, "Mayday, Mayday, Mayday! This is *Sailing Vessel ZELDA*!" She had our undivided attention immediately.

She and Terry had started their trip back across the Med from Turkey, and been anchored in a very small place at the north end of Karpathos for four days waiting for the seas to abate. Looking between rocks and out the opening they determined it was time to go, so pulled the anchor, left the anchorage and started moving down the western side of the island toward Kasos.

Within an hour Terry, a previous heart attack survivor, suffered a massive heart attack. He had gone out to raise the mainsail and collapsed during his effort. Marie immediately went to him, performed CPR and inserted a nitroglycerin pill under his tongue. No response. She couldn't locate a pulse and assumed the worse. Unable to move him from his position, she lashed him to the mast and began radio contact for help.

Although there was no Coast Guard response to her Mayday call, two fellow cruisers did answer, even though they were not close enough to help. That's when she sent out the single-side-band call. And what a lucky break for her that day! The radio propagation worked extremely well all day long, which was not always the case. Propagation was quite often problematic.

All the cruisers, spread out in Greece and Turkey, sat glued to the sound of her voice and the tragedy unfolding, and feeling somewhat helpless, yet badly wanting to help. With all the resources, surely someone would come up with the right answer, and soon. With no cell phone coverage where she was, she depended on her radio. Without the single-side-band, she would have spent the day alone. She had all our attention, thoughts and prayers. No one else talked on that radio all day, leaving it open for her to feel our collective presence.

Tom, on *Sailing Vessel PRECEPT*, tied up at a Greek marina, walked to the Greek Coast Guard office just down the dock after hearing the problem. He made it his mission to make sure they were kept up to date with Marie's position, and acted as a relay for her until Athens Rescue Coordination Center could talk to her directly (and that took a while). It turns out Greek Coast Guard does not monitor Channel 16, the International Distress Channel; they listen to Channel 18, with repeater stations relaying messages all the way to Athens. We also learned that ports monitor Channel 12, not 16. The Coast Guard also listens to the single-side-band system, but with different frequencies for morning and afternoon. Needless to say, this would be very confusing and in an emergency, another stress factor. We all learned something valuable that day and hoped we would not have to use it.

While waiting for new communication, I relayed the Mayday information via VHF radio to Steve and Pat on *Sailing Vessel EQUUS*, and they in turn went over to tell Susan and Bob on *Sailing Vessel MEG*, both located in Marmaris Yat Marin. They would come up with a plan to help as well.

Marie is a longtime sailor. She announced she could sail the boat to the next port, but would need help in getting in and tied up at Kasos. When the Athens Center talked to her, finally, they wanted her to go around to the large port of Pigidhia on Karpathos. She had already studied that as an option, but decided that the port of Kasos, only 12 miles away, would be her choice, as the other one was twice as far.

With that as her choice, Athens said they would send a fast boat from Pigidhia to meet her near Kasos, and the port police in Kasos would also rendezvous with her for assistance. So we all waited while she sailed south, steering from the outside cockpit, and moving often inside the boat to monitor the radio. Each time she came on the radio, we knew she was still alert and working the problem.

Three hours after her call, she approached the port. The Port police vessel was waiting for her just outside the breakwater. They had her take down her sail while waiting for the Coast Guard to arrive with a doctor on board. The seas were very rough, and with the sail down, the boat wallowed while waiting. When the CG boat arrived, they could not transfer the doctor directly. He went first to the port vessel, then over to *ZELDA*. He confirmed that Terry had died, then went forward and threw up—"right on the new deck" Marie said later. Only then did someone come on board and assist Marie into port to tie up.

The Coast Guard removed Terry onto their vessel for a ride later that afternoon to Karpathos. After an overnight there, he would go by ferry to a funeral home in Rhodes. Marie spent the rest of her time that day dealing with paperwork—telling her story to a woman who spoke English, who translated it to Greek to someone who wrote it down line by line, who in turn read it to the port captain. Very tedious.

Terry had wanted to be cremated when he died. This could not happen in either Greece or Turkey. To fly him home for cremation would be costly. She wanted options to think about. Cruisers went to bat there too and learned that Bulgaria or Italy would be the closest places doing cremations, but permissions were needed and fees were involved. So she decided to bury him in Rhodes and the U.S. Consulate in Athens suggested two funeral homes for her to contact. She chose one, and later learned Terry can be exhumed in 5-6 years, at which time she can take him to the States for cremation as he wished.

Marie asked Denis to contact Terry's son and daughter in the States, as her cell phone still did not work. Afterward she began to worry about *ZELDA*'s safety. That port was open to the weather where winds and waves would bash her about if left for too long. That's where Bob and Susan come into play. They had told Denis they had reservations on the 4 P.M. Marmaris to Rhodes ferry, and could be there to meet Marie, Terry, or both, or just wait for further instructions. Denis relayed this to Marie. She said, "Wait," but they didn't, making their way to her on Kasos Island where the three of them moved *Zelda* on to Crete, the next island, and a safer place. The body of water between Kasos and Crete is a notoriously wicked one. That day it was as quiet as a mill pond.

With *ZELDA* safely secured, Marie could turn her thoughts squarely back on Terry. Stella, her funeral home contact, helped her with the plans, yet charged her a healthy fee too. The people in Karpathos who held his body and routed it on to Rhodes wanted 4,500 Euros for their service. Stella talked them down to 1,000, but that appeared still too steep. (4,500 Euros equaled $5,400 U.S.)

He died Monday. By Thursday Marie was in Rhodes, choosing a burial site. The cemetery was divided into three parts—Greek Orthodox, Roman Catholic, and "other." She walked through the "other" section first, later telling me, "I couldn't leave Terry there. The markers are falling down, the weeds are taking over, and it looks terrible." The man in charge of sites took her to the Roman Catholic side. (She had been raised Catholic; Terry was Unitarian.) They walked along an olive tree lane. Terry loved olives. She spotted a place without a marker and asked if she could have that one. After checking his notebook, the man with her said, "No, someone is still there." Oh well, the next row had a magnificent pine tree spreading over several spots. "Can I have that one?" "Yes." Nearby she also noticed a unique rusted pipe arrangement for a cross with an engraved heart attached. That inspired her to design one similar to it for Terry. The cruising community had now been notified of the funeral time and place in Rhodes.

That afternoon Marie, Susan, and Bob spent walking all over town looking for flowers suitable for Terry. By the time they returned to the hotel, Steve and Pat from *EQUUS*, Brent and Tanya from *WILD WIND*, and us from *TEKA III* were there to give hugs and support. We had taken the 4 P.M. Marmaris-Rhodes ferry, leaving our boats in the marina. She looked exhausted, but is a very strong woman, and as long as she had decisions to make, she kept making them.

After breakfast the next morning Marie gave us all assignments. Steve and Pat went looking for more flowers; Brent and Tanya to find a Robert Frost poem on the Internet; Denis and I to the ferry to meet 6 people coming in on the morning Marmaris ferry. Everyone would meet at the cemetery about noon. The cruising community is just wonderful. Spread out among the Greek islands and in Turkish ports, everyone who could, scrambled to find access to a ferry for the trip to Rhodes. Fortunately Rhodes is a prime ferry destination, and our trip to the port netted us eleven people for the service and to give support to Marie. All of us walked to the cemetery, going first to the Greek Orthodox chapel, then to the Catholic one. Susan met us there and updated the newly arrived about the death and how Marie was doing. Six other people came with Marie and the minister from the funeral home. Counting the minister 25 people came to Terry's farewell.

When the hearse arrived, four men took Terry inside and opened the coffin up near the front of the small chapel. Everyone sat on simple benches and listened as the minister, visiting from Sweden, wove his talk around the anchor marker Marie wanted to have made for Terry's resting spot under that special pine tree. Bob gave the eulogy; Brent read a Robert Frost poem; Ted, another poem from one of Terry's poem books; short talks were given by Susan, Denis, and me.

I had never spoken at a funeral, and felt intimidated with the open casket. Peeking at Terry took the fear out of the situation. I sensed him communicating to me that he wanted me to tell my stories to everyone. So I did. They included the one in the Azores asking directions to the whaling station, Denis not following Terry's advice in Valencia and losing his wallet to pickpockets at the Falla Festival, and several others. I have missed him.

Most friends left on the afternoon ferry. A few stayed one more night. Marie returned to Marmaris with Denis and me on the Saturday afternoon ferry. She had made arrangements to stay aboard *MEG* with Bob and Susan. Sunday she designed the marker; Monday we set off to find someone to make it; and Thursday she brought the finished cross with anchor and heart to Marmaris Yat Marin.

The engraved heart read, "Terry O. Blackburn, Ph.D.; 1943-2004, Peacefully at anchor." Friday she returned to Rhodes to place the marker, then on to Crete and her longtime home, *ZELDA*.

Marie showed a serene sense of courage throughout her ordeal. The cruising community lost a special friend. Marie lost her sailing soul mate.

And all the women cruisers had a chance to reflect on how we would have dealt with such a serious situation.

Terry Blackburn's marker on Rhodes

The Mysterious Black Sea—Where Few Cruisers Go!*

With equal amounts of excitement and anxiety we awaited the signal from Commodore Teoman Arsay's 63' ketch, MAT. At 10 A.M., 3 July 2004, Teo fired the cannon on board announcing to us and the world that our KAYRA journey around the Black Sea had begun.

KAYRA, known in Turkish as the Karadenzi Yat Rallisi, made a 2,042 nautical mile counter-clockwise circumnavigation of the Black Sea. Sponsored by Istanbul's Atakoy Marina, thirty-seven vessels composed a unique group of modern-day explorers for this grand adventure. We were scheduled to stop at 34 ports along the coastlines of Northern Turkey,

---

* Adapted from my story, "Cruising the Black Sea," *PassageMaker Magazine,* May/June 2005

Georgia, Russia, Ukraine, Romania and Bulgaria during the next two months. The vessels flew flags representing the USA, Canada, Turkey, England, France, Germany, Holland, Sweden, Israel, Antigua and St. Vincent.

The number of people taking this extraordinary voyage ranged from 92 to 120, depending on guests aboard—the oldest person, 70; youngest, about 2. We had one dog and four cats representing the pet world. English was the official language of the rally, but if that happened to be your only one, you missed out on some good conversations, as the airwaves carried French, German, Turkish, and Hebrew all the time.

We had to mesh as a unit and use patience plus humor to help us over the rough spots. There were three groups organized by boat size, each with a group leader, and set schedules for checking in. If people did not abide by that, what could be the reason? Were they off sailing, just having fun and forgot the time for check-in? Or did their VHF not work? Could it be assumed they were asserting independence from the group mode? And was it important to be the first to arrive into port? Or to have the front seat on the tour bus? Our commodore assisted in making the daily routines work smoothly.

Teoman Arsay came to the commodore job with credentials. He had been one of the main organizers and made the trip before; understood cross cultural differences, spoke several languages, had a great sense of humor and sly smile, listened and ruled by being a non-dictator. One of the cruisers called his job, "herding cats." Our printed schedule gave us many details as to dates, places, mileage between ports, times to leave and arrive, but when the whistle blew "long, short, long" we knew the Commodore needed our ear for an important announcement. For example: buses were coming, fuel was delayed, or the time had changed for scheduled events.

Prior to leaving Atakoy Marina, we spent a week there getting organized, from paying our fees for the rally, getting visas for the other countries, gathering flags to "dress" our boats at port, and just getting to know each other.

Additional entertainment came when President Bush and his entourage came for the NATO conference the end of June. Security precautions caused a major lockdown of water and land traffic in Istanbul for all the world's dignitaries attending. Although they closed the highway outside the marina, keeping us more or less inside, the heavy helicopter traffic right over our masts gave us some indication things were up. Sure enough when President Bush arrived at the airport, he deplaned from Air Force One, walked a few feet to Marine Chopper One, and used "the friendly skies" instead of the motorway to move into downtown. After the three-day conference ended,

Marine Choppers One and Two flew over the masts again en route to the International Airport. I waved.

The night before departing and under a full moon, all participants put on formal wear for an out-of-doors banquet with music, speeches, and a wonderful display of fireworks over the water. During the banquet a hand tapped me on the shoulder. The hand belonged to Ms. Tuba Noyan, Editor of *Naviga,* a Turkish nautical magazine. Our commodore had told her I was a writer and she made a formal request for me to write the KAYRA story for her magazine. I would write it in English, supply photos to accompany the text, and she would translate the text into Turkish. This glossy magazine made a nice spread of my story, and the English section in the back allowed two versions of my experience.

After the cannon's boom we lined up according to our number and headed around the corner and into the Bosphorus Strait. It's a 25-nautical-mile stretch of water, which divides Istanbul's European side from its Asian side and drains the Black Sea into the Med via the Sea of Marmara and the Dardanelles. We found it jam-packed with activity. There were large and small ferries crossing and re-crossing, privately owned vessels out for a Saturday spin, fishing boats, northbound or southbound commercial vessels, full or empty, and the constant out-going current from the Black Sea to deal with that day. Also in the equation, a large number of sailboats, tacking back and forth between the two main bridges, narrowly missed each other and sometimes us. We boaters collectively held our breaths and searched for eddies to help us along.

The Istanbul skyline where the Golden Horn meets the Bosphorus wowed us! Topkapi Palace, Hagia Sophia and Blue Mosque stood proud and tall, along with minarets and domes of importance to the Turkish people. From many minarets all across Turkey we would hear the Muslim call to prayer five times a day, beginning at daybreak and ending at dark. That distinctive sound floats through the air, being picked up by similar calls along the way. We would see many minarets and witness daily calls to prayer on our journey to Georgia, almost 700 miles away.

At the top of the Bosphorus we entered the mysterious Black Sea. It measures 630 nautical miles from east to west and 330, north to south. With a schedule to meet, the rule read, "We go if conditions are uncomfortable; not if they are dangerous." We did go once when we really should not have gone, but we all arrived in the next port safely, some more bedraggled than others.

The Black Sea measures 144 miles at the top between the Ukraine and Turkey land masses. As one of our activities in Balaklava, Ukraine, we climbed up to ruins of a Genovese fort, faced south, and the first one to "see Turkey," received a bottle of champagne. Misty fog in the distance and the earth's curvature kept anyone from seeing the far-off shore, but we all captured a bottle of champagne anyway, including a young local woman who posed on a rock for all our cameras.

Along the north coast of Turkey, the Black Sea is really "Green" in places! In the Bahamas green means "lean" or very shallow water. So when we first saw the green water ahead we gasped and rechecked the depth sounder. It registered 110 feet from the bottom of the boat to the sea's floor, which we found hard to believe. It was both an eye opener and jaw dropper. Sometimes there were distinct demarcation lines between black and green. Looking ahead it showed very dark; looking back, a sparkling green. One theory is that lime, washing away from the mountain rock into the streams, flows into the sea to create this dramatic event. And the Black Sea has been fished out, evidenced by the fishing boats coming into the wharf and offering only small specimens for sale.

Accommodations and supplies were issues for the planners for our summer journey. Securing the ships in ports along the way ranged from anchoring, side-tying to the sea wall, or med-mooring. The European boats are used to med-mooring, and it makes excellent use of space. Remember three boats could tie up in 52-foot length if we went in stern first.

Med-mooring in theory is quite simple. In the Med, ports provided a bow line for attachment. In the Black Sea, we used our own anchors. Basically one drops the anchor perfectly perpendicular to the wall and then reverses slowly into the space provided. On reaching the dock, just hand the line to someone ashore to tie up, walk back to the bow and secure the anchor line; return to the stern to adjust shore lines, put a passarelle (gangway) in place, get off the boat, and plug in the electricity. Then you are set. That explanation is too simple.

First of all, how far out does one drop the anchor? Gauging is tricky. You must also remember other people's anchors that are already in place. Try to avoid dropping yours on top of theirs. If the anchor does not set the first time, it means hauling it up again, and a second try. Or in one case, when the anchor chain all plays out and the bitter end rope breaks, you have a serious problem. No longer attached to your anchor, you use the momentum of reversing to squeeze between two boats already in place, tie up, put the dinghy in the water, borrow a grapple hook and spend time "cruising" for the chain. The only time that happened had a happy ending. Our friend returned the grapple hook with a smile, "I found it!"

Of special note in med-mooring is the wind. You have difficulty lining up to begin reversing and miss your assigned slot, or have a close encounter with your neighbor. Keeping one's cool is a must; help from others appreciated. And if we weren't involved in the whole process and could just stand back, it would look like a choreographed port dance.

On *TEKA III*, Denis and I shared the job of med-mooring. After preparing the fenders and docking lines, I moved quickly to the bow and dropped the anchor on cue. Denis reversed the boat. That left no one to toss the lines to shore from the stern until I completed the bow work. Then I scrambled aft, grabbed the lines coiled for throwing, and heaved them to someone on the dock. If I did not give them a quick non-verbal demonstration on how to hook us up to a ring, bollard, or rusty pipe, they might just stand there and hold it. Holding it won't do. They must secure the lines somehow, but the places set up for large fishing boats or commercial vessels had bollards and rings spread far apart and in-between, huge ugly black tires for fenders. Not the best arrangement. All this time the boat is slowly moving to the quay. If I miss getting the line to shore, retrieval is a must. Lines like to get tangled in props.

Once the lines were ashore and Denis felt he could leave the controls, we together finished straightening out the boat and tightening the lines. Sometimes the high walls made it necessary to locate our 10-foot construction ladder, tie it at one end to the swim bridge and climb almost straight up it to get off the boat—scary and not fun. No wonder we preferred to anchor out!

The port people provided us with electricity, but not what we were used to, along with a challenge at every port. Many plugs going into one central box looked crazy and unworkable. Sometimes someone had to figure out the formula, the end result often looking like a "Rube Goldberg" layout. At other times the electric lines ran so far along the dock or seawall that the boat at the end of the line received very low voltage. When we were to leave the boat for a three-day inland tour in Romania, we took a long extension cord and plugged in where we determined the voltage to be high enough for our refrigerator to work in our absence. At our position the voltage had registered only 80 volts; plugging in elsewhere brought it up to 110.

Fellow cruiser, Marvin Day, sorts out electrical problems

If boats needed water and a water hose was not available on the dock, a truck would arrive, drive slowly down the pier and ask at each boat, "Water?" Fuel trucks carrying up to 3,000 gallons would also be available in ports. Since the sailboats had to motor much of the time to meet schedules, they needed "topping off" at all the ports. One fast powerboat was always thirsty. If trucks were not available for fuel, someone would collect empty jerry cans in a van and return them full the next day. Our ship carried 2000 gallons of diesel fuel and could have made the entire trip with the fuel on board, but we did top off in Odessa where they had a fuel barge and a cheap price. Some fuel cost $4.00 a gallon at that time. What it is now is anyone's guess.

Each port had a welcoming ceremony shortly after our arrival. Dignitaries gave short speeches, bands played, folk dancers performed, including grabbing members of the audience at times to participate as well. Their dancing opened us up to traditional ways of the Turkish people. Yet the closer we got to Georgia, the dancing changed in rhythm and intensity. The Commodore asked members of the fleet to present KAYRA plaques to members of the local planning committees, mayors, harbormasters, and politicians.

Turkish folk dancers

After the speeches, dances, and awards, we attended cocktail parties or buffet dinners. The buffet table offered grilled meat, chicken, sausage, lamb, meatballs, tortellini, a barley-based dish, quiche, fish or sardines. A salad of tomato and cucumbers with yoghurt, chickpea soup, and copious amounts of bread were always on the table. In Turkey they do not eat pork, but in the other countries we had pork often. A sample cocktail gathering included a large hors d'oeuvre spread of meat and cheese open-faced sandwiches, pastry shells with different delicious fillings, deep fried croquettes, meatballs, salmon, and vegetables. Wines in Turkey and Georgia were good; Ukraine, variable; Romania and Bulgaria, okay. Fruits and vegetables were available at local markets for breakfast or lunch on board, but with all the food presented to us, we did not need to cook often. In fact, gaining weight over the two months became a potential problem.

Everywhere we went people were not afraid to use their English, especially in Turkey. Children would gather around, asking, "What is your name?" "Where are you from?" "How old are you?' It would have been a treat to watch their next English lesson at school and hear what they had to report. Everywhere the KAYRA went, people came, as well as print and TV media. At Samsun, Turkey, one of the two Abyssinian cats on the sailboat, *ATTITUDES,* posed and slowly sauntered down the gangplank when he saw the cameras rolling, with the style of a movie star. Another boater reported that her son checked the Internet one day, only to realize the woman he saw in the pink dress dancing at a KAYRA function was his very own mother. At the Turkish Naval city of Eregli (pronounced Irili), Denis made the plaques speech, comparing Eregli to his home port of Seattle, a big Navy facility. I spoke quietly with a gentleman in uniform during the cocktail time. The man standing next to him seemed interested in our English conversation, yet said nothing. At a pause in our talk, the officer introduced me to the silent man as "my love father," his father-in-law. I think that is a wonderful title.

At our 18 stops in Turkey, 2 in Georgia, 1 in Russia, 9 in the Ukraine, 2 in Romania and 2 in Bulgaria, we took local tours to learn about those cities and also went inland to play tourist as well.

We have many memories of places in Turkey. Here are some special ones. Turkey was ruled for many years by the Ottomans and in Safranbolu, a World Heritage Site, we observed features of the still-lived-in old Ottoman buildings. Outside, they purposefully built each home so it did not block the view of its neighbor. Inside the kitchen was a pole to indicate the house's position. If you could place your hands around it and easily twist the pole, everything was okay. If the pole did not move, it meant the house had a settling problem. That seemed like an unusual engineering feature. The pole twisted for me that day.

Also, Greece and Turkey had intermingled populations over time, witness the proximity of the Greek islands on Turkey's west coast. Everything changed in the 1920s. Greek troops had occupied parts of Turkey after WWI. However, under the leadership of Mustafa Kemal, a War hero, the Turks ousted the Greeks and as part of the peace settlement the parties agreed to the exchange of populations. Around 1.25 million Greeks were returned to Greece and 450,000 Turks went back to their country. Refugees on both sides significantly affected both countries. Mustafa Kemal is known as "Ataturk" and revered after 1935 as "Father of the New Turkish Republic." Along with statues of Ataturk everywhere across the country, we also experienced how Greek Orthodox monks once lived in a Byzantine Monastery high atop a mountain outside Trabzon in eastern Turkey. It took us 45 minutes to climb up a steep trail and reach this perch on the cliff. No one lives there now, but our visit made us realize what a remote life it offered. They really had to be self-sufficient to live there, high in the sky. Their courtyards and chapel depicted religious scenes in still-colorful frescoes—a very peaceful place.

In the capital, Ankara, history came alive for us at the archeological museum, compliments of two college professors, our knowledgeable tour guides. On our way back to the boats and the Black Sea, the group had an up-close-and-personal tour of some ruins from the ancient Hittite peoples.

In Sinop, after a full day of activities, we witnessed fireworks out over the water. During that event my sister in Florida and I were talking on my Turkish cell-phone. "What was that?" she asked. When I told her, "Fireworks," she responded, "Sounded like a terrorist attack to me." This is the sister that did not want me to cross the Atlantic because of icebergs.

Everywhere we went in Turkey we felt like honored guests. Their smiles and friendly "Merhabas" (hellos) showed an interest in us as visitors they would not see if we had not come to their country. The Turkish Coast Guard shadowed us all along their coast. On land, Polis and Ambulancia crews followed along to be of assistance. We had a wonderful time in Turkey.

On to Georgia. There we were victims of thievery at the first port, Batumi. Boats were boarded while we were on a tour in the daytime, with sets of tennis shoes, cell phone and soccer ball taken. Then during the night, someone cut the davit lines to a dinghy and quietly slipped away with dinghy and motor. No one bothered our boat.

An uncomfortable overnight train took us from the port of Poti inland to the Capital, Tbilisi, for a day of sightseeing. There, Mother Georgia's statue faces King Vakhtang's (the town founder) across the river. She holds a sword high in her right hand for Georgia's enemies to see, and a goblet of wine in the left for their friends. A 6th Century church, Sveti tskhoveli reportedly has part of Jesus' robe buried in the church's foundation.

Old churches, including a wedding in one, sulfur baths, Persian fortress ruins, and the long, hot train ride stood out as highlights. Georgia felt poor. There were refugees, beggars, men with tools by roadside waiting for work, plus large empty factories and unused farm land seen from the train. Empty boxcars lined the train tracks coming into towns, ripe for graffiti, yet there was none. We wondered if they even had the paint to do such a job.

Our life at sea between ports took on a new dimension at this point. Our first overnighter took us from Poti to Sochi in Russia. When we left Georgia all boats had to stay at least fifteen miles offshore due to political unrest between Georgia and Russia. Patrol boats were in the area to make sure this order was carried out. Denis and I had done overnighters before, but some boaters had not experienced a night passage. All went well, with the exception of one close call when someone fell asleep at the wheel and had to be awakened by a VHF radio call before they got into trouble.

Memories of Sochi, Russia, focus on port officials. The immigration woman staunchly wanted to have our passports for review and stamping immediately. She even said she would board us, "If you hold my hand," by stepping on our unsecured, wiggly ladder just as we worked on securing it. Somehow she made it, but soon after that others boarded and wanted their paperwork too, now! Thunderstorms, water in the harbor surging in and out, boats relocating within the harbor for safety, kept us all busy until evening when the Sochi Yacht Club invited us to a wonderful evening of food and stirring Russian music. The next morning we had another musical event at a tea garden in the hills outside of town.

After the 128 nautical miles to Sochi, we had another long stretch to do—248 this time. It took two nights and a day at sea to reach Yalta in the Ukraine. At first the wind blew 20 knots out of the west, creating seas of six feet or more on the nose, but calmed down during the second half. We found the Black Sea to be similar to the Mediterranean. Winds caused short, choppy seas, which made the ride very uncomfortable until the wind moderated.

Once in Yalta we found a place of no smiles, massive paperwork, interesting palaces and recent history, fireworks for the President's birthday in the middle of the night, plus an almost international incident. I had soaked clothes in a bucket on the way there. After giving them a quick scrub, I threw the soapy water overboard, intently watched by a port authority as I did so. He grew livid and red-faced as he yelled at me! If the Commodore had not stepped up in my behalf, I am sure I would have been fined on the spot. (Or taken away in handcuffs even!) Apparently he did not believe I had used a non-polluting soap for my wash. His experience was along other lines. To save me, the Commodore pulled out his portable VHF and made an announcement, "All KAYRA yachts, this is the Commodore speaking. Do not do laundry while in port, or shampoo, or shower with water going overboard!" That seemed to satisfy the harbor person.

It also reinforced our stereotype of people from the former Soviet Bloc countries being dour-faced persons who shout easily and demand certain behaviors. We found this in dealing with formalities and were thankful we had the power of the group. It is understood that those countries are not cruiser-friendly to individual boats. At one anchorage, a couple of military men swam out to one of our fleet, boarded and refused to leave until someone told them why we were all coming there. It took a VHF call to the Commodore, who used our Ukrainian liaison to intercede, before they would go away.

The Soviet Black Sea Fleet was all-powerful until the dissolution of the Soviet Union. Balaklava, Sevastopol, and Nicholayev were all closed ports until a few years ago. Balaklava still has its submarine pens, but no subs; Sevastopol has its ship cranes, dry docks and some military ships as testament to the might of the Soviet Navy; Nicholayev, now does more commercial ship-building than military. All were interesting to visit.

Nicholayev is reached by a 45-mile journey up the Bug River. We were instructed to go in convoy, smallest to largest, which started out fine. The current, wind, large ship traffic, and shifting of channels worked against us. Small sailboats, having to use sails to keep up the required six knot speed, lost momentum when the channels shifted and their sails needed readjusting. Everything jammed up. It took all day to make this trip, and then the Mayor totally ignored our appearance, never showing up himself. Someone at the Yacht Club had to work hard to set something up for us to do while we were there. Although we had a good time, KAYRA will probably not go there again.

Odessa, Katherine the Great's seaport city, is a delight. Much to see and do, even though the Opera House, where we had intended to see a famous Ballet, had not finished its renovation. A military band came to the pier and played for us on arrival and departure. It felt like being in "A Victory at Sea" scenario. This city, one of our favorites, warrants a return visit by air someday.

We had two more long sea trips, first the 139 nautical miles from Odessa to the Danube River and Izmail where we would check out of the Ukraine. At the newly dredged channel into the Danube we met our pilot boat, who promptly grounded the Commodore's boat. That didn't give us a lot of confidence in his skills and ability to get the rest of us to Izmail without a similar occurrence. The Danube had a 1-2 knot adverse current for our trip. We found the trip less interesting than expected, very hot, with little to see along the shores, except an occasional group of locals to smile and return the waves of strangers boating up the river in convoy.

American flags were in demand in Izmail. The port's flagpole had need for one. The Mayor requested one for his office; and the next day the Immigration Officer who came on board to return our passports also asked for one. We were happy to oblige in each case from our stock of flags on board.

We continued on the Danube into Romania, where we boarded local tour boats for a trip into the Delta. Along the shore were many birds, people camping and fishing, plus other local boats coming our way, passing us in a super-narrow space. Everyone laughed at these close encounters—us and them.

Our last sea trip of 153 nautical miles took us from Sulina where we exited the Danube to Mangalia in southern Romania. After our very "dark and stormy night," being tossed about in gale-force conditions, we happily tied up at Mangalia's wall. During the voyage most boats took on water, even 63-foot *MAT*, with its high semi-enclosed steering station. Winds at his position kicked up to 50 knots in gusts during the gale.

At first we pointed *TEKA III*'s bow in a rhumb-line from Sulina straight for Mangalia breakwaters. As night progressed, we decided that even if there were fishing boats and nets closer to shore, we had to change course to be more comfortable. The angle for the course change put us beam-to the sometimes five to six foot seas, even in depths of only 35-feet just five miles offshore. That demonstrates the wind and sea phenomenon. It doesn't have to be deep to have high waves, or have a big fetch (a long distance for the waves to build with the wind). With both paravanes working hard in the water, we still tossed back and forth until we could make the downwind turn and get a better ride. The winds were 30 to 40 knots, seas still high, but we were not so uncomfortable.

Denis went down to rest. I snuck us through an anchoring field outside the busy port of Constanza, Romania. I targeted each anchored ship on the radar, evaluating movement or not. All were staying put. We were so close to shore that all the neon lights just sparkled from town. But wait! Those three, a red, a green, and a white on top were moving right toward me. I pushed the "Acquire" button on the radar. While I waited for feedback as to speed and course of the ship my eyes saw coming out of the port, I got nervous. Yes, it was moving my way. When the information because available, I knew he traveled at 10 knots and in two minutes we would make contact. I put the engine into neutral, abruptly turned the boat to starboard, hesitated to make sure the larger vessel had not also turned, and then poured on the coals. Denis woke up and asked me what was happening. I pointed outside to the stern lights of the container ship gliding past us. Then my knees started knocking really bad.

Settled safely in Mangalia several hours later, we boarded buses for our "Dracula Tour"—three days/two nights in the Carpathian Mountains and Transylvania countryside. What a beautiful drive! At Dracula's Castle we learned the truth. Hollywood had it all wrong. Dracula did not have huge canine teeth with which he ripped a neck open and sucked out life's blood. King Vlad, Dracula's real name, reigned for six years in the mid-1400s. He ruled over less than half a million subjects in Transylvania, but according to reports, killed 40,000 of them. If he did not impale them, he used some pretty vicious torture methods, which resulted in death as well. In Bucharest our guide gave us a history lesson about Romania, with not such good marks for the Communist ruler, Ceausescu, whom the people revolted against in 1989. She called that particular time as "the dark chapter." On the outskirts of Bucharest we enjoyed walking through a living museum showing different styles of houses from four Romanian regions in the mid-1800s.

And driving through the countryside we witnessed houses featuring several towers in the architecture. She said each tower represented a male child in a "well-off" gypsy family.

At a sponsored dinner one night in Bucharest Denis had an accident involving his steak knife. As the waitress started clearing the table, his knife was knocked down onto the wooden bench where we sat. With the handle embedded in the bench, the pointed end stood up, a dangerous situation. Without looking, he reached down to retrieve it and impaled himself in the mid-hand. Everything seemed to move fast after that. People moved out of the way on our side of the table. Denis said he felt funny and leaned over onto my lap. Someone handed me a fan. Someone else went for the doctor in our group at another table. He came, checked Denis' weak pulse, and the guide called the ambulance. When it came, doctor, guide, Denis and I went to the nearest Emergency Room for evaluation and treatment. I rode up front and just to impress me (there was no traffic), the driver put on the sirens.

The staff took him in right away, cleaned the wound, and asked if he had recently received a tetanus shot. He said he didn't remember the date of the latest one, but because he had been a career Air Force officer, he had received many shots. Now retired, he kept his shots up to date while he traveled far and wide. The guide heard this and we became the recipients of "payback." When the Dictator had closed off their country and the people were starving, the USAF flew in chickens. She remembered this life-saving event, and here was her chance to do a good deed in return. She paid for the ambulance, the Emergency Room fees, the pharmacy, and taxi back to the hotel. No questions asked. After the hospital staff bandaged Denis' hand, they sent him to the casting room. In such a trauma, isn't it better not to close all the air off by putting the wounded area in plaster? Denis thought so, and signed a special paper refusing a cast, for their records. The hand problem followed us back to the States and surgery at the University of Washington Hospital. His hand is better, but not best.

Heavy rain, thunder, lightning, plus 20-knot winds from the northwest accompanied us on our 49-mile trip to Golden Sands Resort in Bulgaria. Rain and wind hindered docking. One sailboat's prop caught on the underwater buoyed rope to use for med-mooring. When one boat is "dead in the water" in a small environment, others are definitely affected. The entrance had a heavy swell coming in from the weather, so others waiting to come in had to float around beyond the breakwater, one for three hours. It took that long for all of us to get inside, be assigned a spot, assisted into that spot and the next boat called into the harbor. The next and last port in Bulgaria, Nessebar, had none of these problems, thank goodness.

Back to Turkey, land of minarets, mosques, and "Merhabas!" (hellos). We stopped at only two ports, including one where we "roasted" the

Commodore, before whisking down the Bosphorus to Istanbul. Going south with the current this time, we watched the knot log climb up to 10 and 11 knots at times. Fasten your seatbelts!

We all had an unforgettable KAYRA experience. Of course the Fleet had problems to deal with along the way. Boat problems included contaminated fuel filters; blown headsails; electrical problems when a radio, starter or alternator needed repair or replacement; problems with a water system; a lightning strike "knocking out" radar and autopilot systems; plus weeds on a prop that called for a tow to the next port to clear and check for problems. We had none, and did act as a rescue boat for the one with weeds on its prop, pulling it to the next port.

People problems had quite a range. Many had stomach virus, at least ten at one time without the same source of contact. A suspected heart attack sent one man to the E.R., then a flight back to Holland. Laryngitis, a hurt back, a swollen leg, seasickness, a fall leading to an overnight stay in a Bulgarian hospital with a seriously bruised hip, and Denis's impaled hand rounded out the bad karma.

We arrived back at Atakoy Marina on day 64, with a "Well Done!" feeling, having logged 2,042 nautical miles. As one cruiser said at the beginning, "We paid our fees to join the rally, but purchased much more than money could buy!"

The Black Sea Rally is imprinted forever in our hearts and minds. We could not have done this trip alone—too much bureaucracy to deal with, and no language skills on our part to communicate. We appreciated all the work that went into making the trip such a success. Cheers to Atakoy Marina and especially you, Commodore Teoman!

Middle East Escapades

The Middle East! Most Americans, including us, were afraid of traveling there, but here we were planning to do just that! For the months of May and June in 2005 we would take our boat to some exotic ports of call there, and travel inland as well. Previously the Eastern Mediterranean Yacht Rally had sponsored an organized trip for up to 100 boats to visit Cyprus, Syria, Lebanon, Israel, and Egypt. Yet, no one that we knew of had done such a trip alone!

Joining us on *TEKA III* were our friends and seasoned cruisers, John and Joan Brair, from *SEASCAPE*. They brought along Tipper, who became "Chief of Security," guarding the boat at all times, and "Physical Activities Director," making sure her people had daily exercise walks or Frisbee activity, as well as, "Good-will Ambassador," making friends for America. A buddy boat, *CONESTOGA*, carried two new friends, Bob and Betty Hershey.

We had studied our guidebooks, provisioned the boats, made a schedule and gotten excited. There are a lot of logistics involved in such an extended trip with stops in multiple countries. Syrian visas were the first order of business. Americans had to obtain theirs through the Syrian Embassy in Washington, D.C., which required certain documents to be mailed in and processed. Bob, Betty, Denis, and I received ours that way. John and Joan had stayed in Turkey that winter and attempted to get their visas in Ankara, with no luck. When that did not materialize, the marina in Lattakia, Syria assured them their visas would be available on arrival. So off we went on the morning of May 2, 2005 to begin our Middle Eastern experience—first port of call, Girne, North Cyprus!

Cyprus is a "divided" island, with Turkey claiming the north and Greece the south half. On a land tour across to Nicosia, the Capital of Southern Cyprus, we found the famous "Green Line" drawn on the pavement, visibly marking the border. Of course all six of us had to have our photo taken straddling the line with the barbed-wired wall behind us.

Other remnants of the island's history included a Crusader's Castle in Girne, Capital of Northern Cyprus, once the home of Richard the Lion-hearted back in 1191—the Third Crusade. Castles are always cold places with high rock, heavily fortified walls to keep the enemy out. It is not a place I would like to sleep in. Standing on the ramparts one could easily keep an eye on the city outside the wall and anything arriving by sea. While we were there, we saw ferries coming in from southern Turkey bringing military replacements, as Turkey still keeps an active force on duty.

Boats were not allowed to go from North to South Cyprus, as the island is truly divided into two governing areas. We left directly for Syria from Girne, and fifteen hours later, arrived at Lattakia—to be the only two boats at the marina. Does this tell you it is a favorite vacation spot for cruisers, or not?

At the marina three men arrived at the boat, sat down under the shade of a covered picnic table to look over our boat papers, crew list and passports. John and Denis found it quite interesting that one man opened up a notebook and spent a lot of time running his finger down the list of boats (not in alphabetical order) that were "questionable." This took more than a few minutes, but he did not find *TEKA III* on the list. Satisfied, they all boarded, took a good look around, commented on the family photos in the aft cabin, asked about the papers for Tipper, took our passports and left. Where they went, we did not know. We knew we were totally in their hands. Without passports we could not leave or even move around. Having a passport in hand for identification or a special permit amounting to the same is critical. So we waited. Finally they returned to the marina.

But, they could only check four of us into Syria—the four with visas. No visas appeared for John and Joan, so they were in limbo. They stayed in limbo for the next week, anxiously anticipating each day that word would come from Damascus they had been cleared by the Department of Immigration. Until then they could not leave the marina. They insisted the rest of us not lose any touring time while waiting for them. We did play tourist, hoping they would catch up, but it did not happen, and they sadly awaited our return to the boat. They never stepped one foot out of the marina the whole time we were in Syria. Since John grew up in Lebanon, and they had both visited parts of the Middle East before, their hopes were to see Syria on this trip. Alas, it turned out not to be.

If they had gone with us, here's what they would have seen first—the famous Castle named after General Saladin. An impressive fortress, now in ruin, it had been used first by the Crusaders, then by the Islamic soldiers after the Crusaders left in 1188. This castle sat perched on a hilltop with 15-foot walls to protect those inside, and deep ravines all around below.

Saladin, a crafty soldier, divided his troops so that half could keep the crusaders busy at the most suspected point of entry, while the rest bombarded another wall with catapults from a hilltop across the valley. The fort fell to Saladin. Looking up from the ravine bottom one wonders how anyone could climb up in the first place, and fight after that.

On our way into the desert for a visit to Palmyra, we stopped at the best preserved of all the Crusader fortresses in the Middle East—Krak (castle) Chevaliers (French for Crusaders). An English-speaking guide sold us his services at the main gate, escorting us all through the extremely large multi-floored castle from the basement storage to the defensive ramparts. Richard the Lionhearted spent time there, evidenced by the famous lions carved over one of the moat entrances. There were dining halls, huge kitchens, storage areas, meeting rooms and living quarters for the knights. Also stables for their horses. It felt like a small village self-contained and well fortified— well positioned at the top of a hill protected by steep sides and only one entrance. Again, not my cup of tea.

Many schoolchildren were there that day and couldn't resist calling out to us in English, "Hello," "How are you?" The women with these kids, one their English teacher, tried their English on us too, giggling as they did.

From the ramparts we could see St. George's Monastery in the distance. It is amazing how many paintings there are in Europe and the Middle East of St. George and the dragon scene. I wish I had been taking a tally. St. George is young in many paintings and the dragon is small; in others he is much older and the dragon is larger. The result is the same: George won each time!

In the monastery we met men who told us about their family members living and working in the States. Many Syrians have moved to America over time. I remember as a youngster in Jacksonville, Florida interacting with a Syrian who ran the small grocery store near our house. And several Syrian families belonged to our First Presbyterian Church. We found there are positive feelings about America and Americans, but they see the U. S. government quite differently. With the Bush administration's focus on Syria being part of the "axis of evil" and a major supporter of terrorism, Syrians wanting to visit family in the U.S. find it is almost impossible to obtain visas. Personally we felt friendship with the people.

Driving into the desert past a large Army installation, complete with many satellite dishes along the perimeter, we thought about the problems between and among the Arabic countries, plus how close we were at that point to the Iraqi border. And wondered just what the future held for everyone involved. There has not been total peace in that part of the world since people first moved there.

Arriving at Palmyra, an early staging post for caravans traveling between the Mediterranean countries and to the Silk Road in China, we immediately reflected back on our 1995 adventure on the Silk Road. We began that trip in Xian, China and went west via various modes of transportation from train to plane, ending up in Islamabad, Pakistan. Camel caravans were the original eighteen-wheelers or container ships! They called them "ships of the desert" for a reason.

The Roman Palmyra ruins date back to First Century B.C. Are they impressive! Columns everywhere, some complete with their Corinthian type carvings at the top, others in chunks lining the streets, all gave the distinct impression of what they were for—doors, arches, walls, porticos for temples. Sitting at one end and staring into the distance gives one the dimension of the place that used to be there. The city was originally built by Solomon around 2000 B.C., making it 4000 years old, one of the oldest cities of the world. It linked Mesopotamia with northern Syria and the Mediterranean. While there we did not realize how far back the history went. Imagine, Solomon's Temple 2000 years before the Romans!

Ancient city of Palmyra

The best part of visiting Palmyra is getting up early and watching sunrise over the limestone columns, accenting the grand street as well as the other ruins. An amphitheatre, agora (market), church, forum, and Temple of Bel were easily seen and not much imagination needed to put people in the picture. Populations of people lived in the Temple of Bel until 1928 when they were asked to move into the villages nearby for their safety. Sunset, seen from a hilltop fort, offered another opportunity to see the colors change yellow to pink and shadows lengthen over the scene. We paid a man to guide us during the day and explain things since there were no informational signs posted in the ruins. For sunrise and sunset trips we went alone to quietly absorb the ambience.

Transporting ourselves from the ancient to the modern, we drove on to Damascus, a sprawling city with lots of traffic and many people hustling and bustling around. This is a city with religious significance to both Christians and Moslems.

From our background of Bible stories we remembered Damascus as the place where Saul, the persecutor, became Paul, the persecuted. We searched for and located the little chapel where Ananias took Saul in and cured him of his blindness. In that basement chapel behind the small altar are three paintings side by side. One shows Saul knocked off his horse and blinded alongside the road; the middle one has Ananias administering to him; and the last painting, Paul being lowered by a basket into the river just outside the town walls, as he now was a victim of persecution. Fellow Christians helped him escape. We could not find that spot on our map, but did stop at a nearby shop and talked to the owner. He told us he had played the part of Saul/Paul in a German documentary 10 years ago and presented us with his business card showing him in his robe for the part. Quite interesting.

Umayyad Mosque is the most important religious structure in all Syria. I had to wear a full-length brown robe with hood. Shoes off, we entered the courtyard and reverently walked to the mosque entrance. Many people were there. We learned some had come on buses from Iran. Inside, groups sat around on the floor listening to their leader, quoting or singing verses from the Koran. In one area is a small basilica dedicated to John the Baptist, considered a prophet by Moslems as well as Christians. John's head is supposedly contained in a casket inside the green tinted room. Outside the mosque again, we sat to watch people coming and going and a pigeon dropped a blob on my borrowed burqa. We left.

The best ice cream in the world is made in the souk (covered market selling everything) in Damascus. It is better than "Ben and Jerry's" and better than "31 flavors." They sell tons of it, some through the open window into the souk passage, some in the inside seating area. The cones are huge and the servings generous. They make it right before your eyes in many large vats. One could easily get fat with daily portions of Damascus ice cream. The flavor that day was pistachio.

Mary enjoying a small ice cream cone

Outside the souk, we watched as women had difficulty getting onto an escalator wearing their burqas. Their frightened looks and tentative steps portrayed their fear. Many may have never seen an escalator before. We quickly walked around them to get on the escalator ourselves and were almost to the top when one lady screamed and fell backward. The man accompanying the group of women rushed to push a stop button. By then all the ladies were near panic. Apparently she either lost her footing when the step moved up, or her long dress caught somehow. The ambulance siren started in our direction within minutes, but we did not stick around to be part of a staring crowd.

On the drive back to Lattakia from Damascus we intently focused on what we saw outside the car windows. A platoon of soldiers, near one of the Christian convents we visited, smiled and waved while jogging with their automatic weapons, and what looked like rocket grenade launchers. Bedouin tents had colorful laundry hanging out on a line. Roadside vendors along the road sold things from strawberries to cigarettes. Large trucks carried huge loads of rocks or marble. A small pickup with a self-assured brown and white cow standing in the back section passed us, with the cow looking over the cab top to view her travels. Not to be missed were many photos of the former and present Presidents of Syria (father and son). One person asked if we had many pictures of George Bush along the roads. After all, that was his experience. Denis commented on Bill Clinton smiling from his book cover, displayed in all the Damascus bookstore windows.

In our hotel we felt we were being monitored by different people at different times. They would strike up a conversation in English just to find out more about us. The desk had probably already told them who we were. On the street one man came up behind us and asked us something in English. Neither Denis nor I had said one word during our walk up to that moment. It made us very curious as to their intent—being friendly or monitoring us for some reason.

Two events, however, left a bad taste in our mouths for this visit. No visas for John and Joan, which actually imprisoned them in the marina. And the fuel scam. Before we scheduled our departure from Syria, Denis calculated the amount of fuel we wanted to purchase and paid the marina office to order the fuel truck. Parking their truck on the pavement near our boat, the men brought a hose onto our boat and put the nozzle into the fueling compartment alongside the pilothouse wall. They then turned on the meter for the diesel to flow from truck to boat tank. Denis monitored the in-flow from the engine room tank sight-tubes. When their meter said they had emptied the truck, the men pulled the hoses back on the truck, refused to give us a receipt, and drove off. We stood amazed as they brushed off all our complaints that we were not full. Denis calculated we were cheated by one-third—receiving only 510 gallons, having been charged for 766. A complaint to the marina office netted nothing. They said the truck meter said what it said, therefore we were wrong. John had been watching the dial and it said all the fuel had been delivered. What could we do? We wrote a letter to the other American boats coming into the marina soon and told them to have a jerry can available for "testing." They did, and found the dial to be faulty, dismissed that truck and ordered another.

The voyage to Jounieh, Lebanon began with flat seas but turned into lumpy ones about 3 A.M. After 124 nautical miles we checked in at Jounieh, then proceeded to Holiday Beach Resort to tie up for ten days and explore the country top to bottom, side to side. We had a special in-country homegrown guide! John had been born in Palestine, but grew up in Lebanon. Not only did he speak the language, but his German mother had spent many years as a tour guide for Germans visiting Lebanon, and he had learned from her about special places.

Before that road trip we did a unique "Memory Lane" walk of Ras Beirut. Joan, an American teenager there with her parents, met John in Beirut over 38 years ago. We found the hotel where they met (he worked the desk there), the jewelry shop, his church, her church, and lastly his neighborhood. John's family house still stood in place, alas, now surrounded by high rises. The best part came when John went into the local grocer's to buy some bottled water and the grocer's son, now running the store, remembered him, calling him by his "nickname."

Other highlights in Beirut included viewing the assassinated Prime Minister Hariri's coffin at the mosque next to Martyr Square, plus rows of posters showing the mass demonstrations demanding the Syrian Army leave Lebanon earlier that year. One photo showed a placard saying, "Vive La Syrie en Syrie!" We also witnessed many buildings still standing, but bombed out or bullet ridden, from the years the Lebanese refer to as "terrible times," internal civil war and the Israeli invasion. Will there ever be peace in Lebanon again?

Political signs in martyr's square, Beirut

Our north-to-south route covered the towns of Bylbos, Tripoli, Sidon and Tyre. Our alphabet started in Bylbos about 1000 BC. The Phoenicians turned Egyptian hieroglyphics and symbols into a twenty-two letter script, which the Greeks later switched into a left to right reading and writing format. On the day we visited Tripoli's famous Crusader Castle, its walls were being used for a rappelling exercise by the Lebanese Army. Sidon's sported a Crusader castle about 200 feet offshore, connected to land by a stone bridge, and easily protected. Tyre, with Israel in sight to the south, had two sets of ruins. Al-Mina, an old port with a large harbor, and Al-Bass, with its 20,000 seat hippodrome for chariot races, had marble columns, sarcophagi, and paved streets one end to the other. We climbed up into the stadium and pretended the races were scheduled for later that day.

Al-Bass also had a close neighbor, Hezbollah Party soldiers. Signs everywhere proclaimed, "We are ready!" We sat at an outdoor café table and listened to some military music from a nearby kiosk. Denis went over and asked about it. They sold him a CD of Hezbollah Army music, and tried to sell him a video of Hezbollah soldiers car-bombing Israeli vehicles. He passed on that one.

West to east let us explore The Cedars, a national treasure where the remaining Lebanese Cedar trees live and breathe at 6,000 feet. These old trees, mentioned in the Old Testament, are the remnants of a vast forest that once covered the mountains of Lebanon. The original Temple of Solomon in Jerusalem was built of cedar; also, many sarcophagi in Egypt. Slowly but surely, the tree population dwindled. While these old cedars are protected, it will take a long time for the new ones to mature. John had owned a landscaping business in Santa Barbara and commented on the tree trimming technique to be less than perfect for protecting the trees.

The scenery, driving west to east across Lebanon, is spectacular. To get to Baalbek we had to cross over the ski area; at one place people skied across what we saw as the road, but in winter the road is closed. Sheep and their herder added color to the scene on the road ahead of us.

The Phoenicians built a temple dedicated to Baal in First Century BC, where sacred prostitution and insatiable blood lust were part of their cult worship. In 6th century AD Emperor Justinian ordered all pagans accept baptism and ordered some of the buildings destroyed to prevent secret rites occurring. The Arabs came after the Byzantines and converted Baalbek into a citadel. Many invasions, sackings, lootings and earthquakes over time have caused a lot of damage, but what is left today is impressive.

At Aanjar near the Syrian border, we were escorted through the ruins by an Armenian "Tom Cruise look-alike," who spoke quite good English. This was a walled town dating back to 700 AD as an inland trading route. Only "royals" actually lived there. Merchants coming and going took one of the 600 stalls along the promenade to barter their goods, and then move on. Aanjar flourished for 50 years. The last Prince fled to Spain, where he built the famous Alhambra, a place we have also visited on our travels.

From the car windows in Lebanon we saw over two dozen types of trees, another 24 species of flowers (as tallied by John and Joan), people in local and modern dress, shops featuring replacement "car fronts" for BMWs or Mercedes, just standing at attention right outside the mechanic shop; men at Army checkpoints who just waved us through; old Army tanks left in a field and flowers growing all around them; upcoming election political ads, including one showing the winner smiling (maybe they had already placed that one beneath the "Vote for me" one). We mustn't forget out daily hunt for manaeesh bread, and ice cream throughout Lebanon. Manaeesh bread is a pita dough baked on a round hot stone. After baking, it is then coated with olive oil and spread with zattar spice mixture (thyme, oregano, marjoram, sumac berries, and other things), then rolled into a taco-shape for easy eating. Scrumptious!

After farewells to the staff, we left the marina and set our course to an offshore waypoint 15 miles off the Lebanon/Israel border. Time of departure: 6:15 P.M. on June 1, 2005.

The Israeli Navy rules the seas around their country and wanted instant contact with all vessels within 25 miles of the border. Joan and I were on duty that night. John and Denis slept. The first call came over the radio to us, but the coordinates did not exactly fit our location, so we did not respond. No other boats showed up on the radar. In a few minutes the call came again, "Calling the fishing vessel at ___latitude and ___longitude. This is the Israeli Navy." I answered this time. "This is *TEKA III*. We are not a fishing vessel, repeat, not a fishing vessel."

What kind of radar or infrared satellite images were they using to see us in that profile on that black night will never be known, but the interrogation began at that point. It continued throughout the night and included us, Israeli Navy patrol ships, Haifa Radio and Harbor Control. When we entered the bay, a harbor patrol boat escorted us to an out-of-the-way place to go through the Immigration process.

For starters they wanted to know names of persons on board, nationality, country of birth for each, destination in Israel, and port departed from in Lebanon. John became our issue. Although he was an American citizen, and had been for 38 years, his birthplace was Haifa—at that time Haifa, Palestine. With the boat tied up to the concrete wall, we watched as several marked cars parked and personnel from them stood around, looking very official. We had to sit on the bow, like "ducks in a row" while the main officer called the shots. She allowed Denis to get off the boat and then only to give her the six passports. (Four people were on our boat, a sister ship carried two more Americans.) There we endured more grilling, mostly between the lady on shore and the Brairs, quietly perched on the boat's bow.

She argued quite a while with John about him being born in Haifa, Israel. He corrected her each time, "Haifa, Palestine." Israel, Palestine, back and forth until he said, "when I was born, it was Palestinian." Looking at his age on the passport, she had to concede on that one.

"How did you meet your wife? She is American."

"In Lebanon."

To Joan then, "What were you doing in Lebanon?"

"My parents lived there."

"Why?"

"My father worked in the oil business." All this time we minded our P's and Q's, trying not to appear nervous or agitated, even though we were. Joan said they had been married 38 years and spent that time in Santa Barbara, California until they went world cruising on their boat.

The interrogator knew the boat was ours, so asked us, "Where did you meet these people?"

"In Spain."

"Why are they with you?"

"We needed experienced crew."

Then the focus changed. "Where did you come from before here?"

"Lebanon."

"Why were you there?"

"Being a tourist."

"Who did you see there?"

"A brother of a friend in the U.S."

"What is his name?" As soon as we gave it, they asked for a spelling and one of the guys started talking into his microphone under the shoulder lapel. "Are you sure you did not see anyone else?" "Yes."

"We are boarding to check what you have, so please, Captain, be our guide while the rest of you wait here." That completed, we started to breathe a bit more deeply. After we received our passports back, we felt even better. It is not the experience I enjoyed, and don't want to do any time again. We may have been watched the entire time we spent in Israel, but I tried not to be aware of it.

That introduction to life in Israel lingered as we attempted to find a space in the marina. Supposedly we had made prior arrangements, but alas no one could find a record of them, and no one wanted to be helpful either. Finally some boaters tied up in the marina stepped in, waved us into an empty spot and later lent us a cell phone to call Herzliya, our next stop to check on our reservation with them. Cruisers are good problem solvers. By calling, we learned the marina there would be closing earlier on our arrival date, so we had to adjust our departure time from Haifa.

From Herzliya, just north of Tel Aviv, we took land trips to Jerusalem, Bethlehem, Nazareth, and Jordan while the boat stayed securely tied up. Young people, men and women, were everywhere in their military uniforms, carrying weapons all through the city of Jerusalem. We were confused at one point as to how much the bus would cost to take into the old city. I solicited information from a young lady in Army fatigues, who also waited at the bus stop. She just shrugged and said, "I don't know. I ride free." On the bus, a young man in uniform got up to give me his seat. No one else did.

Our trip to Jerusalem coincided with "Jerusalem Days" and settlers from the countryside had been bused in for the event. Many of them sported orange armbands supporting the West Bank and Gaza settlements. They all sang loudly as they paraded into the old walled city and made their way to the Wailing Wall, where activities were scheduled, and security tight! Armed men in civilian clothes escorted school age groups. They looked serious too.

My experience at the Wailing Wall turned out to be more emotional than I thought it would be. First, the wall is an extension of the Temple of the Mount, like an outside synagogue. It is divided with about 2/3 space for men; 1/3 for women. The wall is very warm to the touch, partially due to its exposure to the sunshine, and partly due to the many hands that continually touch it. Many notes are left in the cracks. The woman next to me had her whole upper body pushed up against the wall, her face to me, and she began to sob heavily. Watching her made my tears come too. Multiply her behavior many fold and remember you have to approach the wall with head covered, and retreat without turning around, you get a picture of what happens there. I watched to learn protocol that day, but our guide the next day explained it this way, "No one turns a back on God."

Gethsemane Garden, where Jesus prayed until his sweat turned to blood, the Church of the Holy Sepulcher with its Stations of the Cross, the rock at his burial crypt that split at his death, and the Ascension Church all touched us as places from our Christian background.

Our bus ride to Bethlehem gave us some interesting points to ponder. Twice we were boarded by the Israeli Police. They checked the passengers' papers and at one stop made several men get off the bus. John told us later those men were Palestinian and probably did not have the right papers.

We weren't allowed to ride the Jerusalem bus into Bethlehem proper. We had to get off, climb up a hill and wait for another bus into town. We just followed the crowd to the bus which drove into a parking space, loaded us, backed out, and dropped us off somewhere near town center. We continued to follow the crowd to walk into the main square and the Church of the Nativity.

In Bethlehem we learned that several religions share the Church of the Nativity—Greek Orthodox, Armenian, and Roman Catholics. We never learned that as youngsters in Sunday school. They have set schedules for services and it seems not to be a bother to share. Beneath the altar is the place of Jesus' birth, symbolized by a 14 point circle—the 14 generations between David and Joseph. Before leaving the underground area, the local guide took us to a large open cell with skulls piled high, reminders of the babies Herod had killed. Birth and death in the same place.

Lighting a candle in the Church of the Nativity

Nazareth and the Sea of Galilee are settings for other Bible stories. There is a stunning chapel dedicated to Mary's visit from the archangel—Basilica of the Annunciation. The most fascinating and unique feature was floor to ceiling paintings from many countries showing their unique and individual perspective on how Mary learned from the angel she would give birth to Jesus. St. Joseph's Church, right next door, could not hold a candle to her basilica.

At the north end of the Sea of Galilee, we found a church dedicated to the "Sermon on the Mount," built by none other than Mussolini. It is circular and depicts the Stations of the Cross, one by one, along the sides of the chapel. Quite close by is Peter's House, below a round chapel which could be "The Upper Room," at the ruins of Capernaum. At the Church of the Bread and Fishes we touched the rock where Jesus placed the bread; the chapel is built around it.

In addition to the above places in Israel, we had the opportunity to visit a Palestinian refugee camp in the West Bank with a man from "Alternative Tours." Two young men met us at the cafeteria, answered all our questions, took us on a walk around the premises, and shed light on what it is like for them to be a "4th generation refugee" as both their families have been there since the camp opened. Eleven-thousand people live in less than one square mile. When Palestine was divided to make a new Israel after World War II, some Palestinians were rounded up for the camps. They were told to lock up their homes, bring their keys, and they would return shortly. Not so. For the first ten years they all lived in tents, then a one room building for 9-10 people. These were single story only so the soldiers guarding the camp could see everything. Housing is better today. They have water and electricity, a school for boys and one for girls, a medical clinic opened from 8-12 daily with one doctor available, yet it is still a refugee camp. There is a mural painted along the walls going up four stories depicting "keys" left dangling and unclaimed still today. So much for the promise to "return shortly."

We were amused with some of the children following us and saying something in Arabic we couldn't understand. John finally interpreted that they wanted us to take their pictures. As restricted as they are, they know about digital cameras, posed as only kids can do, and then giggled when shown the picture before running off to whatever they had been doing before that.

The young men told us the Israelis show control by coming into the camp during the night with loudspeakers, demanding all males between 15 and 45 assemble at the school. There they are taken away blindfolded for questioning. It seems spies in camp keep the soldiers fed with information about problems, so in order to stay on top of security, they have to act.

Leaving the camp we drove out to view the settlements and the walls. These walls are not straight. They zig and zag around property still owned by Palestinians. By not allowing access to homes and fields, they can say the Palestinians aren't using their land, so the land is confiscated, the fence moves, only to make another zig zag down the line. It was frustrating to see how the transfer of goods occurred. At designated roadblocks trucks backed up to each other and hand to hand passing of boxes kept the right people on the right side of the border.

We cannot see an easy fix to the Israeli-Palestinian problem, but are appalled at how the Israelis, restricted to ghettos themselves in the past, have taken the same approach to ostracizing the Palestinians and confiscating more land in the process, witnessed by or denied by the whole world. It is a sad situation.

But in Jordan the atmosphere is upbeat. A poster greets the visitor: "Discover the legend; explore the history; and experience the hospitality." We did all of that in a week's time with our rental car driving from the northern border crossing with Israel to the southern one at Gulf of Aqaba.

Each day we saw a new piece of history to wander through and learn about. Or experience the hospitality of the people. Once we got lost and even after making larger and larger circles attempting to find a sign to our destination (signs were in Arabic characters and in "English"), we remained lost. Stopping at a mechanic shop, I asked for help.

Several men came to the car and almost in unison said, "Go straight to the next intersection. Do not turn left. Do not turn right. Go straight to the next intersection. Do not turn left. Do not turn right. Go straight. At the next intersection, turn right and you will see a sign." They were right too. However, shortly after that we took the wrong exit from a traffic circle. Without wasting time I had Denis stop immediately when I saw a man reading a newspaper outside his fruit stand. I approached the man, who put down his paper and asked in perfect English, "How can I help you?" I told him I was lost.

He told me to go back to the traffic circle (roundabout) and take the bus. "No," I said, "I have a car." He asked where the car was and if I had a driver. So I took him to meet Denis. He told us both what to do to "get found again." Then he took my arm and said, "Come." We walked back to his fruit stand. He grabbed a plastic bag, picked up two apples, two bananas, two pears, and two oranges. Handing it to me, he said, "There. Next time you get lost, we'll have tea!" What a delightful memory!

Petra, the famous Rose Red City, is overwhelmingly the major attraction for visitors to Jordan, visited by about 300,000 people a year. Everyone you meet when discussing Jordan asks, "Have you been to Petra?" Its name, Rose Red City, refers to its spectacular colored sandstone rock caves and tombs that change colors with light and dark, as well as the different coloring in the sandstone layers. It looks like a mosaic of artwork in nature. Petra stayed a secret, well kept by Bedouin, until the early 19th century. We walked through the canyon leading to the spectacular "Treasury" twice our first day there—once in the daytime, and once at night, following candles on the desert floor whose reflections on the walls gave an unusual feeling to the awesome experience. At the Treasury, a Bedouin elder talked to the group about life in Petra, then and now. He mentioned something that stayed with me, "Jordan has a unique position in the Middle East. It is surrounded by 'noisy neighbors'!" Our hike earlier that day took us with our guide to a monastery, the trail winding 800 steps up the mountain, with people along the way selling souvenirs or refreshments for the heat of the day. It truly was a fascinating place. Now with the Indiana Jones movie, Petra can come alive without your making a trip there.

The carved Monastery was worth the effort!

Speaking of movies, we stayed overnight at Wadi Rum, Lawrence of Arabia's desert, taking a four-wheel-drive car with Bedouin driver to explore the sands in the afternoon, watch sunset, eat a meal in a Bedouin tent, and get up for sunrise after sleeping on mats in a tent set up for guests (on the sand). At breakfast the cook served us, sat down to visit, and commented about the stillness and quiet of the desert. "No cars, no trucks, no helicopters, no missiles." Well said.

The only animals we saw were camels, and they were there to make money for their masters by giving rides. Camels have the longest eye lashes, biggest feet and haughtiest look about them, in my opinion. I have met them up close and personal in far western China, in Tunisia, Syria, and now in Jordan. I have passed on all occasions to test drive one. There is a limit to my sense of adventure, would you believe?

A friendly camel at Wadi Rum

It took 25 hours to go by sea from Herzliya, Israel to Larnaca, South Cyprus. All during the trip we heard the Israeli Navy calling vessels at this or that location. Bob and Betty on *CONESTOGA* headed to a different port than us. We kept our two hour report-in schedule until we thought we couldn't hear each other. Well, turns out we could. Just before midnight, Bob's voice came loud and clear over the VHF radio with this message, "This is the *Sailing Vessel CONESTOGA* calling the vessel off my bow. What is your intention?" He did it more than once. We waited and then contacted him ourselves. His report: a boat had shadowed him, speeding up when he did, slowing when he did, but never speaking to him. Finally the other boat shone a spotlight on him, and then left. Was it an Israeli gunboat? A fisherman? A pirate? Who knows—but it sure was spooky! Bob's position was 80 nautical miles off the Lebanon/Israel border, so go figure.

In Larnaca we had to deal with authorities so Tipper could leave the ship and relieve herself. 25 hours is a long time not to go to the bathroom, and she had never let herself go on a boat, ever. After much discussion and showing of papers, and the government vet coming to the boat to "see" the dog, they agreed for a port fee of $60 U.S., she could have marina privileges. Too late. She peed on the boat. Later Joan reported that Tipper got a bladder infection from her experience.

Back to Turkey after the winds subsided to make the crossing more tolerable. There we parted company with the Brairs and joined up with our

San Diego family to do ten days of sun and fun on the southern coast of Turkey.

Turkish Tidbits

Izmir, Istanbul, Cappadocia, Marmaris, and Dalian episodes, plus long-distance bus rides added spice to our adventures in Turkey.

Izmir on the Aegean (west) side has two tales to tell. One, my military ID had to be renewed just a few days after we first arrived in Turkey—late September 2003. Denis is retired Air Force, and I needed to keep my ID card up to date, not only to be allowed on military installations, but for medical coverage, should it be needed. It is important that this card not expire. A lot of paperwork would be required to start over again for a new card, e.g. birth certificate, marriage license, and sponsor-applied paperwork. This we did not want to do, so found out what our options were for renewal. If we were not stateside, we could do it at any military base worldwide, or through an American Embassy or Consulate's office. But it could not be done more than thirty days before expiration. There was an Embassy in Istanbul and an Air Force Base in Izmir, Turkey, but for the last thirty days before renewal, we would be at sea working our way through the Greek islands. It became imperative we reach Marmaris, our port of choice in southern Turkey, before 25 September to complete this transaction.

Secured at the Marmaris Yacht Marina dock, we boarded a long-distance bus into Izmir, found a hotel, and called the phone number we had for the U. S. Military Pass and ID Office. They gave us directions and appointment for 10 A.M. the next day. Just to make sure we could find it, we went on a reconnaissance check of the vicinity that evening. The building was nondescript, except for the huge concrete blast barriers along the entrance side. The door did not look like a real door. It blended in very well with the façade. I asked at a Turkish security checkpoint around the corner. The man on duty confirmed I was in the right place. On our arrival the next morning, two GIs (noted by their haircuts and military bearing) in civilian clothes stood nearby and I asked about the door. They pointed to it and said, "Push that one. Security personnel will check you in from there." And they did. All set with my new card, we reversed our trail and headed back to Marmaris. No time to sightsee this trip.

The other tale from Izmir is my "Turkish Bridge." One of the anchor teeth in my original bridge had decayed and the tooth next to it had minimum support to offer, so the new bridge had to span five teeth instead of three. That was the analysis of the female dentist in Marmaris, who had been recommended by another cruiser. When I initially arrived at the dental office she took care of me, but because she was busy running a political campaign, she passed me on to her new assistant. He ordered and installed the bridge. So far I'm the only one I know in America with a Turkish bridge, constructed in Izmir, installed in Marmaris.

Turkish carpets are a sought-after souvenir, and there are many carpet salesmen throughout the country. We bought our first carpets in Istanbul in the 1980s. Over twenty years later, young carpet salesmen in Istanbul or Marmaris followed me on the streets, pushing their wares. When I told them I had bought carpets in Istanbul probably before they were born, they replied frequently with, "Well, they are old now!" We had no intention of buying more carpets until we visited Cappadocia in central Turkey by rental car in 2004. There we found two throw rugs for the pilothouse, and an area carpet for the future home in our lives. Never say "never," right?

Cappadocia, in central Turkey, is one of our favorite places. Hasan Huseyin, our guide for the unique landscape of caves and fairy chimneys, had been born in one of the caves. His cave is now transformed into a Bed and Breakfast in Goreme, complete with Honeymoon suite and hot tub, where we stayed on our last night there.

The Cappadocian landscape is formed by the erosion of a very thick layer of volcanic ash formed into a soft volcanic rock, called tuff. Hard volcanic rock rests on top of tuff layers. When erosion wore the tuff away, it left stone-like columns, resembling chimneys. Early inhabitants of that area believe these formations represented chimneys for fairies living underground. Even today the imagination does not take much effort in arriving at the same conclusion.

"Fairy chimneys" in Cappadocia

This tuff made it easy to carve rooms, staircases and other living quarters, and has been used for thousands of years as homes for people in that part of Turkey. Faded frescoes from the Byzantium churches still showed on the cave walls. Many caves were "peopled" until the 1950s when they were deemed not safe and sound to live in anymore.

After touring the caves and walking among "fairy-chimneys" in the Open Air Museum of Goreme, we drove to Derinkuyu, which means "deep well." It is the biggest, most popular and best lit of the underground cities where people lived, beginning around the 7th century to stay safe from Arab marauders. We took a walking tour down and around and down some more, viewing niches for living, going to school, worshiping, or storing food. Heavy millstones, recessed into the walls along the way, were ready to roll into place and seal off parts of the living areas for further security. The fascinating thing about that visit was the lack of smell, knowing many people and animals had lived underground there for extended periods of time. Air intakes must have been cleverly installed.

Speaking of smells, we also toured a Caravanserai in central Turkey. These places provide a place of rest for camel caravans on their treks through the desert, like a "Motel Six" for travelers of that time. The sandstone colored building, still standing, is huge. Its entrance is tall enough and wide enough for camels with riders and packs to pass without a problem, either coming in or going out. Inside, the lower area is to house, feed and rest the camels. Having a lot of camels in one enclosed space could be quite aromatic. Upstairs, the men sleep, cook and eat. In the center of the whole building is a winding staircase up to a small room where men could go with their individual rugs, not missing the daily calls to prayer.

Whirling dervishes wowed us with a performance in a room at the Istanbul Train Station. Men and women, dressed in full-length white gowns and wearing red, very tall Moroccan-type hats, danced for a small audience. How they could spin and not get dizzy is a feat that I cannot explain just by watching them. As they started to spin, their heads tilted slightly to the right side. With eyes closed and feet marking a small pattern on the floor, they rotated without losing balance or stepping on their own feet while moving about the room to the music played by a small group of musicians nearby. Their heavy gowns extended out from the body, adding to the mesmerizing effect of their performance. They belonged to a certain sect in central Turkey. In December each year they staged a big performance in their city, but at other times, went to cities throughout Turkey to dance.

Just for fun in Marmaris, I joined a group of women cruisers for a visit to a Turkish bath (hammam). Inside, we first went into a large room to rest and relax on heated marble platforms (most of us wore our swimsuits). Located along the wall were marble washbasins with flowing cool water and a silver bowl for collecting water to pour over ourselves. As our bodies heated up, skin began to flake. The cold water rinsed the dead skin away. We repeated the hot seats versus the cool rinse off until one-by-one we were called over to the washing table. There a young man dressed only in a red and white sarong tied low over his abdomen gestured for me to lie on the table while he soaped up his huge sponge mitt. He first soaped my back and legs, after which he motioned for me to turn over. By that time the men working the spa had learned we were American, so my man asked, "Where are you from in America?" When I said, "Seattle," he threw up his soapy mitt in the air, jumped backward and exclaimed, "Supersonics!" My city's basketball team was famous in Turkey! After a soaping, another man rinsed me off before we headed to the showers. After showers, we all rested in a hot tub drinking tea, followed by a massage—four to a room to make the ladies more comfortable, each having a man doing the massage. This cultural experience, at a reasonable cost, took about three hours including a pickup and return to the marina. I had another Turkish bath on the Black Sea trip, but it did not measure up to this one. And it was interesting that in a Muslim country, where men are not allowed to touch women if they are not related, that these men apparently felt no compunction about their interaction with us.

Every week on Market Day in Marmaris, we grabbed our pull-along trolley and headed to the market for fresh fruits and vegetables. The market took up about a city block inside a concrete building close to the town center—food vendors on the bottom floor and clothing upstairs. Before the actual market were small alleys with people selling everything from barrettes to bicycles, jewelry to jogging gear, plants to pots, and everything in-between.

Inside, people jostled for space to look at the displays, pull their trolleys along behind them, push baby strollers, dodge people with canes, all to get close to the counters to shop. Vendors were both men and women; the women wearing traditional scarves from their village. They called out their specials to people parading by; at the same time chatting with their neighbors on either side of their table. The concrete floors were uneven, aisles narrow, and sometimes wet from sellers splashing water on their displays. If one had a claustrophobic tendency, this would not be a place to get tangled up in, but for those who enjoyed the adventure, it made quite an experience. Denis loved markets and we frequently them in every town or village we went to on our journey. If he saw something he did not know about, it became "target of opportunity time" and we most likely took one home. Vendors would try to explain verbally or non-verbally how to prepare such an item—raw versus cooked. No recipes were exchanged due to the language barrier. However we had along with us two lady cruisers with Macedonian and Arabic cuisine backgrounds and they helped.

The displays were super-colorful and invited you to buy something. Our trolley spilled over after about an hour. We had grapefruit, oranges, cantaloupe, squash, eggplant, carrots, potatoes, lettuce, tomatoes, wild broccoli, red and green peppers, onions, cucumbers, okra, green beans, lemons, spinach, cilantro and mint for sure. Often we added bananas, strawberries, blackberries, peaches, plums, and various cheeses. Only to repeat the process the next week. What an adventure!

I need to introduce you to the souvenir many people collected—the "evil eye." We have two on the boat. Both are about 4 inches wide of colorful ceramic, with a very large super blue eye in the center. Their mission is to ward off evil. I positioned mine so one covers the boat from bow to stern, the other, port to starboard. I felt safe.

And I needed that extra help once. I almost lost the anchor and four hundred feet of chain in 96 feet of water near the Dalian River. We planned to anchor and stern-tie to shore, then catch a local boat for a river trip, and end up at the famous mud baths. My job was to let out the anchor chain while Denis reversed the boat toward shore. Our son and grandson waited in the dinghy to grab the rope and tie it to a tree on shore. A very large problem developed when all 400 feet of chain came out of the chain locker.

As the chain started off the boat, it gathered speed at such a rate I did not secure the brake in time. Only the rope attached to the last link at one end and the bottom of the locker at the other kept us from losing everything. Thank goodness for a tight knot!

When I realized the scope of the problem, I waved violently at Denis in the pilothouse from my kneeling position at the bow, indicating he needed to leave the controls and come forward. He didn't believe what he saw, but his brain kicked into problem-solve mode right away. With the assistance of a block and tackle system he designed on the spot, the anchor chain began to slowly wind itself back on the winch. Again, the only thing that kept us from losing it all was a very tight knot at the bottom of the chain locker. The evil eye worked that day!

Of special mention is the transportation used when we left the country for the States each year. We could not cruise during the winter months, so had the boat pulled out of the water and stored on shore until our return the following spring.

Marmaris is on the south coast of Turkey. Istanbul is on the north. Most international flights land and take off from Istanbul. An airport 30 miles away from Marmaris had flights in and out of Istanbul, but with weight restrictions for luggage, made it unworkable for us.

So here's what we did. Packing any boat equipment that needed repair and a list of items to buy for the boat, some clothes plus personal items for our home stay, and laptop, we first took the dolmus (small bus) from the marina into town. There we purchased tickets for a long-distance bus ride (14 hours) to Istanbul. Buses were air-conditioned, with relatively comfortable seats for me and not so great for my 6'2" husband. An on-board attendant provided snack service during the trip. About halfway into the trip, the bus stopped at a company-owned restaurant with cafeteria food service and very clean rest rooms. We often ate a delicious soup to hold us over, and had a chance to stretch our legs. Since there were many buses coming and going out of the large parking lot, it became important for us to remember our bus number. I think also the bus driver had his eye on us too, being the only two foreigners on his bus. In Istanbul, a taxi took us to hotel for a rest before returning to the airport and an overnight overseas flight to Seattle. A shuttle ride home allowed us to crash in our own bed many hours after we began this trek.

Coming back we had to repeat all these same steps but it took a lot more energy since we had to bring back parts and equipment for the boat, such as a repaired desk-top computer, new electronics, bilge pump, plus nylon lines and ropes. For that we lugged four large, sturdy suitcases loaded to their maximum weight of 70 lbs each. At destination after unloading, we gave the suitcases away, only to repeat the process the next year. It must have been quite a sight to see a couple in their mid-sixties dealing with all that luggage. Checking the four heavy bags relieved us of everything except worrying that something might be lost. We had the foresight to inventory each bag in case we had to identify the one missing and its contents. Once that happened. That one had new computer equipment in it, but nothing was taken during its absence from us. We just delayed our trip to Marmaris by a day so it could be found and delivered.

On our next trip back to the States we chose to fly out of Izmir with their once a day flight to Germany, rather than leave from Istanbul. We not only had a shorter bus ride on the outgoing trip, but were successful in arranging a car to meet us for a ride back to Marmaris from Izmir, eliminating a lot of lugging heavy suitcases around.

Exotic Istanbul, a blend of modern and traditional, sits atop a bluff overlooking the Bosphorus Strait, an extremely busy waterway for shipping between the Black Sea and the Mediterranean. The Bosphorus also separates the European and Asian sides to the famous city. A tourist's five senses can be overwhelmed quite easily.

First the ears. Beginning at dawn, the first call to prayer from a minaret, which floats across the air over the city, is followed by four more calls before the day is finished, after sunset. When the calls are sung by a man on the scene through a microphone, it has more impact than when a recorded version is played, but the result is the same—people stop for prayer. Men pray in the mosques or their shops; women pray at home.

Then there is the Turkish language, melodic to listen to, but hard to speak. We tried to learn some words, as we did with all the other languages we encountered, but never took official lessons. Fortunately for us the signs were often in English as well.

Eyes worked overtime to take in the beauty of such buildings as the Blue Mosque and Aya Sofya, monuments to the rich history of a Christian and Muslim country. Istanbul was originally called Constantinople.

The people dressed mostly in Western garb. Women rarely wore scarves on their heads in the city, but did in the countryside. Men wore suits and ties. Well-behaved children tagged along with family groups we passed on the street. People walked, drove cars, or rode public transportation, including boat taxis back and forth between the two sides of the Bosphorus to get around.

A Grand Bazaar, with its many vendors, stood waiting to offer tourists anything and everything it seemed. Hawkers on the street, either in official stalls, or just hanging out, wanted to separate you from your money, especially carpet salesmen. Stopping to have tea with them usually ended up with a sale. That's how we purchased our first carpets twenty years ago.

Sense of smell is captivated by the local restaurants with their displays of cooked foods in glass cases just inside the restaurant doorway. If one didn't know what a certain dish was, he need only to ask before purchasing. Or just follow the aroma, pick something, and enjoy. Eggplant is a favorite vegetable dish and there are multitudes of ways to prepare this vegetable, each colorful and exotic. That's the fourth sense, taste.

The Blue Mosque, with its six minarets, many domes, and blue tiles inside, stands out as one of Istanbul's special sights. As a mosque, it is easy to imagine the stone floor filled with men shoulder-to-shoulder on their mats facing Mecca as they prayed five times a day. A wall partitioned a special place for the women to pray. It all has to be imagined, as visitors are not allowed inside during prayers, but one can touch the floor and feel its holiness. We did.

Nearby is Ayasofya (Hagia Sophia), considered the largest Christian church ever built until St. Peter's Basilica in Rome. When Mehmet the Conqueror took the city from the Byzantines in 1453, he proclaimed it a mosque. It served as a mosque for almost 500 years. Ataturk, the Father of modern Turkey, made it a museum. It has only one minaret and a wide flat dome, considered a "daring engineering feat in the 6th century." Both are spectacular and have wonderful gardens surrounding them. A very nice touch.

In 2004 we marveled at the Blue Mosque and Ayasofya as we passed below them on the Bosphorus Strait on our way north with the Black Sea Rally. Quite stunning!

Get Ready: Crossing the Mediterranean

Decision time! Do we return the same way we came? Or do we go through the Red Sea, on past India and Thailand, then cross the Pacific Ocean to make a complete circumnavigation?

We spent a lot of time studying the pros and cons of the latter one. Weather-wise and "other-wise" it made sense to turn around and work our way back across the Atlantic. Typhoons, pirates, and adverse head winds were the main issues. Even if we worked our way successfully through the different weather systems from the Indian Ocean to the Pacific, a trip across that ocean probably meant going north to Japan first, before heading to the Aleutian chain in Alaska. Timing for that meant a summer event, with a high incidence of fog to deal with, right in the shipping lanes. But before even considering the weather, pirates operating in the area between Somalia and Yemen made our hair stand up on the backs of our necks. We heard stories about cruisers who had traveled through this treacherous area, holding their collective breaths, and keeping a close diamond formation to protect each other's back and side.

In March 2005, an incident occurred that ended up without loss of life, but certainly could have gone the other way.[*] Two American sailing vessels, *MAHDI* and *GANDALF*, were moving from Oman to the Port of Aden (30 miles off the coast of Yemen). The Captains observed two outboard-powered boats, three men in each, passing their stern going about 25 knots at 9 A.M. They returned in an hour, just looking things over. At 4 P.M. two different boats, four men in each one, approached. Their profile was different, so they were not the same as the morning ones. Coming very fast toward the Americans, they separated, one firing into the cockpit of *MAHDI'S* port side. The other one fired at *GANDALF*. Those pirates meant business. The boat that fired on *MAHDI* then swung up to the stern, apparently to board. The *MAHDI's* Captain loaded his 12 gage shotgun with 00 buckshot and started shooting into their boat, forcing them to keep their heads down. After 3 shots, the pirate's engine started to smoke. The captain

---

[*] Adapted from noonsite.com story, "Violent pirate attack on two yachts off Yemen

on *GANDALF* rammed the other boat amidships, almost cutting it in two, and turning it over. *MAHDI's* Captain turned to shoot at the boat behind him, but the boat turned to head toward *GANDALF's* stern. Two men stood on the bow with the intent to board. *MAHDI's* Captain turned the shotgun on them, knocking them down. When the boat veered away he shot the driver, who did not fall down like the other two. The two American boats kept going at full speed and as soon as they were out of rifle range, they looked back and watched both boats drifting, disabled.

The pirates made a mistake by trying to board. If they had stood off a bit and just fired with their automatic weapons, the outcome would have been completely different. The Americans' "Mayday" calls summoned a commercial ship in the area, which came to sail alongside them until dawn to make sure they were all right.

We first heard about this incident over the single-side-band radio news, and then in Herzliya, Israel, both boats pulled into the marina and tied up at our dock. They were lucky. Having a weapon on board, knowing how to use it, and the guts to do so, saved them. Few cruisers carried weapons. We didn't.

So the best bet for us turned out to be choice number one.

Not looking back after that decision we pointed the bow west, revisiting some of our favorite anchorages in Turkey on the way to Symi, the first island in Greece. Clark and Joan Scarboro rejoined us for their third cruise on *TEKA III* with us. With them on board we dropped south from Symi to the Greek island of Crete, explored it from east to west, crossed back to the Peloponnese peninsula of Greece port-hopping to Methoni, and then a 48 hour+ crossing to Catania, Sicily.

At our first anchorage in Crete, meltimi winds kicked up and held us in port for several days. We capitalized on the free time to rent a car and explore the island, giving us a good overview of the land from the mountains to the beaches. Outside Iraklion in the central section is the Knossos Archeological Museum displaying the ancient Minoan culture, a Bronze-age civilization flourishing between 3650 B.C. and 1100 B.C. By exploring the Museum and surrounding buildings, we witnessed part of the ancient culture through its art and architecture. Tragedy occurred to the Minoans 3500 years ago with a huge volcanic explosion on Santorini (Thira), the Greek island 60 miles north of Crete. This explosion, considered the largest one in the history of civilization, ejected 60 cubic kilometers of material into the air, and resulted in a huge tsunami, which wiped out all the coastal settlements on Crete. Shortly afterward, a weakened Minoan civilization was easily taken over by the Myceans.

Back on the water between Iraklion and Khania we overheard the military at Souda Bay Naval Base call a freighter at a certain position and ask that ship's Captain to change course to avoid a military exercise. By the time we arrived in the same area, we expected and received a similar call. We had to move our course south of the intended one, decrease speed, and then go into a holding pattern until they notified us the Exercise was over. We saw Navy jets zooming in and out on practice bombing runs, but they were too high to identify. The control people at the Navy Base notified us of the all clear with, "*TEKA III,* you can proceed on your original course. Thank you."

Only then did we really see the aircraft! They passed in formation right over us on their way back to Souda Bay airfield. It gave me a stirring feeling to watch them, wing-tip to wing-tip at close range—our U. S. Navy flyboys in action! I called it "the sound of freedom."

In Khania, on the west side, we entered the harbor and could not for the life of us figure out where to tie up at their docks. The inner harbor seemed much too small for our size boat and we hesitated to go there, yet no one on boats in the other marina area popped out of their vessels to see us or offer assistance. Our only hope was a man in a white uniform carrying a clipboard, walking the concrete sea wall. He looked official. I whistled and screamed to no avail. He just shrugged his shoulders. We worked our way closer and he finally figured out I had to be dealt with, so put his clipboard down, walked over to a spot, pointed to it, and in pantomime told me to "park here." We did. We had been told a long time before entering Greek waters that some Greek authorities were not friendly, almost to the point of being quite rude and uncooperative, yet had not come across any. Until then. This man wanted the captain, Denis, to come immediately to his office and do the paperwork. We managed to finish our med-moor and secure all the lines before he had to leave. I expected Denis to return and tell us about his negative experience, but he came back with a smile. He reported the man was very pleasant and did not give him a hard time at all.

I certainly enjoyed watching the tourists come by every day in their horse-drawn carriages touring the harbor up close and personal right behind our med-moored position. We could see all the action from the cushions on our aft deck. One horse wore a straw hat with cutouts for his ears and seemed ever so happy to be clip-clopping along on the cobblestones of old. He posed for my camera.

Leaving the west end of Crete we were indeed headed home with the bow pointed west. NATO warships radioed commercial ships along our way from Greece to Sicily. After making contact, NATO ship #72, asked where the commercial ship had come from, where it was headed, and what cargo it held. I would note their position on our chart when they called someone: "…

ship 5 miles off my port bow at latitude___, longitude___." That way I could compare our position to theirs with some credibility. During the first night they were ahead of us, but during the day we were ahead of them. They had rerouted south of us to check ships in another quadrant. We never had a chance to see that ship, until we were coming into Rota, Spain a few weeks and about 1500 hundred miles later. A VHF radio call went out that "Warship 72 is leaving Rota Harbor; any concerned traffic should call them on Channel 16 or 13." And there it was!

On the island of Sicily, and before the Scarboros returned to the States, we did more land touring, this time on the south side of the island, after we drove all around Mt. Etna in the northeast corner. Siracusa, a sea city, proved interesting, but the Greek Temple mid-island that we missed on the first land trip, proved disappointing since we had traipsed through so many Greek ruins between the first trip and this one. I can see how people get jaded with too much of a certain feature in history and landscape.

From Sicily to Gibraltar we had some interesting encounters with ships at night. The first one came on the radar at twelve miles off the port side, roared past our bow at a super-speed, and became a flash in the pan shortly after that. We suspected it might have been a smuggling ship because it ran fast and without lights right in a line between the African coast and Italy. Where was the Guardia Finanza when it could be of use?

The second event occurred over the VHF radio. I had the duty alone. A click over the radio let me know someone had opened the mike. He paused, and then burped loud and long! Not once, not twice, but three times. It gave the impression that this man, perhaps a bored fisherman wanting to be obnoxious, keyed the mike to make a statement. After the third time, I picked up my mike and said, "*Buon giorno.*" He never said another word.

Number three and four were between the Balearics and Barcelona. Denis had a rule that any ship coming within two miles of us had to be reported to him. Two did. The first one worked out all right. I called him when his course of three miles directly off the port side started to change. It looked as if he would cross my bow, according to the trajectory on the radar, but I wanted to hear it from him. I called. He answered. He would be crossing the bow but with room to spare, so no problem. In the middle of the night it breaks the monotony to speak with someone "out there" and I learned he was a car carrier headed to Barcelona from Tokyo. He had been at sea a long time.

The last one followed the same pattern as number three, but by then I was in a new position when he changed course from ninety degrees off my port side to coming right at me. I called. And called. No answer. If I did not change course, or he did not either, we were in trouble. I woke Denis up.

Shortly after we began working out solutions, the other boat changed course to pass behind me. As he passed, I determined it was a small cruise liner. Who knows why the person on duty did not answer my call. It goes back to what I said before, either they cannot speak English, are not awake, or don't care. We missed trouble, but just.

In Menorca we met another long distance trawler, this one flying an Aussie flag. Bob and Margaret on *SUPRR,* a 46-foot Nordhavn, turned out to be good friends over the next few months. Their crew even "saved our butt" at English Harbor in Antigua, us arriving late to a crowded anchorage, with rain, after our Atlantic crossing in December 2005.

In Cartagena, Spain, we met another buddy boat, a 65-foot steel boat capable of crossing oceans, *PAMACEA*. Coming into the harbor I had arranged the fenders and lines for a starboard tie (right-hand side) to the dock. Just as we started down the small channel to our assigned spot, Denis requested I change everything to make a port tie, causing me to scramble to reverse everything in only a few minutes. The boat at the beginning of the dock watched as an American-flagged boat came past them, with Seattle as the home port, and tried to contact us by waving. They were also from Seattle, and here we were halfway around the world from Washington State. I never saw Pam, Neil, or their boat at that time. After we tied up, Neil approached the stern, smiled and said, "We are from Seattle, too." What a small world!

Get Set: Staging in the Canaries

Weather became our focus at Gibraltar, the mouth of the Mediterranean. First we had to make it down to our staging area in the Canary Islands off the coast of Africa, then the 2,764 nautical miles across the Atlantic Ocean to the Caribbean. We collected weather faxes, communicated with our weather guru from the original crossing, and watched the sky.

Marvin Day, our longtime cruising friend, joined us in Gibraltar to take up crew duties. He stayed with us a total of 82 days, down to the Canaries and on across the Atlantic. That's a whole bunch of meals at the Captain's Table, even whipping up some of his special spaghetti for us every now and then. We celebrated his 64th birthday halfway across the big water.

In the Canaries we intended to wait out the official end of hurricane season (November 30) before striking out across the Atlantic. About that time two late season tropical storms brewed mid-Atlantic and went east, not west. There must be something wrong here. We experienced Tropical Storm Vince while in Rota Spain, blowing up to 45 knots and sending waves with white curls on top into the protected marina past the breakwater. We waited, secure at the dock, for a weather window so we could drop south to the Canaries.

The second day out of Rota presented us with a problem. The boat took an independent turn to the right and wouldn't stop. After turning off the Autopilot, Denis went to the stern and stepped onto the swim bridge to see if there had been a problem with the rudder as it now was jammed all the way to the left. He found nothing wrong there. Back inside the boat again, he hastily moved many things aside to slide his body under the aft cabin desk and behind a panel to check for any hydraulic fluid leaks. Nothing. But he did find the problem. The rudder-angle sensor-cable, which interfaces rudder steering through the autopilot, had broken. Probably metal fatigue. So, Marvin hand-steered while I fetched tools and Denis problem-solved, making a new temporary cable from heavy-duty fishing leader. We only lost 20 minutes of travel time and the seas were pretty calm for the event. If the dilemma had happened during the night or with rough seas, the fix might have taken much longer, and been much scarier.

On the trip down to Graciosa, two sets of dolphins visited us, and gannets kept flying over, thinking we were a fishing boat, I guess. Many flying fish were about, including one committing suicide when he flew onto the deck. Over the VHF Denis talked to the Captain of a large tug pulling a semi-submersible oil platform en route from Angola through Gibraltar to Sicily, and on to Egypt. It was an unusual sight.

After 83 hours of travel, and a full moon for our night passage, we arrived at Francesca Harbor, Graciosa Island, October 16, 2005. We woke up the neighbors as we dropped the anchor at 11:30 P.M. just outside the circled group of ten sailboats swinging on their hooks. In daylight we learned these boats flew flags from France, Belgium or Switzerland.

After three nights anchored at Francesca Bay and exploring the small island, we journeyed around to the east side of the next one, Lanzarote. Tying up at Puerto Calero Marina for three weeks, we started trip preparations and played tourist. We would never get this chance again—similar to landing in the Azores. Neither place is convenient for just stopping by.

Lanzarote claims to have over 300 cinder cones. Timafaya National Park covers the six volcanoes that erupted constantly between 1730 and 1736, destroying the best agricultural section of the island, and adding several more acres of land with its huge lava flow to the sea. We took a guided walk (in the rain would you believe?) with a local woman, who said we were special that it rained for us so we could see what peeked up out of the lava beds. All plants lay dormant beneath the surface, waiting for a chance to get a drink and sprout. Since there is very little rain, all plants, especially the grapevines buried in holes surrounded by lava rocks, normally depend on the heavy dew from the trade-wind clouds for moisture.

While we walked down below, we looked up among the peaks and saw tourist buses making their way up, down and around the high landscape, many passengers probably looking down on us trekking along on the bottom. Our experience later with that bus trip was a jaw-dropper! The bus would stop right at the top of a crest with very little pavement on the road's edge. We looked way down into craters or far ahead down and around the bend. At the end of the ride, a man herded us over to where he scooped some tumbleweed into an open pit. It promptly ignited. Then following instructions, we picked up some ground, only to drop it like hot cakes. HOT rocks. Lastly, he poured pails of water into holes, and steam gushed up. We were definitely standing on some active volcanic stuff.

In Las Palmas, the ARC (Atlantic Rally Crossing) had gathered. There were 150 boats ready to cross en masse on Nov 20. This ARC has been going on for 26 years—an organized "pay your money to go with others" crossing from the Canaries to St. Lucia in the Caribbean. No room at the marina for anyone else, so we anchored out. On our six days there we socialized with other people in the anchorage who were also planning to cross independent of the ARC, have the same experience, and save money.

While awaiting departure, we crossed over to Tenerife Island for a quick look-see. At the Santa Cruz Marina about twenty cruisers, not all Americans, got together for a potluck Thanksgiving dinner, with turkey tetrazzini the closest to a roast turkey entrée. We did have cans of cranberry sauce and pumpkin pie mix, so the celebration went well. You don't have to bake a whole turkey to have a feast.

Two days with a car gave us access to the whole island. One day we stopped to see the special museum at La Laguna along with its famous church, Iglesia de Nuestra Senora (Church of Our Lady), where I lit a candle and whispered a prayer for our voyage (similar to the church on Gran Canary where Christopher Columbus and I also prayed); and La Orotava, a village with old world charm in architecture, balconied houses and narrow streets, nestled on the hillside of a 10,000 foot volcano. Huge poinsettias—tree-size clumps of them—grew alongside the road and called out for a photo to capture their size and color. On another day we grabbed sweaters when we took off from the marina to visit the volcano, Tiede. Pine forests were plentiful and we picked up some special pinecones for Christmas decoration around our cloth Christmas tree purchased at La Laguna.

Weather appeared to be changing. We took advantage of a good day and returned to Las Palmas. Nancy, Marvin's wife, who came to visit during our stay in the Canaries, had to catch a return flight to Galveston. Our son, David, would be coming in a couple days after that. We needed to be in place. Tropical Storm Delta arrived the day after we did in Las Palmas. We had tied every which way to the dock for the 35-knot winds from the south, and heavy surge coming in from the marina breakwater. That night the wind shifted to the northwest (180 degrees). Several boats received damage by being blown back into the dock. We had repositioned ourselves forward so nothing happened to us.

Cruisers pass on information through a daily get-together over the VHF at a certain time each morning. The Cruisers' Net reported that Santa Cruz, where we had just been on Tenerife, had experienced 40-60 knot winds and heavy rain with T/S Delta. Dock damage had hurt several boats, including one with a crack in her hull sustained from banging into the sea wall. The wind and seas broke the floating dock loose from its moorings and squashed all the boats tied up at that pier, with one falling on the next until the inside one, *IOLANTE*, felt the brunt of it all. (Repaired, she not only made the crossing, but continued all the way to Mexico the next year). On Lanzarote, where we had recently tied up, part of the sea wall near the bathrooms had fallen down at the Puerto Calero Marina; the roof blew off the maintenance shed; two boats out of the water had fallen over—all with 60-80 knot winds. *PAMACEA* had sat that one out in the marina. So guess we were very lucky in our Las Palmas marina.

This storm gone, we watched Tropical Storm Epsilon start to form right in our projected path. Every year people plan to start their crossing at the end of the hurricane season. This one did not want to end. Epsilon was storm #29. And it, with Vince and Delta, formed mid Atlantic and headed east, not west, the normal pattern. Still December looked like the best month and it would allow people to be on the other side for Christmas and New Year's.

We picked up our son, David, at Las Palmas airport about 6:30 P.M. Saturday, December 3. He said he looked down from 35,000 feet over the Atlantic to see the sea just a-churning near France, Portugal and Spain. Whereas we only saw a Low Pressure Center on the weather fax on board, he saw the real thing from his airline seat and reported it really looked nasty. However, that one was probably Delta as it continued northeast, and not our upcoming one, Epsilon.

We would meet Epsilon along the way!

Go! Heading for Antigua, Almost 3,000 Miles Away

Denis, David, Marvin, and I left Las Palmas about 10 A.M. on Sunday, 4 December 2005. We calculated a 16-day/night journey to English Harbor, Antigua on the Caribbean side. There is no place to anchor in the ocean so we go 24/7 until destination. Daughter Dawn and son-in-law Larry made an "on-line tracking system" on our website (www.teka3.com) for interested people to follow along and "see" us at sea. Each day at noon, Denis sent an email to her via the single-side-band radio with our latitude and longitude position, plus other information—e.g., the weather, fishing reports, or mammal sightings. She looked forward to being a kingpin in our operation. After all, if her brother could be "crew," she could be "operation central." Both good positions filled with capable people.

Many sailboats went south to Cape Verdes, a 7-day trip, to rest, refuel and break up the crossing into smaller parts instead of one big leap. Only three powerboats made the crossing (*PAMACEA, SUPRR,* and *TEKA III*), all starting from the Canaries. They were specially designed as long-range trawlers who could carry enough diesel fuel for the trip. In fact, we still had half a tank on arrival in the Caribbean, having about 2000 gallons at the start. Altogether I think there were fifty boats heading west at about the same time frame, but we never made visual contact with any one of them. Plotting them on the paper charts let us know just how close we might be to each other, but that's about all.

Our days were full. Along with the ability to pick up ten weather faxes a day over the single-side-band (SSB) radio and computer set-up, we had four radio times for check-ins with others. Our informal 50-vessel "Atlantic Crossing" Cruisers' Net met twice a day (breakfast time and dinner time) over the SSB. In addition, we kept up with the other powerboats at scheduled times each day. I started tracking on the paper chart—about 25 boats nearby at first; which filtered down to 6 over time, as people spread out. It became a game as to who would be in the Caribbean first. Some were headed to Barbados, others, like us to Antigua. When sailboats did not have wind, they conserved fuel by just drifting, or used their engines to keep on target. As a powerboat, we could run our engine 24/7, giving us a bit of an advantage. Just to keep the record straight, however, we have been passed on the ocean by sailboats under full sail. One even called us on the radio to say how impressive an event that was to him and his crew. We heard some sailboaters announce over the VHF they were going swimming while "becalmed." It sounded like fun until one person reported seeing a shark.

Each morning boaters exchanged weather information gleaned from many sources, reported positions and conditions, and shared information, good or bad. Good: how many fish caught? Bad—how many got away! One boat hit a sleeping whale and headed to Cape Verdes to check for damage. Another one got a fishing net caught on the prop, but released it easily.

The day before leaving Las Palmas, we learned that 30 rowboats (two men to a boat) were to be in our path, rowing for 100 days across the Atlantic to the Caribbean. That made me nervous. How would I see them at night? We never did see one, but heard Rowboat #24 calling a sailboat close to them. I never heard an answer. We saw that rowboat later in Antigua. In fact, several of these rowboats from that race were tied up at the small dock there. Each boat had messages scribbled all over them by the rowers, indicating their psychological state over the voyage. It seemed like a good idea at the time, and a grand adventure, but no one seemed to be gung-ho to do it again, soon.

On Day 2 out of Las Palmas, we tried the new sails David had brought with him from San Diego. Denis had been concerned about potential problems with the rudder or prop putting us out of commission in the middle of the ocean crossing, and with Marvin's help, had designed sails just for *TEKA III*. A sail maker in Texas produced them and shipped them to David for special delivery. The day we pulled them out of the bag we had ten-knot winds behind us. With the sails in a wing-on-wing position, engine in neutral but autopilot still engaged, the boat moved forward at 2.8 knots of speed. That's quite good, considering the flopper stopper weights were in the water, which at normal cruising speed cause a half knot loss of speed. The set-up looked like Christmas Angel wings! Feeling so good about the initial test, Denis really wanted to try the system again when the winds increased to twenty knots, but we didn't do it. Maybe we should have. Just to see the outcome.

TEKA III sailing for the first time ever

I sent a photo of *TEKA III*'s new sails to SSCA (Seven Seas Cruising Association). We joined that organization in 2000 in Maine, and in 2001 applied for "commodore" status, having met all the requirements—living aboard, being long-distance cruisers (22,480 nautical miles under the keel up to then), and responsible citizens on the water. Two sailboat couples sponsored us, as was the rule. However, and this happened to be a big "however," we were a powerboat! Needless to say we protested their decision, claiming the organization did not call itself, "Seven Seas Sailing Association." It fell on deaf ears and until 2008 no powerboaters became commodores until *CLOVERLEAF*. The couple on board had a background of sailing before turning to power, so that might have made a difference. The Commodore Committee did not ask us if we had any background in sailing. The word, "powerboat," presented the wrong picture, and rang the wrong bells.

After successfully trying our sails, we watched as Tropical Storm Epsilon appeared in the picture. Weather faxes showed it forming mid-ocean, but not traveling the usual way—west toward the Caribbean. It seemed to be unable to definitely set a course. It moved west, stalled, moved slightly east again, all the while churning up the sea. If it decided to move east on a grand scale, instead of the expected westward pattern, headlines in African newspapers could have read, "Tropical storm ravages western Africa, going the wrong way!" Our weather router wondered if it would start west and hook around to the east toward us as we traveled west. With that in mind, we dropped our course further south. And kept an eye on it!

Winds at first were from northeast at 10-12 knots, increasing to 18 to 20 knots from the north that evening, with eight foot waves from the northwest. The next day the wind shifted to east-southeast 9-15 knots, with waves of six feet. Two days later, Epsilon had stalled enough that a cold front overtook it, dissolving the potential for a bigger storm, but our waves increased to fourteen feet and the winds increased to 25 knots in advance of the cold front. The fifth day, the winds changed course to northwest, topping at 15 knots, yet the seas refused to lay down that fast. Waves were between nine and fourteen feet, then down to ten the next day, continuing to decrease a bit each day until we reached destination.

At the halfway point we celebrated not only that event, but Marvin's 64th birthday with turkey, dressing, mashed potatoes, gravy, cranberry sauce and a glass of wine. For dessert we had coca-cola cake (made from scratch!).

With four of us on board the men took three-hour stints at night watching. I had no responsibility there, but because I felt involved too, I got up when I felt the need for a reality check. My main job, "galley magic," kept me occupied a lot of the trip. These guys rewarded me by eating everything on their plates. Maybe the fresh salt air added to their appetites. I know it did to mine. No one gained weight though. The motion of being on a boat, which constantly moves, seems to have a significant effect on burning calories.

Fish, fresh fish, constituted the main meal each day. For the first half of the trip, we couldn't seem to keep up with the catch of the day, an abundance of mahi-mahi (also called dolphin fish on the East coast). What we could not eat, we froze, until we just had to give up fishing for a while. By the time we started up again, something had happened to the luck. Larger fish took the lures and broke the lines, disappointing the fishermen. But the excitement of the fight kept the blood running! David had one fish on that took off with his line so fast he had a hard time holding the rod, until the line broke. At another time we had a billfish on, and when he jumped out of the water, the line broke. The fishing did keep us entertained, involved, and fed. No doubt about it as an on-board activity.

Sunrises and sunsets are spectacular out at sea. We saw many. Also moonrise and moonset of the full moon. The moon rose late on Saturday, Dec 17, off the stern. With it came a "moonbow" off the bow. The phenomenon made one's mouth drop.

Equally awesome, were the mammals of the sea that crossed our paths. Dolphin, Pantropical Striped ones, and Atlantic Spotted ones, came several times to play around the boat. One morning about 9:20, David walked by me in the pilothouse and pointed off the bow. There, two fins in line with each other showing out of the water became a mama and a baby whale. They swam at the surface for a minute, dove, surfaced once more, and then we never saw them again. I said, "Is the mother showing us off to the baby, or the baby to us?" Another time a pygmy killer whale surfaced and "blew" not too far off the starboard bow. Both times we made identifications with our dolphin and whale book on board, compliments of the Whale Museum at Lanzarote, in the Gran Canaries.

In addition, a meteor filled the sky about 5 one morning. What a burnout! Only Denis witnessed it as it happened on his night watch. Too bad for the rest of us.

Three hours before reaching Antigua we could see it as the day started to fade. By the time we arrived at the entrance it had turned dark, quite dark! No moon! We entered English Harbour carefully as the entrance lights, marking rocks on one side and shoaling water on the other, were not working. Two range markers, positioned on shore for further guidance in entering, weren't working either. Using our radar and a light from *SUPRR* to line up on the channel, we cleared the entrance, and gasped as we saw boats anchored all over the place—not only in the appropriate anchoring field, but also right in the channel. We needed help, so were happy when our friends on *SUPRR* already in the anchorage, showed the way by shining their spotlight at us.

The minefield of boats ahead of us meant we had to hurriedly bring in and store our flopper stoppers. Once we decided on an empty spot to anchor, our anxiety level shot way up. We had a new problem. Although *SUPRR* kept the spotlight on to guide us, boats we were passing in the anchorage also turned on their spotlights, which decreased our night vision. Fortunately they quickly turned them off when they saw we were not going to collide with them. Then it started to rain—heavy rain! The crew in *SUPRR* donned slickers, dropped the dinghy off the transom, jumped in and headed over to assist. They pointed out a "hole" and stood by to watch while we anchored. We were so grateful for their physical presence, and presence of mind to calm us in our time of need. Cruisers are special people.

We had violated a common rule of cruising by going into an unknown port at night and almost got into big trouble. Luckily we didn't hit anyone in the process.

Our crossing went well, however our buddy boat, *SUPRR*, suffered serious damage after its flopper stopper paravane went wild, hit and bent the prop when they were about halfway across the ocean. They had to reduce speed due to vibration, but they made it to Antigua on their own.

We did hear of a sailing vessel, *FIRST LIGHT,* suffered rudder problems, such that the couple had to abandon ship after attempts to work something out failed. Fortunately another sailboat was able to take them on board. Later we learned that broken-down boat floated all the way to Barbados and washed up on the beach. On another crossing in a previous year there were two deaths reported. One man fell overboard with his lifeline attached, and drowned because he could not get back into his sailboat while it continued on its way. In the second case, a storm wrecked a boat. The people were rescued by a ship. As the woman climbed up the rope ladder, she lost her footing somehow and fell back into the water. They never could locate her in the rough water. Very sad in both cases.

After clearing with the authorities in English Harbour, Antigua, we moved the boat from its anchorage to a marina and promptly flew to Tacoma first, and San Diego next, to get hugs and smiles from all the family. Job well done by *TEKA III* and Mr. Gardner and the crew! Merry Christmas!

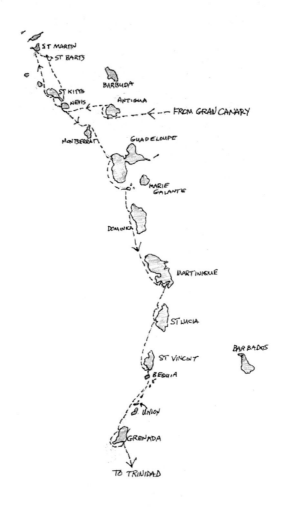

Rainbows and Green Flashes
in the Caribbean Islands

The "Theory of Threes" awaited us immediately after returning to the boat in Antigua. Losing things or fixing things seems to occur in threes. If I am on a losing streak, it takes missing three of them to take off the hex. Problems the same way! Leaving Jolly Harbour Marina for our first anchorage, we tried to lower the flopper stopper arms. They moved only so far. Then we heard a cracking sound, originating from the starboard side teak railing. We had forgotten to untie the additional lines put in place for leaving the boat in the marina. Okay, we fixed that one with "Gorilla Glue" and screws. On entering Deep Bay anchorage, the micro commander (the electronic unit that shifts gears from forward to neutral to reverse) refused to change gears from "forward." To anchor you must have "neutral" and "reverse" working. We made a U-turn back out to deep water and Denis went to work. It only took a few minutes and the micro commander functioned again. Ready to anchor now, with forward, neutral, and reverse responding appropriately, we went back to our chosen spot. There, problem #3 showed up. The windlass clutch on the Delta anchor had frozen up. The anchor chain would not budge from the winch. That meant a trip to the engine room for a rubber hammer. With brute force—hammer and muscle—everything came loose enough to drop the hook. The theory of three completed!

Gary and Diana Whitney arrived from San Diego and after we figured the weather would not abate for us to go north a bit to Barbuda, we headed west to Nevis Island. What a ride! Twelve-to-fifteen-foot high waves piled one on top of the other at our stern, to the point we felt the next one would just come on board. Watching from inside the pilothouse, the churned up seas behind the stern looked ominous. Our flopper stoppers worked with beam waves that rocked us sideways, but they could do nothing for waves that wanted to intrude over the stern. Twenty-five-to-thirty knot winds blew all the way across. This eight-hour journey seemed scarier than crossing the Atlantic. Fortunately no waves came on board and the boat rode just fine. Rounding the south corner of Nevis and anchoring on the lee shore with palm trees lining the beach felt great. Showers kept passing, creating beautiful rainbows! And I began to relax again. Gary and Diana went for a swim to shore to check things out on Nevis.

We cruised by every island in the Leewards Chain, but did not stop at each one. Some left us with vivid images—like Henry, the Set-Up-Taxi-Man, who earned his money on St. Kitts. He took us on a special driving tour of his island, plus an exhilarating and interesting rainforest hike. Henry enjoys showing off his island, blowing his horn at everyone he passes. It seems there is a code for horn-blowing. I couldn't figure it out, so waited for an opportunity and asked for an explanation. What was the difference between one, two, and three toots? Two toots were unique. It was a way of asking, "What's up?" After breaking the code, we listened more carefully and those two toots did indeed sound like, "What's up?"

After the Whitneys left, we pushed on to St. Maarten/St. Martin, anchoring in Simpson Lagoon on St. Maarten. Local lore has it that the Dutch (St. Maarten) and French (Saint-Martin) colonists decided to settle their on-going land disputes by having a Dutchman and a Frenchman stand back-to-back at one end of the island and then walk in opposite directions around the coastline. The island's boundary line would be established at the end of the day, whatever spot they finally met. As it turned out, the Frenchman walked much faster than the Dutchman and consequently the French side ended up larger than the Dutch one. The Frenchman had quenched his thirst along the way with French wine, while the Dutchman drank more potent Dutch gin, thus accounting for his much slower pace. A bit of history trivia for this stop! While there we watched the Seattle Seahawks play in the Super Bowl on television, complaining loud and long about some of the referee calls. But we were proud of our home team, making it to the Super Bowl.

The volcano on Montserrat erupted "big time" as we passed it on our way south. Its spectacular display needed 3-D to capture it on film. But the eyes could take it all in and we kept riveted to the scene all along the whole island as we passed. Ash, clouds, lava spilling down the canyons made a truly spectacular image.

Some excitement occurred in the Les Saintes anchorage south of Guadeloupe. Marvin, our sailing friend, would have been proud of us starring in that day's "Harbor TV." He pointed out often how the anchoring dance per se could be so entertaining. We of course could not laugh too hard at others' antics, as perhaps the next day would be our turn to provide the interest for others.

Friends on *DESTINY* called us over to anchor next to them as they saw us approach. We dropped the anchor, but after reversing the boat to set it, found ourselves too close to the boat behind us. They also let us know they did not appreciate our encroaching, so we pulled up and started a circle to try again.

While doing that, two things happened. First, another boat pulled up and anchored in that same spot—just drove up, dropped anchor, and relaxed. We, on the other hand, had our arms out and 50 lb. weights in the water, so we had to watch everyone in the radius of our turning circle so no problem would occur. Yet one did. The port-side weight tangled with a Swiss boat's anchor chain, climbing up his chain as we kept going in our circle, then flopped off the chain near the boat's bow and made a humongous crash. The Swiss boat's owner came dashing out. We stopped, and later checked with him to find out he had suffered no damage to his boat. Whew!

Now we had to find another spot. Many boats were there and to make sure we did not bother any others, we located a large area to anchor, away from most other boats. But we were right in line with the waves coming into the anchorage, making it uncomfortable, even with the flopper stoppers in action, so moved again. This time the second incident kept us on our toes. We lowered the anchor and used the boat's engine in reverse to set it in place. It did not set; it dragged, having tangled with something on the bottom. That something, we found on bringing the anchor back up, was a huge chain. We could not lower the anchor until the chain was dislodged, and for that we needed assistance from an additional person working at the water level. Fortunately, the owner of *DESTINY* had brought his dinghy over to check on us. With the anchor in mid-air, he and Denis worked as a team to unwrap the chain from it. I stayed inside the pilothouse to move the boat forward, if needed, to take off any pressure. It took some time, but they finally released the chain and dropped the anchor in another spot, hoping that chain would not still be in the way. At the bottom of Les Saintes Bay it waits for other boaters to try their luck at anchoring there. Too bad we couldn't leave a sign, "Don't anchor here!"

Many cruisers had praised Dominica, "the nature island," and especially a local guide, Martin Carriere. We went to check things out, intending to stay only a couple of days, but stayed for eleven. Between socializing with other cruisers through Sundowner parties and dinghy drifts, we toured the island with Martin. The Coast Guard came aboard once and after doing their inspection, sat down and asked us one question no other authority had in our ten years of traveling—"How long have you been married?" They convinced us we needed to stick around to experience carnival activities.

The carnival there existed mostly of parades, one in the morning, and another at night for three days. We went to shore the first morning and found a good place to observe the people passing along the parade route. Only a few wore costumes (most dressed in street clothes), and nothing as elaborate as magazine or television images of other carnivals with huge headdresses, lots of ruffles, skimpy clothes and high heels for the women. The music, projected through extra-large boom boxes on flatbed trucks preceded the people on foot. Its beat captivated the couples linked together as they passed—glued so close to each other their synchronized swish and sway gyrations presenting an almost "X-rated" scene. Everyone smiled, laughed, drank and drank and drank, bottles of beer in hand as they moved down the street. After the morning parade came rest time, before the evening parade, more music and more drinking—that time we listened from the anchorage.

One of our favorite images from Dominica, "Green Flashes," occurred right at sunset as the sun dropped into the Caribbean on the horizon! Watching through binoculars made it even more visible. It is only momentary, but it can be witnessed. Many people only see one, we saw seven.

Dominica offered some of the best fruits in the Caribbean

On our way to a port on Martinique, we passed a unique piece of history—"Diamond Rock." It is a 573-foot chunk of limestone on which the British in 1804 landed troops and cannons and registered it as a British War Ship. From that rock, 107 men controlled all traffic, including an eighteen-month blockade of Martinique. The French ended up floating several barrels of rum over from the mainland. The British sailors imbibed heavily. The French were then able to take Diamond Rock on June 1, 1805. The Brits fled to Barbados where they were court-martialed for deserting their ship. And today when a British ship passes HMS Diamond Rock, the crew stands at attention and salutes.

Our daughter, Dawn, and her family scheduled a visit for Tobago Cays, part of the Grenadines. They flew to St. Vincent's island and we met her plane, after an unusual mooring experience in the cut between St. Vincent's and a resort islet. The current between them ran about four knots. No room for error if you missed tying up among other boats already in place. We had made arrangements over the radio to pay for one of Charlie Tango's buoys, with his man Sparrow waiting for us in his dinghy near the assigned buoy. The exercise took a while. I passed the rope through the bow opening when we got close enough. He missed it. Our boat moved away from him with the current, so we had to maneuver again. The second time he caught the rope, but I did not get it secured on the boat, and we had to try once again. Third time charm. But after Sparrow retreated to his dock, and I began to do some laundry in a bucket on the aft deck, the boat started to come loose from its mooring. My line on board had untied. Sparrow raced out to us in his dinghy, shouting, "The line!" Once Denis and I realized what he was shouting about—the boat moved so silently we were not aware of its drift—we started the engine and went forward again. This time we arranged two lines between boat and mooring buoy and it worked. But what an ordeal! Not one I wanted to repeat either. We stayed overnight and the next day picked up the family for their time on board, and left.

Tobago Cays was the highlight of their adventure, but first Dawn had an anniversary surprise set up for Larry. We all were sworn to secrecy—Denis, granddaughter Megan and me. Dawn could not wait and spilled the beans a day ahead of time. Then I told Larry we were <u>all</u> going to the resort on Canuoan—massage, hot tub, good food—the works. He almost bought my April fool's joke. Following that, Dawn and Megan told him the real story—there was no resort. Now he appeared totally confused. However there really was one; they went ashore; the rest of us were anchored right out front of their cabin and wished them "Happy Anniversary."

In the Grenadines anchorage we swam and snorkeled over the reefs. Clear water, lots of coral, good light, multitude of colorful fish, it felt as if we were in an aquarium. Turtles swam in the anchorage area too. Everyone, but me, went with a local boatman and his fast craft to the island just outside the reef, where Johnny Depp filmed, "Pirates of the Caribbean II." My unique experience came when I think I encountered a rich and famous couple on the beach. Denis, Dawn, Larry, Megan and I went by dinghy to a small island near our boat to walk up a trail. The trail petered out and it became a bushwhack. At the top we watched a fast and fancy runabout come up to the beach below us. Two men jumped out, put up an umbrella, two chairs, table, and raked the sand from that point back to the water. Not too much later the boat returned with two people in it, who disembarked and walked to the setting under the umbrella.

When we scrambled down the "trail" I walked over to the couple sitting there and asked if they knew anything about a real path up to the top, saying we had trouble on our trip. The woman, still punching numbers in a cell phone, said, "No, but help yourself." She pointed to the other side of their seating arrangement. The man hid behind a newspaper and did not speak. I excused myself for intruding and went back to my group. They had smirks on their faces as I approached. "Do you know who you were talking to?" they asked. "No," I said. My mouth fell open when they answered, "Bill and Melinda Gates [of Microsoft fame]." Well, maybe it could have been. In thinking about it, they did resemble photos of the Gateses, and we had seen their mega yacht, *ICE*, in a couple of places on our travels down from Antigua. So…

Grenada still showed damage from the last hurricane. All the churches in St. George's are missing their roofs—definite feedback that hurricanes leave a lasting impression. Why the churches is not known.

We witnessed the missing church roofs when we had to go into St. George's town and mail our revised Income Tax for 2004. The IRS challenged our 1040 Return—two years later, and we had to scramble. On a boat, many miles away from the filing cabinet with all the data to support a tax filing, what does one do? Dawn's address was the IRS one for us, so she received the challenge in her mail. She read us the three issues involved, plus the statement implying we must pay the IRS about $5,000 by a certain date—less than a month away, plus penalties if not paid on time.

Fortunately for us, son-in-law Larry, was able to create a program for us to use the Internet and call up our 1040 information and work through the issues. The little marina near our anchorage had Internet facilities. We spent a great bit of time working on this problem and after the dust settled on these three challenged items, learned the IRS actually owed us money. We submitted all the paperwork from St. George's through International Mail and waited. The deadline date came and went. We sent several follow-up letters and finally received a check for the amount we deemed they owed us.

By this time we had secured the boat in Trinidad for the upcoming hurricane season and returned to the States. I am thankful for modern-day communication to assist in working out problems vs. the old post office system when you are (1) out of the country, and (2) on the high seas.

Before we left for Trinidad, we heard a "Pan Pan" call (a non-threatening distress call) over the VHF radio. A steel powerboat over 100 feet long had gone aground on a reef at the south end of Hog Island. The drama took several days to be resolved. At first, a barge, a dive boat and several local boats, plus dinghies bearing cruisers, gathered to help. The powerboat sent lines over to the barge and dive boat. Both attempted to pull the boat loose. The barge had to retreat home after his starboard engine overheated. The dive boat stayed, but had to send one of its divers down to cut a rope tangled on its prop. Advice came from many. One suggestion: drop the anchors and chain to lighten up the bow and make the boat more maneuverable. Another: transfer fuel to another boat. Or, blow sand beneath the hull to push it up and perhaps over the reef. Or, get a large tug. By day three the boat sat there listing slightly to port, and good-sized waves were lapping at its side. Finally a very large tug did manage to pull him off the reef. We left Grenada looking back at a sad situation, knowing when the reef released the boat, extensive repairs would be necessary.

We later heard of another vessel's drama. Cruisers on a catamaran traveling between the island of Grenada in the Windward chain and Isla Margherita in Venezuela met with misfortune. The woman had gone below for a few minutes, leaving her husband at the wheel. When she came back on deck, she could not find him. After checking around outside, and dropping back inside, calling out for him all the time, she realized he must have gone overboard somehow. She immediately hit the man overboard button on the GPS, which locked in the location at that point in time, then began circling the area, making ever larger circles. While circling she radioed the Venezuelan Navy, who sent a boat to assist. With nothing found after extensive searching by both vessels, she discontinued looking. Distraught she continued on to the next port. Along with accidents and illness occurring, "man overboard" is not wished on anyone cruising. And the feeling of helplessness, coming up empty after searching, leaves an overwhelming feeling of "why?"

To reach Chaguaramas Bay in Trinidad, we had to enter through what is called the "Dragon's Mouth." If tide and current run fast against each other, in this mini-strait, the resulting standing waves can come right over the entire boat. Some boaters have had that experience and recommended that we time our arrival at slack tide so the ride will be much easier. We did just that and arrived at Coral Cove Marina, *TEKA's* new summer home with no problem.

Cruising Pirate Waters—The Southern Caribbean

Coral Cove Marina, *TEKA III*'s home in Chaguaramas and Jesse James Members Only Club belong together in our Trinidad memory book. The travel lift at Coral Cove with smiling Calvin its driver in charge, gently moved us out of the water in the launch area and even more gingerly trucked us to our resting spot alongside the fence in the boatyard. We weighed over 40 tons and the lift's tires seemed a bit worn, but we made it. Between the security shack and the marina office, we felt someone would be looking after the boat indirectly, if not directly, during our six-month absence in 2006.

Jesse James (yes, his real name) and wife, Sharon Rose, operated a special land-travel service for cruisers. Its official name was Jesse James Members Only Club; but you did not have to join to participate—all cruisers were automatically members. He also referred to it as his "Maxi-Taxi" service. In his small fleet of vans he or his drivers did pickup and delivery for provisioning at local grocery stores or markets, doctor appointments, going to movies, or highly recommended trips beyond Chaguaramas to experience Trinidad.

Denis and I joined one such trip, which took us across island to the Atlantic side, about three hours long, as the roads are not fast ones, to meet some very special leatherback turtles "doing their thing." Arriving there we met some self-appointed rangers (local men who looked after the turtles each spring when they came on shore to lay eggs). Walking from the parking area down the beach in the moonlight, with waves crashing nearby, we spotted a large turtle with a tripod positioned above her. The rangers were to weigh her with this tripod—its three legs surrounding her and the strap slipped beneath her. At the time we arrived she had glazed over and seemed in a trance. We bent down and touched her shell, which did actually feel like leather. Her position was over a large hole dug by her huge back flippers. She lay over 100 eggs while we watched, after which she covered the hole, diligently. It took quite a while, but when she moved away, you could not tell the sand had been disturbed. What happened next blew me away! She crawled about ten feet ahead and maybe ten feet more to the side, stopped and began digging another hole with her huge flippers. Was she going to lay more eggs? No! This would be her decoy nest. She stayed there a few minutes, before aggressively piling the sand back into the hole, without a care for deliberation. The ranger explained that poachers would zero in on that one and perhaps miss the real one when they were on the lookout for eggs, or later on, baby turtles. We reverently watched as this 747 lb. mama leatherback turtle (that's what she actually weighed that night) slowly made her way back into the sea, never looking back to what she left behind. Next spring she would return to do it all over again. The baby turtles would hatch in June and other cruisers would take Jesse's van back to the Atlantic side, and on a moonlit night watch them scurry into the sea, those who made it.

We returned to the boat in late fall. Bottom painting began, along with other chores, large and small, to prepare for relaunch and our trip west to the Panama Canal. For Thanksgiving we went with Jesse to the Culinary Institute's Thanksgiving Feast, a way for the cooking school students to demonstrate what they had learned. The menu was turkey and the fixings, but we were disappointed it turned out to be rolled turkey, sliced to serve. The real roasted turkeys, brought into the room under dimmed lights and sparklers for decoration at the beginning of the feast, were not the ones they carved to serve. However, we enjoyed the evening and were gracious guests.

Denis and I also made time to stay overnight at a world-renowned Bird Sanctuary—Asa Wright. Trinidad and its neighbor island, Tobago, have many colorful birds of their own, plus they are situated on the migratory path between South America and North America. Asa Wright Nature Center, a 720-acre bird sanctuary, claiming 430 species of birds, is located on the north side of the island, accessible by car up and over the mountain. It has been there 31 years drawing birders from all over the world. In 1998 it won the *Islands Magazine* Eco-tourism Award.

The old estate house, now made into guest housing, features a large veranda off the back overlooking the garden below and jungle beyond. Other cottages nearby also offer accommodations, but we lucked into staying in the old house, making it convenient to pop out on the veranda any time to observe the flutter of color and watch the birds feed. Birds are best seen early in the morning or later in the afternoon. So at 6 o'clock each morning members of the Center's staff bring coffee and pastries on the veranda to early risers. As many as 25 species can be seen right there before breakfast. There are many hummingbirds, honeycreepers, thrushes, motmots, tanagers, kiskadees, toucans, oropendolas (cornbirds) and of course bananaquits galore. The bird feeders on the ground and on stands are furnished with leftover fruit and bread from meals served to guests during the day. Mangoes, bananas, and papayas added more color to the already colorful scene.

Birders trained their powerful binoculars into the distant jungle to locate a bird calling from the dense trees or on top of bare branches. We were impressed with their field glasses and long-range cameras capturing the abundant birdlife near and far. They knew many birds by their calls. A naturalist stayed on the veranda much of the time to answer questions and point out particular birds to novices. A nature walk with one of the resident naturalists also gave us opportunity to really watch the birds in their environment.

Also, the jungle area directly across the main road from Coral Cove Marina provided more birdlife—this time, orange-winged parrots. Every morning just after sunrise, and evening, about sunset, the treetops would erupt with zillions of brilliant green parrots, screaming away in chorus. They started their day together and finished it together. Where they went during the day is anyone's guess. Their routine went like clockwork. It reminded me of the kookaburras in Australia. They woke everyone up within earshot in the early morning with their laugh. One laughed and others followed, until you chimed in as well. That old Girl Scout ditty ran through my head, "Kookaburra sits on the old gum tree, merry, merry king of the bush is he. Laugh, kookaburra, laugh, kookaburra, gay your life must be!" Wonder if there is a ditty about parrots?

After the painting, waxing, and cleaning were completed on the boat, Calvin came with the travel lift again and took us back to the launch ramp. Once in the water, we were happy to see our special crew come walking down the dock. Hugo Carver, of Knight & Carver, who built our boat in San Diego 25 years before, accepted our invitation to "do a leg" on his boat before we got back to the U. S. Every year we would meet up with Hugo and Marjie Carver in San Diego for lunch and keep them abreast of *TEKA III*'s adventures. Although Hugo had been on the sea trials, he had never been on a real trip, and we could use his skills as crewmember. It became a mutual admiration society event, enhanced by his bringing requested items for the boat, plus some nuts and chocolates in his suitcase to butter up the captain and first mate.

Boat ready, crew aboard, paperwork done to clear out of Trinidad— time to go! We ignored the "don't start any trip on a Friday rule," but only went to the next island to test out all the systems, December 1, 2006.

Hugo stayed on board from Trinidad to Cartagena, Columbia, 963 nautical miles, and departed in time to spend Christmas with his family. His seagoing adventure allowed him to be reunited with one of his creations, feel truly salty again, cool off with a daily swim (the weather was super-hot and humid), assist the captain with numerous boat jobs, remove the many flying fish that committed suicide during night passages, take tons of photos, and give us the "hippy dippy" weather report (a la George Carlin) each day. He made me giggle me when he appeared in the pilothouse with a serious look on his face, yet a twinkle in his eye, and asked if I felt the bump when we went over the last Omega line (a line on the chart).

He used his manners, freely discussed serious and frivolous subjects, shared sea stories, and complimented the cook on her attempts at gourmet presentations. Three weeks went fast; no lashes or keel-hauling were threatened or performed. We gave him an excellent grade for his time with us.

Venezuela, first country west of Trinidad and home to modern-day pirates, made us nervous. Pirates operate today in areas south of the Red Sea off Africa, in Malacca Straits off Malaysia and Indonesia, and in South America, mostly Venezuela and Columbia. Pirates operated in the area between Grenada and Isla Margherita, robbing and assaulting cruisers. Even a murder. A boat choosing not to stay in a marina is at risk. According to our information, many idyllic anchorages can be found off the coast of Venezuela, but are avoided today for safety sake. Pirates would board anchored boats to steal and plunder, day or night. Reporting these activities to the authorities did not seem to work, as they took no action to catch the pirates or even seem to care. We never visited a marina or anchored near the mainland for that reason. For the three days it took to cross the coastal waters of Venezuela, we stopped overnight to rest near coral atolls, never getting off the boat, while keeping a vigilant eye on our surroundings, and encountered zero problems.

The ABC islands—Aruba, Bonaire, and Curacao—belonging to the Netherlands, offered us a chance to rest up before our long crossing to Cartagena, Columbia, which was a two-day journey. We spent a few days each in Bonaire and Curacao, but skipped Aruba. Paul Allen (of Microsoft fame) had his 420-foot mega-yacht, *OCTOPUS*, at the dock. It loomed large in our visual field as we approached the docks at Bonaire. Being one of the largest and fanciest yachts in the world, it even has a submarine aboard.

Leaving Bonaire, with flopper stoppers in operation and trailing fishing lines behind the boat, we were approached by a C-130 aircraft. The pilot made an announcement as he neared us, "You are fishing illegally. Stop now. You will be fined!" So Denis reeled in the actual fishing lines, and over the VHF confirmed he had. That didn't seem to satisfy the pilot as he made another turn and came right at the pilothouse level to get another look. I went on deck and did my "this is only a balancing act" by waving my body back and forth with arms extended. He must have accepted my performance as he flew off. But before the next island—Curacao—a helicopter swooped down on us and hesitated, hovering in the air quite close to the aft deck where I stood. It is really intimidating to have an aircraft that close—so close you can see the pilot, hiding behind his shiny helmet, knowing he is armed and the aircraft is probably as well. Soon he left, but we felt anxious and mad at the way we were treated.

Winds coming down from the Andes in Columbia, beginning at Punta Gallina (Chicken Point) and on towards Cartagena, could cause some awful sea conditions for boaters close to shore, so we chose to stay twenty miles out. There were places to hunker down along the Columbian coast between Punta Gallina and the Rio Magdalena, but not knowing what pirate activity brewed there, we chose to make a direct run for Cartagena. A sailboat friend told us later in Cartagena that he chose to stay close to shore, not anchoring though, and had to deal with winds up to forty knots during his passage.

Rio Magdalena in northern Columbia races out to sea some twenty miles, mixing with the salt water as it does so. When we passed it in the late daytime on our way to Cartagena, we could see a definite demarcation line. The river's current is felt many miles out from the mouth. I suspect when storms brew in the Andes Mountains on land and uncontrolled water roars down the river, anything in its way will go with it, even out to sea—mud, houses, cars, old refrigerators, etc. Fortunately it had not rained prior to our passing, yet after we passed out of the river's force and darkness enveloped us, something hit the boat quite hard. It definitely startled me, on watch duty, but did not wake Denis or Hugo. I checked the instruments and listened for extra noise as the shaft turned. Nothing seemed out of normal, so I kept going and watching the dials.

Cartagena, Columbia is rich in history, starting as a port in 1533 where gold and silver were shipped to Europe. The old section is walled with gates connecting old and new parts of the city. Inside the walls is the famous fort, Castillo de San Felipe de Barajas, which took 150 years to build. Tourists today spend time marching up the different levels of the fort, standing at the battlements, or dropping down into underground passages to move from one section to another. With our guide, Duran Duran, I went through one of those passages, but elected not to do the second one. Denis did, and reported I made a good decision to pass. It not only went almost straight down in a narrow pathway, but felt very confining. The extensive views from the fort show how large it really is, and how it could protect Cartagena from the sea pirates during their raids.

Cartagena proper has two entrances by sea, Boca Chica and Boca Grande. Boca Grande is not used because below the surface is a huge wall, not seen until close inspection. Word must have spread fast among sea ships not to use that one. Boca Chica has another surprise for ships, especially those not wanted inside the harbor. Forts stand on each side of the opening. Between the forts, underwater, lies a chain, maybe two, which can be pulled up in time of danger to stop anyone attempting to enter. Once stopped, guess what? Cannons can finish the job.

We followed the well-laid out channel markers into the inner harbor, anchored among fifty other cruising boats from several countries, and stayed a couple weeks to celebrate Christmas. More cruisers were tied up at a couple of marinas there. Everyone contributed something for the potluck holiday meal, and laughed that their family meant 150 of their closest friends gathered to celebrate. My hat went off to the organizers and elves putting such an event together. A call went out over the VHF radio for anyone having cranberry sauce in their ship's stores to please bring it to round out the menu of turkey and trimmings.

Cartagena sunset from the anchorage

One problem in world traveling is keeping the right time on your clock. Our GPS registers Greenwich Mean Time and each time zone from that point adds another hour to the clock. When does one actually cross the next line on the chart? Easily missed, as in our case. Settling in at anchor we asked over the radio about Sunday Brunch at Hotel Santa Clara. We got the answers we needed—where located, how to get there, hours they served, and expected dress code. However, no one told us of the time change and we did not think to ask. Therefore we arrived an hour early for our brunch.

This exquisite hotel had a grand entrance leading into a huge garden just beyond the lobby. To the right of the garden we entered the restaurant, saw the buffet spread, and let the staff know we wanted to do the lunch buffet. They ushered us back out to some seats in the garden area and brought some coffee, saying it would be an hour wait. We did not understand as we had just witnessed a huge spread of food (actually the Breakfast Buffet). But we waited and enjoyed our Columbian coffee, listening and looking for birds in the trees. Then the lunch buffet call came and we ate heartily. After lunch we chose to walk back to the marina, not only to wear off some calories, but to explore by foot the atmosphere of the old city—narrow streets, flower-filled courtyards, unusual knockers on doors, colorful walls on houses, red-tiled roofs, beautiful balconies everywhere.

Vendors with carts full of wares stood at street corners. We were in search of *luz con batterias* (lights with batteries, not plug-ins) for my cloth Christmas tree. I had some ornaments to tie on the branches, but the two-foot tall tree called for some lights as well. Hugo searched every time we went out for these "lights with batteries." We found many strings that plugged into wall sockets, but none with batteries. (He mailed a set to me at my Seattle address, when he returned to San Diego, for my next Christmas on the boat.)

Arriving back at the boat we were due to meet up with friends from *ANNAPURNA* to catch up on news, but they didn't show. Only when people finished playing Mexican-Train Dominoes at the other end of the restaurant area, and one lady announced she had to go home and prepare a dish for the 5 P.M. gathering, did we learn the truth. Our watches said 5 already. It in fact was only 4. Everything that day made sense then.

On another one of our walks through town, a mime adopted us in Simon Bolivar Plaza. He had his craft fine-tuned. Dressed in baggy pants with suspenders, tennis shoes, long-sleeved shirt and funny Buster Brown type hat, he slipped up next to me, sized me up to mimic my walk, and stayed with me for a whole block before picking up another person to trail. He had very expressive eyes—deep, dark brown, and a sad expression, mixed with eyebrows lifted in great surprise to make you wonder what he was thinking. We met up with him several times in that plaza.

Our sightseeing, beyond walking around and taking photos, included the Cartagena Cathedral, Iglesia de Santa Domingo—the city's oldest church, the Palacio de la Inquisicion, a museum dedicated to horrific torture instruments from the Spanish Inquisition, and touring the living quarters of the Priest they called, "The Slave to the Slaves." He spent his time ministering solely to the slaves of Cartagena, hence earning that special title. None of the torture instruments looked especially user-friendly. In fact, most down-right nasty. Walking through the quarters and garden of that Priest generated a very positive feeling—to offset the other reaction.

Another lasting impression of Cartagena focuses on a Christmas bus tour through some of the barrios. About fifty cruisers sat on wooden benches facing the front of the bus, with the side-curtains rolled up for an open-air experience. We waved at and shouted, *"Feliz Navidad,"* to everyone we passed along the way. In addition to seeing the really extensive and beautiful decorations at the big mansions, the bus stopped at different barrios (housing areas) so we could get out, mingle with the locals, and enjoy their lighting scenarios. People gathered on front porches to socialize and be part of the festivities. At one point early on in our trip we passed a group of schoolchildren, both boys and girls, dressed in red and white outfits with stocking caps dangling over their ears. We of course were singing Christmas songs in English. Being carolers they responded to our songs with one of theirs, in Spanish. It gives me goose bumps to write this as it was a stirring event—a feeling of Christmas within a feeling of Christmas.

When a person thinks of Cartagena, Columbia, it would possibly be focused on the cartel, drugs, drug lords, and danger. We found another image. And the message being sent out is that Cartagena is for honeymooners, family vacations, and adult adventures. I also heard that the city is safe because that's where the drug lords take their families. Straying very far from Cartagena to interior Columbia might be a different story, but we certainly enjoyed our time in that unique and special city.

The day after Christmas we struck out toward the Panama Canal, stopping after an overnight voyage at one of the San Blas Islands. We had spent time there on our original trip in 1999, and although the islands are pleasant, we needed to press on to the Canal, where our daughter, Dawn, would join us as crewmember.

Hello, Pacific!

Almost eight years after leaving Colon, Panama, heading East—eventually to the Mediterranean—Denis again radioed Cristobal Signal Station on the VHF.[*] They granted us permission to enter Colon Harbor, anchor in "The Flats," and begin preparations to re-transit the Canal. The date: January 1, 2007.

This time we did several things differently from the 1999 transit. First, we used an agent to complete the paperwork versus doing all the legwork as we did before. And, rules had changed for transiting from the Caribbean to the Pacific side for pleasure boats. Instead of completing the transit in one trip, it now meant a definite overnight in the lake, plus using two advisors. One started the afternoon trip with us to travel through three Gatun Locks and tie up for the night at a special buoy in Gatun Lake. The next morning a pilot boat met us to deliver the second advisor for the last part. Advisors were provided by the Canal as part of our fees. However, our two line-handlers were now to be paid for two days of work, plus bed and board. They slept on the aft deck cushions.

On the first trip the line-handlers got on in the morning, did their job, ate a hearty lunch on board, and disembarked in the evening. This time no tugs were available, so we had to "center tie," with two lines going from the ship's bow to the bollards on shore and two from the stern. These had to be diligently tended to as the boat ascended 85 feet going through three locks to the lake and then down to the Pacific Ocean on the other side via three other locks. That is where our line-handlers earned their money—experience counted.

By January 10, we had completed all the paperwork through Tina McBride Agency, hired two experienced line-handlers (Dracula and Rudy), resupplied the ship, and picked up Dawn at the Panama City airport by taxi. Dawn and I, as the other line handlers, met the Canal's requirement of four for the transit. We spent the night at a hotel in Balboa before heading back across to Colon by taxi the following morning. Getting up early, we walked

---

[*] Adapted from my story, "Return to the Panama Canal," *PassageMaker Magazine,* Feb 2008, pp 152-160

along the promenade and saw several ships start their transit from the Pacific side. We studied the *TEXAS*, a high-profile carrier about 500 feet long with a bright red hull, which did not look like a normal container ship. After some investigation, we decided it was a "tween-decker" ship, because of its many compartments between decks for cargo. An interesting follow-up to watching it disappear under the Bridge of the Americas at 7:30 A.M. was seeing it pop out of the last Gatun Lock on the other end at 4:30 P.M., making the entire transit in the average time of nine hours for large ships.

This time the fee for our boat was $850—$100 more than last time. The Canal, begun by the French in 1881 and completed by the Americans in 1914, is due to expand even more with a third section for super tankers. About 14,000 ships pass through each year, paying fees according to vessel type, size, and cargo; average toll, $54,000. On May 30, 2006, the container ship, *MAERSK DELLYS*, paid $249,165 for its passage. In 1928, Richard Halliburton, an American adventurer, swam the canal and was charged 36 cents.

After our first advisor, Ricardo, joined us in "The Flats," Dracula and Rudy took time to give Dawn and me a good briefing on how to do the lines going through the locks. The two of them would prepare our lines in ready for the "monkey fist" throw from shore. I worked with Dracula on the bow; Dawn with Rudy at the stern. Getting a mindset as to the proper action required, I felt very tense. Even as experienced as I was, I still felt nervous. I knew everything had to be done right the first time, with little room for error. And spotting two large alligators on shore near the first lock added to my dry mouth. A bit of humor occurred when we spotted the huge neon-lit finger pointing to "our lock." It felt like "this way, Stupid!" No problem, actually, as we followed a banana freighter, *CHIQUITA ROSTOK*, inside the chamber. Within minutes, the men ashore started throwing monkey fists at us.

Four men individually heaved a light line with a heavy knot at the end (the monkey fist) toward the line-handlers. We had to be extra alert to catch it and not be hit by it. Missing it meant another throw and wasted time. We tied that monkey fist to the prepared lines and the men on the wall pulled all of them off the boat to their position on the wall, securing each on a large bollard. We tightened the lines to bollards on the boat, in preparation for retightening as the boat ascended. Then the lock gates closed, a whistle blew, and water came in—fast. Fifty-two million gallons of water rushed in from the sides and bottom of the chamber, creating lots of turbulence. As the boat rose, lines had to be tightened in sync to keep the boat straight in the center. As any of the lines slackened, the handler had to quickly release the heavy 7/8" rope from its position, adjust it to keep the boat straight, and wrap it tightly again. This procedure occurred several times in each lock. Denis' job was to stand by the controls and keep the boat lined up.

The three Gatun Locks were in sync, so when the chamber was full and the gates opened, those men on the wall took our lines and just nonchalantly walked forward to the next chamber, and dropped them over the next set of bollards. Denis moved the boat at the same time. The new set of gates closed. We retightened and repeated the process for this chamber, and one more.

We approached these locks at twilight. By the time we popped out into Gatun Lake, it was dark, very dark, after being in the well-lit Canal for over two hours. We had no GPS point to follow, only the directions of the advisor. It felt creepy to be the only boat and not knowing exactly where the large steel-mooring buoy assigned to us actually awaited. Here we were anxiously peering into the dark for some shape to show up, when Rudy and Dracula, who knew its position all along, shouted, "There it is!"

Two large fenders placed mid-ship separated our hull from the buoy. Bow and stern spring lines were tied to prevent the boat from banging against the buoy, making noise during the night, or possibly damaging the boat. A launch came to fetch Ricardo, and the rest of us settled in for a spaghetti dinner with chocolate pudding for dessert. Quite worn out from our day, it did not take long to fall asleep.

Howler monkeys woke us up early. As the day brightened, we saw we were not alone, as several container ships were anchored nearby. Another rule: if the ship does not make the Gatun Locks before 6 P.M., they wait until morning to continue. Our new advisor, Carlos, jumped off his launch onto the deck about 7 and gave us some special news. Extra water had to be released from the lake and it looked as if we would be taking advantage of this and going through the last three locks quickly, and by ourselves. So we cranked up the speed to cross the lake doing 8 knots, but before we knew it, the plan changed. Something had happened to the lock entering the lake, so all traffic had to go through the one we were to use going out. Our speed dropped to less than one knot, and we began watching from the stern for the small cruise ship that would share the three locks to the Pacific with us. We also caught a glimpse of the Smithsonian Tropical Research Station tucked in a corner of Gatun Lake.

Many ships passed us on our trip to Pedro Miguel Lock, all heading toward the Colon side, some with their tugs behind or ahead of them. Being so close to them made us feel small, and that's just the "Big Toots." Passing the Culebra Cut (the Continental Divide section) and its many layers reminded us of the hardships the workers endured while digging that ditch. The jungle on both sides of the Canal had to be conquered as well, mosquitoes and all. The records show that about 27,500 workers, French and American, died from disease or accidents during the Canal's 33 years of construction.

Carlos received word through his communication connection that we would be shown on the Pedro Miguel Webcam as we entered the lock. Many tourists go by bus or van to Pedro Miguel Lock from Panama City and watch the canal traffic from its roof. We could make out people up there as we approached. Dawn whipped out her cell phone to contact both her husband, Larry in Tacoma, Washington, and brother, David, in San Diego. She and I had one eye looking for the camera as we approached to take another set of monkey fists from the men on shore, this time both of us working bow lines. David told us later he saw us and the cruise ship behind us. Not knowing who saw what, she and I waved furiously after we secured our lines. Going down in the locks is much easier on the hands than going up, plus we felt a mastery over the situation by then.

Mary and Dawn having a good time going down, with Carlos looking on

Passing under the Bridge of the Americas, Dawn rang the ship's bell to announce our arrival to the Pacific Ocean. She had brought along a Tacoma News Tribune newspaper front-page headline for a photo "op." With the bridge in the background, she held the paper in front of her and I snapped the picture, which the newspaper did publish after her return to Washington.

She can now add a new skill to her lengthy resume: Panama Canal Line-Handler.

Over 40 ships waited on the Colon side to transit, take on water or fuel. More than that number swung at anchor on the Panama City side, as we reunited Dracula and Rudi with Tina and said our "Goodbyes." Our expenses covered the transit fee, agent fees, line handler charges, cruising permit, visas, line rental, moorage while waiting on Colon side, transportation back and forth to Panama City to the airport, plus miscellaneous items. The total came to over $2000, much more than the initial transit.

TEKA III has now been through the Panama Canal six times—four with her original owner, Rod Swanson, and twice with us. She is a seasoned ship.

Before Dawn went home, we returned to the Perlas Islands south of the Canal, featuring sand, shells, and so much surf we could not land our dinghy in many places. We also spent quite a bit of time attempting to locate the exact setting for the TV "Survivor" series filmed in the Perlas. We spotted several sites that could have been a camp, but we were never quite sure. We also enjoyed watching the Booby birds and Pelicans swooshing and diving for their catch of the day, especially at Viveros Island. Pelicans have such a dare-devil way of diving—enough to give the one watching a headache, as the birds dive straight down and make such a noise on contact with the water—"splat!" The other unusual thing to watch is how they siphon the water out of their huge bills once they settle down on the surface with their catch. Getting rid of the water leaves only the tasty tidbits to swallow. Then the process is repeated. Add a whole passel of pelicans diving and fishing at the same time, it becomes a very loud activity.

Pelicans are Dawn's favorite water bird. I am glad she had such a positive experience watching them before her trip back home. We left her back in Panama City with our agent's driver for a trip to the airport following the Perlas experience, and never looked back as we motored away. Here is her story, in her own words, of the long and trying saga of getting home from Panama:

Leave TEKA by dinghy at 10:20 a.m. Arrive at dinghy dock and breathe easier after bags up on dock, no longer at mercy of the salt water spray or a tumble into the drink. We are met by Tina, TEKA's agent, and "Jeronimo," our taxi driver for the day. Jeronimo takes Mom and Dad to the Grand Terminal where they will shop for supplies and we say a quick goodbye.

Jeronimo doesn't speak much English and I speak almost no Spanish so we give up after a few minutes of trying to chit chat on the way to the airport. His driving is frightening, lots of quick stops, fast starts, cutting in between traffic while moving fast and going around slow traffic via the right-hand ditch. But we make it safely to Tocamen, the International airport, at 11:30am.

After I check in, I rush upstairs to a souvenir store to quickly buy a few things since I wasn't near shops during the trip.

Getting through security and immigration is easy. I have 2-½ hours until departure, so wander around a bit. Discover all the shops are either duty-free liquor, perfume or polo shirt shops. Not like U.S. airports with magazine/book stores, coffee shops, fast-food and souvenir stores. I find the one small restaurant and sit down for lunch. I had trouble getting served (none of the single men had any trouble getting the waitress's attention), and the grilled cheese sandwich was awful.

I wait at the gate and begin to worry when the plane hasn't arrived by boarding time. I feel confident, though, since I have a 2 hour 40 minute layover in Houston. A little delay won't hurt me...

The plane finally arrives and we board ½ hour late, around 3:30. The plane is noticeably hot inside. After passengers are scolded by the flight attendant to sit down so we could leave because of the tardiness, we are surprised to not move back from the gate. We begin to get very hot and time passes with no information. About 15 minutes into the wait, the Captain tells us we have a problem with the a/c system, which has an impact on the de-icing equipment. He says we need de-icing to get into Houston since it is 28 degrees and snowing there. They work on the plane for 1 hour while we suffer almost impossible heat. We depart the gate, and move toward the runway only to do a U-turn. The Captain announces the problem has returned.

We are all asked to de-board the plane at the gate and wait while they work on it. An hour or so later we board the hot plane again, wait again, leave the gate again and turn around...again. Arghhhh! They again ask us to de-plane and wait. It is impossible to leave the gate when traveling alone because you do not know if an announcement will be made to board the plane or do something else that you will miss. So, instead of trying to eat

*dinner at the restaurant (assuming we will eat on the plane), I eat my Oreo
snack pack Mom gave me to hold me over.*

*By 7 pm they announce they need 2 hours to fix the plane so have
rescheduled departure for 8am tomorrow morning. They ask us to check in
at 6am and wait in line if we need hotel accommodations. They reported to
us that the next three days of flights out of Panama were all sold out. The
earliest they could guarantee selling us seats out were for 8 days later. So,
we have no choice but to go to a hotel and try again tomorrow. Ugh.*

*While waiting in line for hotel instructions, they call for any single
women traveling alone. Two of us at the end of the line, me and a gal from
Denver, come forward and are given instructions. Lucky they did this, for if
we had waited our turn, our room situation would have been worse. More
on that later. They sent us all back through immigration, we then got our
bags, went through customs and found the Continental agent. At first the
agent wouldn't give me and my Denver pal hotel check-in sheets because we
wanted our own rooms. The Denver gal rushed over to another younger
single women (who spoke Spanish and English) and decided to room with
her. I was left alone. I finally got the agent to give me a hotel sheet and made
my way with the rest of the passengers onto the shuttle to the hotel hoping
my bags made it in the back trailer.*

*I waited again in the check-in line at 8:30 p.m. Was given a room key, a
dinner voucher, a breakfast voucher, and sent off. Found the room with the
help of a hotel employee who pointed me up the stairs at one point and left. I
hauled up the bags since there seemed to be no elevator, or he didn't
understand my request for one. The room was ok, not near as nice as the
Comfort Inn I stayed at the first night in Panama (with Mom and Dad), but
a major problem was it didn't have any towels in the room. I went down to
dinner in the restaurant, but again had trouble getting served. Something
about being a single female who can't speak the language seemed to make the
waitresses ignore me. Finally got someone's attention who when seeing the
voucher and learning I didn't speak Spanish just asked me "fish, pork,
chicken." I said fish. 45 minutes later the food finally came. I ate quickly, left
a tip and went to the front desk. They were so busy with customers I never
got a chance to ask about the towels. Called housekeeping when I returned to
the room but no one answered the phone. Finally decided to just use the
souvenir towel Mom had given me that I was glad I found room to add in*

my bags to bring home. Falling asleep was hard for I didn't feel secure alone in the room with only a little doorknob lock.

Five hours later, at 4:45 am, I woke up and headed toward the shuttle. Since the hotel restaurant didn't open 'til 6am, our airplane check in time, our breakfast voucher was useless. Arriving at the airport I was surprised to see a huge line of our passengers already waiting. It took 1 hour 15 minutes waiting in line to get checked in again. They gave me my boarding pass for a connection in Houston so I was happy the nightmare seemed to be coming to an end.

I went through security and immigration again and hit the gate. Immediately I knew something wasn't right when the flight crew was sitting in the gate area and the Captain was telling people that he knew as much as we did (as in nothing). We then noticed the plane was still outside but the gate was not against it and it was obviously still under repair.

There were no announcements from the Continental gate crew for the first 2 hours we were there. We learned from passengers who had waited to line speak to the agents, that the plane was still being repaired and no timeline was known. It was at this point in the return trip that I noticed the passengers were becoming a community. Many waited together and dined together the night before. The more outgoing ones were talking up a storm to everyone in the gate area. We learned about some interesting events from these passengers. They told of the young men who got drunk on their duty-free liquor while we waited on the plane at the gate yesterday. They talked about the fight that broke out in one of the hotel rooms where two male strangers were asked to room together. Four policemen had to come to deal with the conflict. One of these men was no longer waiting to board the plane they said. As noted before, I was lucky to get the "women traveling alone" call the night before because we were near the end of the line and the couple behind us was asked to room with another man (the wife made a stink and they changed this arrangement). Besides this doubling-up issue, we learned that the latter half of the passengers were sent to a hotel almost an hour away. They arrived there around 11 pm and had to wake up at 4am to get back here in time. So, lucky we got the closer hotel.

When I noticed the gate next to us said Continental flight to Houston 10:20 am, I asked to be put on standby with I'm sure 50 others. We watched with great envy as these passengers piled into the waiting area and began boarding. I think they wondered why we watched them so closely with what must have been angry eyes. We all waited to see if any standbys would get on. They called one passenger; a mother with a baby. For some reason she went running away from the gate after they talked with her. Seems she left her carry-on stuff somewhere else. It took 5 minutes and 3 gate agents to find her and carry all her stuff back. She boarded and the plane left the gate. We were alone again with our broken plane.

Continental at one time told us we could go to the airport restaurant for breakfast. The restaurant was full and the line was long and I didn't want to wait so I grabbed the only other food in the airport, a hot dog from a kiosk vendor not there yesterday. A hot dog for breakfast... that's a first for me. Twice the agents told us the airplane was fixed and it would be ready after an hour of testing. Each time we waited in lines to rebook our flights out of Houston. My boarding pass had so many scratched out flights and seat assignments, you could barely read it.

Finally, all of a sudden they said we were going to Orlando. They announced "we will book you flights out of Orlando once we are underway." The flight crew rushed to the plane only to come back and say, it's going to be awhile. Eventually there was a rush to board the plane at 1:45 and we took off at 2pm Thursday - 23 hours after our scheduled departure time.

The Captain told us we would fly at 23,000 feet because we didn't have de-icing capabilities, which are needed for 30,000+ feet cruising. He also noted Continental agents were busily rebooking our connections as we were flying to Orlando. Two hours 44 minutes flying time to Orlando. Got a nice hoagie sandwich on board, so a decent lunch at least.

Upon arriving in Orlando we were told to go through U.S. immigration, get our bags, go through customs and give our bags back for connecting flight check-ins. Up the stairs we found a U.S. security check point. I forgot to take out my water so they had to search my bag. They then directed us to gate 23 where we found nothing but our plane. No agents. No information.

Frustrating. We were told we would be met by agents to direct us to our connecting flights so we rushed but now no one was there at all. Amazing....

Finally a gate agent came up and made an announcement that they were fixing our plane and we would then be flying to Houston in an hour. We all just laughed. How many times had we been told that same thing? Why believe it now and why can't we just fly home from Orlando? They told us as long as we left by 7:30pm we would make all the connecting flights in Houston. They were confident they could make this schedule so we all waited. Some passengers opted to drive home or stay overnight in Orlando to catch a flight in the morning up the East Coast. While waiting I was so happy to be in a U.S. airport, I was ecstatic to shop at a news store for a magazine and newspaper so I could read more than the book I started the day before and was close to finishing with no other reading available. I also grabbed a snack at the food court, nice to have so many options, and fast service.

We boarded the plane differently, for the first time they just said "board." No rows, no first class first, just get on the plane. I joked with a fellow heading to Seattle passenger I had met that we didn't have to worry about terrorists for no terrorist would put up with what we had so far!

As 7:30 pm ticked by we were informed by the captain that the maintenance crew was delaying us. I could see outside that they seemed to be pulling off the bags for the passengers who decided not to go on the flight. We were missing our window to catch connecting flights in Houston because of these people's bags. Unbelievable. We finally left at 7:50pm and arrived in Houston at 9:05. We had to wait on the tarmac because so many flights were leaving the Continental gates that none were available for us and we had to stay out of their way. The ironic part was these planes were our connecting flights - very frustrating to know they were taxiing out past us. Unsure why Continental didn't hold the flights 10 minutes for us after all we had been through. The agent at the arrival gate told us all the flights had left.

We were instructed to get our rebooking info and hotel voucher at the gate. When I got up to the gate and learned my flight was for 9am Friday and I was on standby, I demanded a flight out that night. I didn't care how I got there; I just wanted to go home. They had to bring over the supervisor for I wouldn't take no for an answer. The supervisor explained all airline options were checked and there weren't any going to Seattle. Red eyes only went from west to east coast not the other direction because of time zone changes. I then insisted I get on the 9am plane, not be on standby. He bumped me up to a guaranteed seat. By then I was one of the last passengers left at the gate so I walked alone to baggage claim.

The long walk was frustrating and arriving to not find my bags was unbelievable. No one meeting us at the gate had mentioned anything about a problem with our bags. Could this get any worse? Checking with the baggage office, having to wait in line again, I learned our bags were in secure storage and ready to be on the next morning's plane. To get my bags would take 1-½ hours and I would have to wait there on site. It was now 10pm so I said no and they gave me a "comfort pack". I found the shuttle pickup site where many of my fellow passengers were waiting. After 15 minutes with no shuttle in site and over 30 others from the plane mentioning they had waited for a very long time, I decided to take a taxi and got 5 others to share it with me. I figured no shuttle could carry all of us... And the shuttle wasn't coming. I learned later the shuttle only fit 7 and the hotel was 20 minutes away. Though the taxi cost each of us $5, it was a good move getting us there much earlier. I checked in and got a restaurant voucher (either for dinner or breakfast - $10, not for both) though the restaurant was closed. Ugh. Just went to my room, found it to be a fleabag hotel, but went to sleep for I had no energy to complain. I had no toiletries, no clothes or even a change of underwear. The comfort pack included toothbrush, toothpaste, comb, shaving cream, razor, and shampoo. Not much comfort.

I got up at 5:30 am and instead of having breakfast as planned at 6, saw the huge line for the 7 seat shuttle and decided to try directly to get on the shuttle. I missed first one. The second came shortly thereafter and was immediately filled by family of 5 and a couple. I noticed it might have room so I asked the passengers and they were willing to squeeze me in. I had one butt cheek on the back seat and that was all I needed. When I turned around I was surprised to see an older couple from the plane sitting in the luggage compartment (because no one had luggage to fill their space, they got creative). By now we were all desperate to get home, so sitting squished into the luggage compartment of a shuttle seemed perfectly reasonable to me. Upon arrival at the airport, I was relieved to get my boarding pass after *handing them a plain piece of paper with computer codes on it that the agent had given me the night before (because of the upgrade I did not have a boarding pass or an e-ticket). I went through security and had a nice breakfast. You can tell I was pretty rummy because Dave (my brother) had left me a message the night before saying "call me early." I did. I called him at 6 am and wondered why he didn't pick up. I realized an hour later that it was 4 a.m. his time… a bit too early. From here on out, it felt like normal travel. The plane boarded on time; we left on time; we landed on time. I felt bad that my fellow passenger from Panama trying to get to Seattle did not make standby. He had to wait until 5 pm to fly back. That just wasn't right. He was retired and understood I needed to get back to Megan (my daughter), so was ok with me having priority. They offered the passengers of the overbooked plane a first class upgrade and a $300 travel voucher to give up their seats, but not many did so, at least not enough for him to go.*

I was pleased to be met immediately by a shuttle express driver when checking in for a ride home. I normally wait an hour (at Sea-Tac), so this was very welcome especially considering I didn't get a chance to change out of my sandals and light-weight clothes. It was very chilly in Seattle. Having to wait outside for an hour was not going to be fun. I happily arrived at the house at 1:30pm Friday, January 19, 36 hours later than I was scheduled to arrive. So it took 2-½ days to get home or a total of 56 hours. I don't plan on flying Continental ever again.

This terrible tale shows how exasperating and troublesome an adventure can become when it suddenly take on a life of its own. It seems such a simple thing to make a reservation, buy a ticket, and meet your flight to connect with family at both ends of a scheduled trip to crew on *TEKA III*. David, our son, also had a giant problem returning from Antigua to San Diego after the Atlantic crossing, so we know her dilemma was not an isolated case. Nothing guarantees a stress-free trip. For instance, if all goes well for the one coming to the boat, what if the boat is not there—as was the case when Alex flew from Canada to Ft. Lauderdale to meet us for the Atlantic crossing? Both ends are susceptible to problems. Flexibility goes along with good planning. Overall we have had good luck meeting our people and sending them off again. That doesn't mean we haven't worried.

Leaving Panama City, we turned the bow north and began the long trek toward the States and Seattle. We had a grand time meeting and spending time with a local man in Bahia Honda we called, "The Mayor." Domingo Gonzales arrived at our stern in a dugout canoe soon after we anchored. We were the only boat there, wondering where everyone else was in mid-January. No boats on the horizon were going north or south. Again, we went for a day but stayed a week. Every morning Domingo arrived to bring us something—shells, produce from his garden, or just a smile. I checked one of our Guidebooks by Captains John and Patricia Rains and found a photo of Domingo. He looked at it and said it was indeed him, but *"viente anos pasado"* (twenty years ago).

Domingo Gonzales of Bahia Honda greeting us

We took advantage of a quiet anchorage and good weather to lower our flopper stopper poles and give them a shiny new coat of paint. It is a several day process and worked out well. In-between paintings, Domingo took us to the village to show us off and let us buy some fruit from the people there; went with us in our dinghy as a guide up the river to visit other villagers; and of course, to his house to meet the extended family and go for a jungle walk nearby. In the second village we passed a policeman dressed in black pants and black t-shirt. The shirt read, "I am not anti-social; I just don't like you." He looked tough too. I also joined in a little soccer game with some young boys on the basketball court. When we did leave Bahia Honda, Domingo inherited our 3.5 horsepower Tohatsu outboard engine, as he needed a new motor for his small craft. Normally the dug-out served him well, but having an engine for his other boat made his trips back and forth to the village much easier.

Arriving in Golfito, Costa Rica, we stayed one night in a marina, which cost us $150 with tax. The cruising kitty could not afford many of those. After that night, we anchored out in the large bay and paid $15 a day to bring our dinghy into the dock for shore privileges. No rat came aboard this time, but we did look intently at the spot where the other one boarded on the earlier trip.

Son David, and number-one grandson, Soren, arrived for a ten-day cruise in Costa Rica and a fishing experience. They went out with a charter captain, who kept telling me before their arrival that he felt they would be so lucky as to break some swordfish record on that trip. They didn't break the record, but Soren caught a 40 lb. mahi-mahi, a mighty fine catch and good eating too.

John Wright, from Fairbanks, Alaska, also joined us as crew there in Golfito. It is interesting how he came into our lives. Recently retired from Alaska Fish and Game, he started looking for ocean-going trawlers for sale. He flew to Portland and checked one there, but did not like it. He phoned his childhood friend, Hugo Carver, in San Diego and asked for his advice. Hugo told him to hurry up and contact us by email on the boat. Perhaps he could go through the Canal with us. John got the email after his Christmas trip to Hawaii, and too late to make those arrangements. However, not to let an opportunity pass by to get a ride on a real passagemaker on the ocean, he contacted us about doing a leg. He was available then and for an extended period of time as winter still had a grip on Alaska until mid-to-late March. We computed he should join us in Golfito and go as far as he wanted to with us. You never know if you will mesh with people sight unseen, but we did. He learned quickly how to work things on the boat, becoming a valuable crewmember. His passion for birds gave him extra points. His binoculars were never far from his eyes, and we were always alert for his "oohs" and "aahs" as he scanned for birdlife in the mangroves, on land, and in or on the water. He did not miss much that moved.

From the boat at the Puntarenas Yacht Club in Costa Rica, bird activity almost overwhelmed us. In four days, with John's keen eyes on duty, we counted 36 kinds of marsh birds, ranging from seven different types of herons to swallows, doves, and sandpipers. Over the seven weeks he spent with us going to Puerto Vallarta, Mexico, he assisted us in identifying 40 other birds species, from the large ones—shearwaters, storm petrels, tropic birds and frigates—to five kinds of terns and three different gulls, to small ones like red-rumped tanagers to swifts flitting across the bow. Pelicans, frigates, blue-footed and brown boobies, and terns rode on the flopper stopper lines for great lengths of time.

Also we counted orcas, a pilot whale, many dolphins, including 16 pantopical spotted ones at once, and a pod of spinner dolphins that entertained us for quite some time one evening on our way to Acapulco.

The marine mammal book said these spinner dolphins can travel in groups of 1000. Although there were not that many, there were several hundred spinners stirring up the water between us and shore. We changed course to check them out, and once we got close, the show fascinated us. These dolphins, most of them the same size or larger than "Flipper" jumped straight out of the water, spun around more than once, and dropped back down beneath the surface, only to do it again a few feet away. Sometimes several leaped at the same time. We watched the show, totally captivated by the performance, until they swam on.

There never seemed to be an end to sea turtles swimming or sunning on the surface, most having a tern on their shell along for a ride. We wanted John to witness a green flash at sunset and the only time it happened, he got sidetracked as a large whale broached at the same time just out of the sunset's line of sight.

At the top of Costa Rica, we holed up in Bahia Santa Elena for four days while the Papagayo winds whistled down from the hills, sometimes getting over 35 knots. We picked the weather window right to pop out of the bay for a two-day and night trip to Guatemala. Winds were heavy at first, then mellowed, then kicked up a bit at the end. Securing the boat at Puerto Quetzal Marina, we took a van to Antigua for a few days.

Antigua provided us with a wonderful colonial architecture city to stroll through with an American-born guide. She had lived there since her teens and really knew the country from its history to politics to the people living there. She shared many stories of life in Guatemala. We also listened to the National Symphony Orchestra, seated on the Catholic Church steps, play Tchaikovsky's "1812 Overture," with fireworks exploding from the church roof at the overture's climax. John, Denis and I sat on the town square grounds along with the locals, hearing Spanish in the air all around us, watching the children enjoy the evening with each other and their families as we listened to the fantastic music. It gave us quite a warm cultural experience. Anytime the "1812" is played, it gives me goosebumps.

We took a day trip into the mountains by van to Chichicastenango for the colorful market and even more colorfully dressed natives. Returning to Antigua we arrived just in time for the Lent Processional, similar to the parade witnessed in Seville in 2002. The main difference here was the size of the floats that were carried (much smaller), and who carried them (women and children). Only very strong men carried the super heavy Seville floats. It seemed to be a special honor to be a carrier. Everyone had a solemn face as they passed, apparently concentrating on the mission and their participation.

We tensed up approaching the dreaded Tehuantepec area just inside Mexico, north of Guatemala. We must have paid our dues the first crossing in 1999, as this time it was a "piece of cake." Everything looked good weather-wise, so we did not stop to check into Mexico at the usual place, Puerto Madero. Hugging the coast as before, to ensure our safety should anything change weather-wise during our passage, we made it back to Huatulco in 49 hours without any problem. After clearing into Mexico with the port captain there, we journeyed by van into Oaxaca for a few days. Coming back down the mountains in the bus, we could definitely see the waters of Tehuantepec churning away. We had hit it just right for our crossing.

Pelicans were quite funny to watch in Huatulco Marina. Tons of baitfish had come into the area, and the pelicans had instant breakfast, lunch and dinner, just by diving off the docks. After eating, they had no qualms about pooping all over the place, leaving their marks for the staff to continually wash down the place.

An interesting experience happened at the next anchorage up from Huatulco. The new rules in Mexico indicated we did not have to see each port captain once we had processed into the country. But not long after the anchor went down in Puerto Angel, a panga came out from shore with four armed Navy men and the assistant port captain in it. He boarded us and wanted to see our papers. Denis told him we had done everything in Huatulco. This did not satisfy him and he took Denis to shore to meet the port captain and do what they wanted. What a sight—Denis sitting on the front seat between two armed men, being escorted to shore with all our paperwork. I should have taken a picture. Once the port captain had used his "hunt and peck" manner of typing a paper on an old typewriter, Denis was free to go. But he did not have transportation back. He stood on the pier and waved at fishermen near the pier to ask for a ride back to his "barco." They agreed to do so for a few pesos. We think perhaps the port captain still had the authority to make contact with those in his anchorage, and needed to file some paperwork to that effect. However, we were never bothered at any other anchorage all the way to San Diego.

Cruisers will know most of the anchorages going north, but non-cruisers will probably only recognize Acapulco, Puerto Vallarta, and perhaps, Zihuatanejo (Z-town). They all have been discovered by "gringos." Foot traffic, land traffic, and boat traffic bear witness to that effect. John's wife, Kathleen, joined us in Zihuatanejo for her Spring Break from fourth grade duties in Fairbanks. She and John both traveled with us from there to Puerto Vallarta, where they caught a flight back to Alaska.

During her time with us, we had three "A" experiences at anchorages. First, Zihuatanejo (pronounced "zee what ah nay ho") harbor sported enough room for many cruisers small like us, but also a huge cruise liner. "Amazing" described the scene. Once they were settled in at anchorage, the longboats suspended from the upper decks were lowered and the clientele climbed on board for a trip to spend some pesos in town. The beach is quite nice and sandy, plus there are multitudes of trinkets to buy and take home. Hence the obligatory cruise-ship stop. Those life-boats transferring people kept up all day, back and forth, back and forth, so everyone would have a turn to shop.

At Bahia Navidad, there is a well-marked channel, with green markers on one side and red on the other of a narrow and winding stretch of water entering a large lagoon for anchoring. These are not permanent fixtures, only buoyed to something on the bottom of the channel. The "A" at this point: "Amusing." Early one morning, with coffee cups in hand, we spied one of the green channel markers floating our way, blinking its set number of green flashes as if it still stood in place beside the channel. However, it was definitely on a "Walkabout" because it kept going past us and others in the lagoon anchorage, ending up in the mangroves, "Off Duty."

At Tenacatita, the "A" stood for "Anxious." A jungle river ride called us to go for a spin. First we had to get the dinghy through the surf and into the river. With the tide in our favor we had little waves to maneuver through, so barely got wet by choosing a good path through the small breakers. In the river itself our dangers came from nature—overhanging tree branches or stumps in the water, and from man—"Yee-Haa" drivers roaring around the tight corners in their fast boats as the river twisted its way through the bayou. We had one close encounter with a local man going at break-neck speed around a blind corner. I am glad his reflexes were quick to adjust enough to miss us. We got mightily splashed by the event, but were thankful we did not get capsized. The big deal overall came when it was time to leave the river at its mouth. The tide had changed, with significant breakers rolling in. We had to judge each wave as we waded through the surf. Once we had the dinghy in deep enough water, we jumped in and started the engine. Back at the boat we watched others perform the same dance.

"Overwhelmed" described the scene at Puerto Vallarta. Boy has it been discovered! It has grown stupendously with hotels, condos, restaurants, shopping centers, marinas, with buses and cars everywhere. We wanted to visit our friend, but no room at any marina, so on to Guaymas!

On the Hard Again

Willie Nelson's song, "On the Road Again!" resonates in my head thinking about leaving my boat "On the Hard Again!" You might ask why we don't leave the boat in a slip at a marina when we are not cruising. Well, we'd worry about it more. It has to be tied good and strong to the dock to deal with whatever comes its way. We also have to locate someone to look after her: make sure the electric cord and power source on the dock are on, so the heaters on board work; check for external visible damage from other boats or people; look for leaks and check bilge pumps so there is not a possibility of sinking, and in general, report to us the status quo.

TEKA III had previously spent time "on the hard" in several places—Jacksonville, Florida; Gaeta, Italy; Marmaris, Turkey (twice); and Trinidad—to wait for us between cruising seasons. This time her "sit-stay" will take place in Guaymas, Mexico.

Weather window open, we took off from Puerto Vallarta and 76 hours later pulled into Guaymas Bay. There we found many fishing boats, the Mexican Navy, a finished-but-not-yet-open marina, small cruise ship area, and a quiet place to leave *TEKA III* for the hurricane season—Marina Seca. There are two Marina Secas in that area: Guaymas, and San Carlos, a sister city just a few miles away. Many Americans flock to the latter community by car or RV to spend winters in the sun. Their dry storage could not accommodate us, so Marina Seca Guaymas became *TEKA III's* home at the south end of the bay away from the main part of town.

Seca means "dry." Gabriel Larios Rizo, the English-speaking manager of this dry desert storage, made arrangements for us to be hauled out of the water at the fishing boat lift operation next door. We picked our tide and watched carefully all the skinny water in our approach. He came out in his kayak, tied it to the stern, came on board, and guided us through the last tricky bit to shore and the lift. There were rocks on both sides and a slight curvature to the entrance channel. At low tide the path became quite visible, and scary. One wrong movement with the wheel, and contact!

The travel lift had moved out over the water, its huge wheels on concrete finger piers, and the driver hydraulically lowered huge straps under the water. Denis drove the boat right up to the wall near the bow keeping it in line with the sides of the lift. Men on the concrete piers on both sides walked along with us, carrying long lines to steady our approach. Once in place, the lift driver started the hydraulics and the two straps beneath the boat were pulled up snug around the keel before we (me still on board) were being pulled up into the air. Clearing the concrete in front, the driver put it in gear and slowly moved along the tracks it had made on the U-shaped launch area and back onto dry land.

The travel lift picks up TEKA III's 40-plus tons

Swaying in the straps, the boat rode from the fishing boat yard onto the dirt street separating it and Marina Seca, through their fence, and pulled up to a full stop in a position three boats out from the office building. Men on the ground started putting huge wood chocks beneath the boat so the straps could be released and she would sit upright on the desert floor and the travel lift could go back to the other boatyard. Metal stands were then placed four to each side, legs on the ground with heavy padded pieces against the painted bottom. A pressure wash took care of cleaning off the marine growth on the bottom of the keel. To add extra security, we placed four tie-downs straps used by trucks for securing loads on their flatbeds. All in all the boat should not move until time to reverse the process in eight months time. We secured our twelve-foot aluminum ladder to the swim bridge so we could easily go up and down into the parked boat, ten feet in the air. This was an interesting scenario to watch, and we all hoped the workers knew their job and the equipment hauling us around had no mechanical problems.

We could stay in the boat while preparing the boat to be left. We could sleep in our own beds, but not able to use the toilets, a "honey bucket" came into use for getting up in the night. Showers in the building next door gave us a chance to clean up each evening and climb into bed fresh. I washed clothes in a bucket the few weeks we were on the hard. Dish water drained straight out onto the desert floor and evaporated quickly.

Guaymas is not seen as a direct recipient of Pacific hurricanes in the summer. Storms can and do go as far north as Puerto Vallarta, and Mazatlan on the Mexican mainland, but lose their punch as they charge up the Sea of Cortez with mountains on both sides, becoming only tropical storms.

Before preparing anything inside the boat, we dragged out the canvas covers for the pilothouse exterior, snapping them into place. In addition to those covers, Denis designed a PVC pipe arrangement, which he covered with heavy-duty plastic to keep off the hot desert summer sun on the upper deck where the dinghies resided. It looked really good and durable after completion. In Trinidad we had a special shrink-wrap made to go across the whole boat for protection from tropical summer rains. It only partially worked. Leaking in places did cause water damage. It seems the boat is happiest when it just sits out in the weather. Sun and sand were issues in this desert storage.

*The boat is held up by blocks and stands with a sun cover,
ready for the summer heat and winds*

Down in the engine room, batteries needed to be checked for water and turned off, heat exchangers drained and cleaned, vents needed closing to keep dust out, and oil changed as necessary.

In general, seacocks had to be lubricated and removed, fresh water tank drained, propane turned off, bow thruster props cleaned and stored, windlass covered, paravane lines removed and stored, all outside cushions taken inside, and electronics removed, then stored out of sight. With the desert heat, we took extra care to put aluminum foil around the salon windows to keep out too much heat and light.

Dinghies on the upper deck had to be tied down and outboard motors flushed with fresh water. Below the keel, zincs had to come off and the prop cleaned of barnacles before they became permanent fixtures.

The reverse happened on our return: all covers came off, electronics reinstalled, dinghies checked (plus inflatable one pumped back up), cushions went back in place on aft deck, parts in the engine room were lubricated, pumps checked out, fuel filter changed in the day tanks, then touch up painting and rust removal on stainless steel areas gave her a sparkling look again.

I started on the food drill before assisting Denis on some of his chores. Refrigeration was shut down, so all that food had to be dealt with somehow. Options to get rid of the refrigerator items included eating them; storing them in the shower for our return, hoping they would still be okay; pay a visit to all the boats in the storage area to see what they might be interested in taking off my hands; or just throw them away. Packaged items are savable, if wrapped carefully. Little critters can get anywhere. Making it hard for them is the key.

Once packed, we took one bus to Mazatlan, and then another to Puerto Vallarta for our journey back to the States by air. I had an appointment with a bride and groom in St. Petersburg, Florida; Denis due back in the Pacific Northwest. These arrangements, to fly out of Puerto Vallarta, could not be changed without a lot of hassle and fees, so we kept those tickets, and bused two days back from Guaymas to meet our flights.

Getting into the taxi for a ride to the bus terminal, we waved goodbye to *TEKA III* for her last "stay on the hard."

Smelling the Barn!

The boat had only "one more leg" to finish our ten-year plan and be home again. All we had to do was get back to her and start the trip. Once started, the closer we got to San Diego, then San Francisco, and finally Seattle (the three Ss), the more we "smelled the barn." We were headed home!

After Christmas in Tacoma we flew to San Diego for a quick visit before crossing the Mexican border. In Tijuana we boarded a long-distance bus for the fourteen-hour journey back to Guaymas, and the boat. Even though it required us to board at 5 a.m. and sit all day, this turned out to be the most efficient and more direct way to go. We could have flown to Phoenix or Tucson and then boarded a bus to Guaymas, but hey, why make a difficult trip out of a simple one?

My siblings laugh at me thinking I am sharing my bus with chickens and pigs. They can't get the image of a sleek, modern, air-conditioned Mexican bus, with video movies to entertain the riders for the long stretches of road through the desert. If I chose to pay strict attention to the audio, my Spanish would indeed improve during the back-to-back films on the overhead screen at the front of the bus. Instead, I chose to watch the passing scenery, read, observe the other passengers, or take a nap. These buses do stop to pick up or drop off passengers at small town bus stations along the way; also allowing riders to use the facilities, or buy snacks for the road. The driver would announce, in Spanish, how many minutes we had at that stop. We were the only non-Mexicans for the whole trip. We felt honored that the driver waved "Goodbye" to us, when we had collected our luggage and stood out of his way so he could back out and leave the Guaymas station.

We have ridden long-distance buses in other countries over the years; the Turkish ones were the best. Although those in Mexico were comfortable to ride, the rest stop facilities were not as clean as we would have liked. We tended not to stray far from the bus other than to go to the restroom, and then re-board. There were vendors selling tacos and tamales at the station, or someone boarded and walked down the aisle hawking his wares from a large tray suspended from his neck. We did not need to buy anything, having brought snack food along for the trip.

Wanting to see our boat with rested eyes, we spent the night in a hotel near the Guaymas bus station, and picked up our rental car early the next morning for our reunion. She had done her "sit, stay!" very well; however, her PVC pipe job looked pitiful. All that heavy-duty plastic sheeting had blown away, leaving just the bare shell of PVC and the string used to tie the sheeting down. A tropical storm had come ashore north of Mazatlan during the summer. From the States we had monitored the storm's path by charting its latitude and longitude as it traveled up the Sea of Cortez. It actually went ashore near Topolabampo, about 35 miles south of Guaymas, but the winds blew up a storm of desert sand, everywhere. After we cleared up the mess of plastic pieces, we moved a whole bunch of sand back to the desert floor. Only then could we consider starting the paint process that had been lined up before we left in the spring.

Between January 4 and February 4, Francisco Javier, the painter we hired before leaving the boat, showed up daily and dutifully wielded sanders, scrapers, fiberglass spreaders, and painting equipment to give the upper decks a grand coat of fresh paint. It took a month as some of the preparation required grinding off several layers of previous coats before priming could occur. Several coats of paint followed. After painting completed we were ready for resupplying the ship, and checking out all the systems.

Denis decided to check the engine on land to make sure there would be no problem once we launched. It is always good to be picked up by the travel lift, driven over to the launch pad, carefully lowered into the water, be released from the straps, and drive away. His idea turned out to be a good one as the engine did not start. So while Francisco finished his job, Denis turned his attention to the engine.

During all that anxiety, an additional problem surfaced. A small, specialized nut mistakenly got dropped into an acid wash and partially dissolved. We had no spare for that one, even with all the spare parts we had on board. We took a sample to a local machine shop. Mexicans impress us with what they can make as needed parts for machines. However, they could not make this nut, as it was a specialized "British" one. Denis called the Gardner Engine contact person he knew in Vancouver, British Columbia. Bad news! He did not have any in stock. If we ordered one from England, it would take weeks to ship it. However, he did have some used bits and pieces in the back of the shop. If we would pay him for his time to do a "search," he'd let us know what he found. "Go for it!" came our command. Well, luck was with us. He had more than one! "Send both," shouted Denis.

To receive a shipment from Canada, we again were lucky. An American woman living in San Carlos had a contact in Hermosillo (an hour's drive from Guaymas), who could help. She ran a small office for Americans to receive mail from the States by someone driving to the border at Nogales, Arizona and collecting mail to a post office box address there. She also accepted UPS packages shipped to her Nogales address. So to get our part took several steps. First, the San Carlos contact found out the day the Hermosillo to Nogales trip would take place. Once our package made it from Vancouver to Nogales to Hermosillo, we had a choice: wait for the next Hermosillo to Guaymas run, or take a drive ourselves. Since we learned a Costco, Wal-Mart, and Home Depot had opened in Hermosillo, the decision to drive became an easy one. Success in picking up the much-needed part, and an additional shopping adventure to boot! All for the need of a nut!

Everything installed and engine running, we were ready for "splashing," a term for relaunching. Tides were the issue. If we were not in place and ready to drop before the optimum time period lapsed, we had to wait another two weeks. We kept a watchful eye on the travel-lift next door as time approached on the calendar. Saturday afternoon it moved to the water and picked up a very large shrimp boat and lifted it out of the water, but moved only a few hundred feet before stopping. Everyone went home for a five-day holiday in conjunction for Guaymas' celebration of Carnival. When they did come back to work, they cranked up the machine, drove a few hundred more feet and blew out two airplane tires. No spares! So they had to make an emergency run to Hermosillo Airport and find some replacements. That took all day. The next morning, our last morning for the right tide, they started work about 8 a.m. changing tires. My heart sank. We needed to go back into the water because people were coming to meet us in two days time across the Sea of Cortez in Santa Rosalia. By noon they had fixed the tires, backed the shrimp boat down to the water, relaunched it, and started in our direction. We unplugged our cord from the electrical outlet, removed the restraining straps, got the ropes ready, put things away in their places, and watched the lift approach. Once the lift's straps went beneath the boat and lifted it a bit, Denis put the last bit of bottom paint on exposed places, got on board via the swim bridge and pulled the ladder up behind him. With me already on board, we were then off and running!

Once in the water, Gabriel, plus other men from the boatyard, shouted directions as we negotiated the shallow water past the rocks near shore. I stood on the bow to look, but as the men on shore could see the whole picture, their directions assisted as well.

We needed to stop at the San Carlos fuel dock, and after fueling, stayed there for the night. The trip around from Guaymas took four hours of pounding the head seas from afternoon winds, quite an uncomfortable ride. The next morning we left before sunrise to avoid the blustery winds due to blow in the middle of the Sea of Cortez later that day. Funneling down from the Colorado River mouth, the winds channeled down the long fetch from upper Baja Peninsula all the way to the tip of Baja. They really blew by mid-afternoon.

After picking up son, David, and friend, Summer, in Santa Rosalia, we turned the boat south and for 300 miles tried to catch a fish. Nothing. The water was still too cold—between 55 and 58 degrees, but we enjoyed the ride, and each other. They returned to San Diego from La Paz.

That same day John Wright, our former crewmember from Costa Rica to Mexico in 2007, flew in from Fairbanks. Off we went for the "Baja Bash," slogging up the Pacific Coast for the entire western side of the Baja Peninsula. Winds coming from the north and northwest have an open field to build and build wave after wave. When you are going from south to north, there's no comfortable way to go around the set-up, just grit your teeth and slog! We were not looking forward to it, yet we paid heed to seasoned advice from our friend who delivers boats regularly from Cabo San Lucas or LaPaz to the States— if the weather looks good, "GO!"

An overnight (25 hours) from LaPaz to Cabo let us meet the dawn at Cabo Falso, a notorious piece of water. It has the reputation to turn back really big boats, so most people pay attention at that crossroad. All was calm. We kept going and did not stop until Santa Maria, another overnighter. Since the weather still looked favorable we had to figure the best attack for the next bit. There is not much to tuck into between Santa Maria and Turtle Bay, and stopping for three nights would perhaps be thumbing our noses into good luck, so off we went again after a nap and a meal.

At night after Punta Abreojos (which means, "Open your eyes!"), the building seas favored our heading toward shore. That ended up being a mistake! The winds really picked up and spray went everywhere from the wave crests. John was on duty (midnight to three A.M.); Denis and I were asleep. The boat went up a steep wave and fell off the top, hitting so hard I got bounced out of bed where I sleep mid-ship. John had just come upstairs from an engine room check. (These are done every two hours during passages, day and night.) So he had no time to anticipate the action coming. Besides it was totally black. The only color outside, when I looked out of the pilothouse window, was the white foam flying by. In checking our position, we were right off Capo Hipolote, the windiest place on the Pacific side of Baja. The choice was to keep bashing until we got past it on our present course, or change direction. We did the latter. Denis slept through it all in the aft cabin. Needless to say, I stayed awake until my watch (3-6) when things calmed down a bit. That was a rude awakening!

Turtle Bay had changed only a little bit since our visit in 1999. Only one other boat shared the anchorage, *BULLSHIP*. We had to stifle a giggle when we first saw it, then really laugh out loud when the man called for a panga to pick them up for shore time. He sounded like a real tough hombre, with a commanding voice, and we hoped he did not mispronounce his name.

After Denis and John went to town, they reported a dusty village with not much going for it. Being out in the middle of nowhere, visiting yachts are their source of money, other than fishing. My memory of the first visit was taking the dinghy in and climbing up a rusty ladder to the pier. We had a successful climb, yet the crew we had on board, Paul Hostika, lost his footing and fell several feet when a piece of the ladder gave way on his way down.

Before we left Turtle Bay, John and Denis lobbied for stopping at the San Benitos, a group of three small islands on the west side of Cedros Island, to see the resident elephant seals. By going that direction we purposefully missed the north end of Cedros, which was all right with me. We had experienced the wrath of that point on the way south and did not want a repeat performance. Remember the wave coming on board and wetting Denis' bed in the aft cabin?

Lobster fishermen, members of a fishing co-op on neighboring Cedros Island, lived on the San Benitos. When the season was closed, they kept a watchful eye for poachers. We were not able to purchase a lobster as the season had closed. Marine biologists often came to study the large herd of elephant seals living there. To get close enough to anchor near the village, we had to maneuver through the growing kelp—large fields of them.

Elephant seals spent their time on land sprawled out on the sand, occasionally moving to be more comfortable perhaps, or going back into the water to find food. Denis and John took the dinghy to shore to get a closer look and take pictures. A local man greeted them and helped pull the dinghy on shore. Everywhere they looked, elephant seals hung out—large males with their huge noses, females with normal noses, and young pups. In one cove they came upon a male in the shallow water, who called and called to a female on the sand. She answered from shore and joined him in the water, offering herself to him when she got close. Denis and John watched quietly as the scene turned from a courting one to a sexual one, both of the participating seals rolling around together in the water. She often bit him on the neck. Denis reported the male had hundreds of scars on his neck. I missed the whole scene by staying on the boat.

A male elephant seal, calling to his harem

With everything in our favor when we left San Benitos, we arrived in Ensenada, the most northern town in Baja late that afternoon. Several items of business kept us busy until bedtime. First order of business was fueling, followed by Immigration for our Zarpe papers (Exit papers to leave Mexico). After tying up at the marina across from the fuel dock, we did a quick change of clothes, and caught a cab for town and our last meal in Mexico. A mariachi band serenaded us during our meal.

The next morning we pulled out of the marina very excited to be close now. America, here we come! We could hear the U.S. Navy ships on the VHF radio as we approached the dotted line marking the border, and even though the skies looked "dreary, bleary" cloudy, our hearts beat strong and fast as if the sun shone down on us entering San Diego Harbor.

Tying up to the police dock on March 1, 2008, we were greeted by a Homeland Security man with a nametag, "Peace." How appropriate! He and his associate came on board, took an official tour of the boat while asking questions like, "How long have you been away?" "What kind of ship stores do you have on board?" In learning we had been on a ten-year journey, they realized we were outfitted to stay at sea for a long period of time. Officer Peace called Immigration via cell phone with our passport information. Considered now cleared back into the country, we needed a place to stay, at least temporarily. Officer Peace suggested we walk up the dock and check on space-available at the police dock, right next to the check-in dock. Bingo! They allowed ten days at their dock and had space for a boat our size that day. After securing lines to the dock we looked up to see son, David and younger grandson, Aeren, strolling down the ramp. That is until Aeren spotted me coming toward him and started running. Smiles, grins, and hugs were the order of the moment for everyone. John's wife, Kathleen, visited us again as well in San Diego, although she took John away from us on R&R until time for her flight back to Fairbanks.

Business for the month in port included time at Knight & Carver's Boatyard for two large jobs and a couple of smaller ones. We did not have to be hauled out of the water, instead stayed at the dock next to some mega-yachts—200 to 300 feet long. I felt very small. It is interesting to spend time at K&C. Some people who worked on building our boat in 1981 are still there. Everyone is happy to see *TEKA III* still out there doing her thing. We saw Hugo Carver several times, and the new Public Relations person did a story on us for the K&C Newsletter. A special honor for us!

Work done, visiting over, and "the barn calling," we started north out of San Diego Bay on April 1. In Southern California we tied up in Oxnard for five days, Monterey for three, and San Francisco for two, to await better weather. We hustled to make San Francisco from Half-Moon Bay before a system blew in and created twelve foot waves across the bar before the Golden Gate Bridge.

Approaching the Bridge, I whipped out my cell phone and reported to my sister in Florida, "We are now going under the Golden Gate!" John called his wife in Fairbanks, hoping to reach her in the classroom and share our big moment with her fourth graders. He had to leave a message though, as class had not quite started. It felt good to tell someone though.

My brother, Bob McCulley, piled children and grandchildren into three cars for a ride to from Sacramento and a Sunday visit with us on the boat docked at San Francisco Marina. They had all heard about the boat for ten years, and this was their chance to see and touch the legendary vessel that had taken me away for all that time. We enjoyed fellowship and food— pizza, pop, hamburgers, and coca-cola cake. One of the teen-age girls looked at the cake and asked what kind it was. Someone remarked it was a meatloaf cake. She turned up her nose at that, only to return shortly after seeing another person chomping away on a big piece of cake, piled high with whipped cream—"I want some!" A good time was had by all.

North of San Francisco we had two potential nasty points to round— Point Arena and Cape Mendocino, the two places that bounced us around in the middle of the night ten years ago. Those are two of the three places where the land mass juts out into the sea. Currents from either side of that land tend to compete with each other as to which side can cause the worse conditions. The other nasty one is Point Conception in southern California, which we have learned to anchor just behind, and leave at first light before things get "busy."

This time we went past Arena and Mendocino in the daytime and had no trouble. However, watching the depth sounder as we passed Cape Mendocino change from 100 feet to 1,000 feet and back again, pointed out why the sea can get so vicious there. Winds howling down from the high country at the points, also add to the wave confusion.

Because the weather is so bothersome and depths so unusual, crab traps are not found in these two places. That doesn't mean they aren't around in places before or after. The fishermen leave their crab trap buoys stretched out on a line, now with toggles attached for easy pick-up to check their catch. Several buoys of the same color strung out in a line belong to one fisherman. Others going in another direction with a different color belong to another crabber. It can be "pay attention" time for quite a while. When the two-to-three foot chop keeps the buoys playing hide and seek in the waves, it's important to stay on your toes and not catch one.

Between Eureka and Crescent City we had to negotiate a minefield of crab pots, even capturing two on the flopper stopper lines at water level. As soon as we slowed down, untangling began, and we were soon free again. Quite frustrated, we agreed to "boycott" crab when we docked. What a short-lived boycott! An additional crewmember, Keith Bystrom, joined us in Crescent City and insisted he buy us each a whole crab from the local fisherman, even though they were expensive. Yummy!

Another one of those things that go bump in the night occurred along a stretch of the California coast about 5:30 A.M., again on my watch. A "Bam" on the port side got everyone up and ready to size up the situation. Scanning through the plastic section of the weather curtain we saw that one of the paravanes, normally riding twelve to fourteen feet below the surface, now hung in the air several feet out of the water. It had tangled with a long-line fishing arrangement.

Long lines, seen during daylight hours, and not seen on night passages, can be set up several hundred feet to a mile apart, with baited hooks below the surface waiting for a strike. There are floats at each end and sometimes in-between to mark this arrangement. The ones at the ends have flags planted on top of the float. When a flag is spotted, the end of the line is known. Where the other end is may not be known. The fishermen return to check their lines on a regular basis.

We spied the flagged-pole marking the end of the line almost right away. Several things had to happen at once. Denis cranked the winch to raise the flopper stopper pole, thus getting the parvanes closer to the boat. John grabbed a longboat hook and worked at untangling the wrapped line. I concentrated on the flagged long-line pole. As it floated close to the hull, I tried to keep it from going beneath the boat. Once the line came loose, we needed to get line and pole all the way to the bow before releasing it. That way we had a good chance nothing would slip under the boat and get us into more trouble. The seas were not too bad, but it was dark and the water very cold. No one wanted to go swimming for further rescue. At the bow when we were sure the lines were totally clear, John let the flagged pole go and Denis slowly reversed so we could drift away. The whole process took about fifteen minutes, but what a hectic time, and what a waker-upper! And when the fisherman came to check his haul, his GPS reading may not have been valid. We had moved the line.

Last crewmember, Don Rennie, on board, we departed Newport, Oregon at 6 A.M. on May 1. We arrived at Cape Flattery late afternoon the following day and anchored in Neah Bay Harbor before dark—a 36 hour trip. Cape Flattery is where I had my "religious experience" in 1998 to know my ship would take care of me. She did just that too. I had wanted to see this special place in the daylight to offset the really black night we tossed about in the waves before. With the tide right, the waves were low, and nothing frightened me. Those years behind the wheel had also strengthened me.

One more stop—Port Angeles—then home to Tacoma. The last morning just sparkled. The sun's rays bouncing off the waters, and reflecting from the snowfields on the Olympic Mountains, made the blue of the sky so blue. The winds stayed low. The current ran with us. We cruised!

Close to home—Dungeness Spit lighthouse and the Olympic Mountains

At the Hylebos Marina dock in Tacoma, Washington, stood our waiting family, Dawn, Larry, Megan and Sashi, the grand-dog, to take our lines, get and give hugs, and watch us plant our feet once again on special ground. When Mr. Gardner, our trusty engine, cooled down, he got a very big, well-deserved hug from me! From our place at the dock, we can see Mt. Rainier, "Mr. Mountain," whose majesty makes me feel unique and wonderful to be alive.

In the Rearview Mirror

I grew up on a street one block long. The sea never crossed my mind as a future experience. In fact, if anyone would have said to me early in my adult life I would ever live such an adventure, I can vividly hear and see my response. No way! But I did.

That is not to say I did not develop a gypsy streak. Traveling for me began in earnest with Denis serving twenty years in the Air Force. We lived overseas for ten years; three in England, and three in Thailand; followed by four more after retirement, teaching in Hong Kong. Taking advantage of access to neighboring countries, we added many passports stamps to our books.

In the U.S. we explored coast-to-coast, camping, backpacking and moving our recreational vehicle around a lot. There is a lot to see and do in our wonderful country.

In essence, it appears I cannot stay put for very long. And I often have the question posed, "When are you going to settle down and be normal?"

Throughout our eleven years of exploring the world on *TEKA III*, many people have told me I was living their dream. I wanted to share my life at sea so others could go along on the adventure, without leaving their comfort zone.

Out on the sea, one can experience magnificent sunrises, fantastic sunsets, elusive green flashes, and the moon plus stars to light the way at night. In touching new and different lands again, one can find exotic foods, new languages, and different cultures to challenge one's senses in other ways.

The ocean's many moods range from benign to boisterous, caused by forces above and below the surface, continuously moving, seen or unseen. The only thing constant is change as the sea goes through its moods, taking the traveler along with it.

It calls one to take the challenge—ride the waves and join in the flow. The hardest part may be leaving the sight of land, or worrying about, "What if...?" Comparing the smallness of one's vessel with the vastness of the open ocean can be intimidating. Learning how to cope with fears and anxieties leads to competence and confidence. Exploring and expanding one's horizons become a personal growth experience that is hard to measure.

Looking back, I can truly say my nautical life evolved over a period of time. I moved from small powerboats to bigger ones, all of them in protective waters. *TEKA III* lured me to sea for a giant geography lesson, and to meet many wonderful people. The sea time from the Pacific Northwest to the waters of Europe and back went by very fast—anticipating, planning, and doing kept me feeling young.

One of the many "sundowners" among cruising friends

With *TEKA III* at sea my husband and I had quite an adventure, sharing some of it with our children and their children, plus special friends joining us for the ride. She kept us safe over 48,000 nautical miles, stopping at forty countries along the way. We felt no boundaries, physically or psychologically, other than those we placed on ourselves. What a journey!

A Post Script, On Life

Life is defined by course, speed and waypoints. Nautical terms as they are, course, speed, and waypoints all can be applied to life's journey in general. Think about it.

The "course" is the direction, adjustable as needed. "Speed," like the wind, is variable and depends on timing, again individually based. "Waypoints" allow mini-goals to be set up, reached; then new ones plotted.

Life is fast or slow. It depends on the person, place, time, activities and expectations.

Life is too short, or way too long, but always needs to be lived.

Life's path is straight and narrow; crooked and convoluted; or circular, turning back on itself—always movement oriented—toward or away from the moment.

We see ahead, look behind, and scan both sides; searching over the horizon, anticipating what's beyond, while observing what may have been missed in passing.

We feel enriched and emboldened or down-trodden and put upon— interactions with others seem to define those traits more so then from within our own selves. One of life's lessons should be learning to love oneself first, not depend on happiness created by others for us.

We are not perfect; yet with all our faults and faulty decisions, we hopefully learn not to make the same mistake twice.

Life is rich in opportunity, with many doors, sometimes unrecognizable as such. Which door to open? Can we just take a peek first? What motivates us to do one or the other versus just passing on by? Risk-taking is scary, yet provides growth in most cases. Fence-sitting takes energy too, but feels much safer. Whichever we do, action is needed at one time or another to move forward. Speed, course, waypoints.

There's daring do and adventure, with a cautious element to moderate events along the way. "Steady as she goes!" Life's unpredictability, versatility, viability make the world go round. Respect for life's forces is very important. Don't try to stare down a big storm. Know your limitations. Pull on your strengths. Stand tall or stay small. Think your way out of trouble, but try not to get there in the first place.

We learn by living and by doing. Choose a course, set mini-goals, go at your own pace. Make your life a meaningful journey!

Feel the rhythm; Trust yourself!

Acknowledgments

My genuine thanks go to the following people whose care and support helped bring this book out of my heart and soul to share with adventurers, armchair or real world.

Readers, listed alphabetically, included Sally Bee Brown, Judy Buskirk, Glenna Kaye, Martha Evans, Winona Knutsen, Larry Kurdek, Lois Ludwig, Summer Pelstring, David Umstot, Dawn Umstot, and Denis Umstot. Their feedback, suggestions, and encouragement meant a lot to me.

Also, Hugo Carver, friend, and builder of our boat, who responded graciously when I asked him to do the "Foreword." I appreciated his kind and thoughtful words, as well as, building such a seaworthy passagemaker that took to the sea with no hesitation.

Larry Gezelius spent hours developing and maintaining our website and therefore keeping our adventures alive on paper, not just locked inside our heads. Denis Umstot took the photos; Judy Gitenstein performed the copyediting; Todd Engel created the cover.

The many cruisers who took the time to stop by our boat, either in an anchorage or tied to a dock, or hailed us on Channel 16 as they passed on the water, to confirm we were the *TEKA III* from those *PassageMaker Magazine* stories. In learning we were, they added to our sense of well-being as fellow cruisers and journey journalists with their warm wishes for more adventures and subsequent stories.

And Dr. Philip Chen, University of Washington Eye Center, Seattle. His vigilant care for my glaucoma condition, and genuine interest in our travels, made it possible for me to "see at sea" and enjoy our adventures.

Appendix

TEKA III Specifications

Designer and Builder: Robert Beebe (Design 141) with modifications by builder, Knight & Carver, San Diego.

Specifications:
Length overall: 52.5 ft.
Beam: 16 ft
Draft: 6 ft
Flying bridge with controls
Constructed of fiberglass with airex foam core
Gardner 6LXB 127 hp main engine (2.5 gph @7.5 knots)
Twin disk MG-509 transmission
40 inch four blade workhorse nibral propeller
Auxiliary power: 58 hp Westerbeke
10kw hydraulic AC generator operates off main or auxiliary engine
Hydraulic come-home with chain drive on main shaft (5 kts at 2000 rpm)
Fuel: 2000 gallons in 5 tanks (filtered before entering the day tank)
Water: 600 gallons
Lubricating oil: 40 gallons
Hydraulic oil: 40 gallons plus 35 gallons reserve
Holding tank: 38 gallons
Paravane stabilizers with retrieval winches
Underwater wet exhaust prevents diesel fumes
Bow thruster: 20 hp hydraulic American Bowthruster twin prop
Hydraulic windlass and power steering
Hydraulic main engine start with electric starter back

LaVergne, TN USA
06 December 2009
166133LV00004B/9/P